THE
PHILIPPINES

Other Titles in
ABC-CLIO's
GLOBAL STUDIES: ASIA
Series

Central Asia, Reuel R. Hanks

Japan, Lucien Ellington

The Koreas, Mary E. Connor

China, Robert LaFleur

Nepal and Bangladesh, Nanda R. Shrestha

Vietnam, L. Shelton Woods

India, Fritz Blackwell

GLOBAL STUDIES: ASIA

THE PHILIPPINES

A Global Studies Handbook

Damon L. Woods

A B C CLIO

Santa Barbara, California • Denver, Colorado • Oxford, England

Library of Congress Cataloging-in-Publication Data
is available from the Library of Congress.

ISBN 1-85109-675-2 — ISBN 1-85109-680-9 (e-book)

09 08 07 06   10 9 8 7 6 5 4 3 2 1

This book is also available on the World Wide Web as an eBook.
Visit http://www.abc-clio.com for details.

ABC-CLIO, Inc.
130 Cremona Drive, P.O. Box 1911
Santa Barbara, California 93116-1911

This book is printed on acid-free paper. ∞
Manufactured in the United States of America

To Shelton, My Brother My Friend

Contents

Series Editor's Foreword

It is imperative that as many Americans as possible develop a basic understanding of Asia. In an increasingly interconnected world, the fact that Asia contains almost 60 percent of all the planet's population is argument enough for increased knowledge of the continent on our parts. In addition, there are at least four other reasons why it is critical that Americans become more familiar with Asia.

First, Americans of all ages, creeds, and colors are extensively involved economically with Asian countries. U.S.-Pacific two-way trade surpassed U.S. trade with Europe in the 1970s. American companies constitute the leading foreign investors in Japan. With the world's second-largest economy, Japan is also the second-largest foreign investor in the United States.

The recent Asian economic crisis notwithstanding, since World War II, East Asia has experienced the fastest rate of economic growth of all the world's regions. Recently, newly industrialized Southeast Asian countries such as Indonesia, Malaysia, and Thailand have joined the so-called Four Tigers—Hong Kong, the Republic of Korea, Singapore, and Taiwan—as leading areas for economic growth. In the past decade China has begun to realize its potential to be a world-influencing economic actor. Many Americans now depend upon Asians for their economic livelihoods, and all of us consume products made in or by Asian companies.

Second, it is impossible to be an informed American citizen without knowledge of Asia, a continent that directly impacts our national security. America's war on terrorism is, as this foreword is composed, being conducted in an Asian country—Afghanistan. (What many Americans think of as the "Mideast" is, in actuality, Southwest Asia.) Both India and

Pakistan now have nuclear weapons. The eventual reunification of the Korean Peninsula is fraught with the possibility of great promise or equally great peril. The question of U.S.-China relations is considered one of the world's major global geopolitical issues. Americans everywhere are affected by Asian political and military developments.

Third, Asia and Asians have also become an important part of American culture. Asian restaurants dot the American urban landscape. Buddhism is rapidly growing in the United States, and Asian movies are becoming increasingly popular. Asian Americans, though still a small percentage of the overall U.S. population, are one of the fastest-growing ethnic groups in the United States. Many Asian Americans exert considerable economic and political influence in this country. Asian sports, pop music, and cinema stars are becoming household names in America. Even Chinese-language characters are becoming visible in the United States on everything from baseball caps to T-shirts to license plates. Followers of the ongoing debate on American educational reform will constantly encounter references to Asian student achievement.

Fourth, Asian civilizations are some of the world's oldest, and their arts and literature rank as some of humankind's most impressive achievements. Anyone who is considered an educated person needs a basic understanding of Asia. The continent has a long, complex, and rich history. Asia is the birthplace of all the world's major religions, including Christianity and Judaism.

Our objectives in developing the Global Studies: Asia series are to assist a wide variety of citizens in gaining a basic understanding of Asian countries and to enable readers to be better positioned for more in-depth work. We envision the series being appropriate for libraries; educators; high school, introductory college and university students; businesspeople; would-be tourists; and anyone who is curious about an Asian country or countries. Although there is some variation in the handbooks—the diversity of the countries requires slight variations in treatment—each volume includes narrative chapters on history and geography, economics, institutions, and society and contemporary issues. Readers should obtain a sound general understanding of the particular Asian country about which they read.

Each handbook also contains an extensive reference section. Because our guess is that many of the readers of this series will actually be traveling to Asia or interacting with Asians in the United States, introductions to language, food, and etiquette are included. The reference section of each handbook also contains extensive information—including Web sites when relevant—about business and economic, cultural, educational, exchange, government, and tourist organizations. The reference sections also include capsule descriptions of famous people, places, and events and a comprehensive annotated bibliography for further study.

—*Lucien Ellington*
Series Editor

Preface and Acknowledgments

During the writing of this book, I have had the opportunity to go home twice, for a variety of reasons: to visit with family and friends, to work with Fil-Am students who are trying to connect with their roots, to do research, to visit the place where my father is buried. The Philippines is home to me even though I have not lived there for more than thirty years now. It is where I grew up, having arrived there at the age of five and leaving after graduating from high school. Later in life, I decided to pursue a doctoral degree with an emphasis on Philippine history. I have taught at least a dozen courses at the university level either exclusively on the Philippines or touching on the Philippines in the context of Southeast Asia. I have given papers and lectures on aspects of Philippine history in the United States, Europe, and the Philippines. Yet for all this, writing this book has been more difficult than I had anticipated. I suppose that the pressures of writing this book would be similar to those of writing about a close friend or family member. Being objective is practically impossible. One is delighted to tell others about that friend, but at the same time wonders what to leave in and what to leave out, what "good things" to include and what "bad things" to exclude. No doubt I have left out what some consider important and included material some believe to be superfluous.

Years ago, I met someone who told me that she intended to become a missionary to the Philippines. The son of missionary parents, I had spent my childhood in Baguio City, in the Cordillera mountain range of Northern Luzon, so I was interested to hear more about her plans. But as she spoke, I began to get an uneasy feeling. So I asked her, "Where do you think the Philippines is?" "Oh," she answered, "right next to Ecuador."

Spread out in the South China Sea, off the coast of mainland Asia, the archipelago often appears somehow misplaced. One can get a sense that it belongs elsewhere. For various reasons, primarily its colonial experiences—as the saying goes, the Philippines spent four hundred years in a convent (the period under Spain) and fifty years in Hollywood (under the Americans)—the Philippines has seemed out of step with its Asian neighbors. The Philippines is the fourth largest English-speaking country, behind the United States, the United Kingdom, and India. In addition, the Philippines is the only Christian nation in Asia, with over 80 percent of the population being Catholic and much of the rest being Protestant, plus a Muslim minority in the south. But the Philippines is a part of Southeast Asia, sharing history, culture, linguistic and religious roots, and more with the region.

Located in the South China Sea is that archipelago which has come to be known in the modern world as the Philippines. It was named *las islas Felipinas* by Ruy Lopez de Villalobos, the leader of the fourth Spanish expedition to Southeast Asia, for then crown prince of Spain, Felipe, who later became Philip II of Spain and who was responsible for the Spanish conquest of the islands named after him. (It is worth noting that outsiders have usually included *islas,* or islands, in the name of the archipelago—thus, *las islas Filipinas* by Spaniards and the Philippine Islands by Americans, but the Philippines is the name used by Filipinos.) Today, in Filipino, the national language, it is known as *Republika ng Pilipinas* (the Republic of the Philippines) or *Pilipinas* (Philippines) for short. Not only named by foreign intruders, but made to be considered as a single unit, with many parts, the Philippines remains a country of enigmas and paradoxes and, above all, great diversity. It could well be that the enigmas and paradoxes arise as a result of expectations, usually by outsiders, of a certain uniformity; but if one expects uniformity, the Philippines will seem a very strange place indeed.

There is no question that cultural influences from outside

the region have impacted Southeast Asia, and this includes the Philippines. The question of how extensive this influence was has been the subject of research and debate. J.C. van Leur, a Dutch bureaucrat in what is now known as Indonesia, concluded in his dissertation for the University of Leiden in 1934 that foreign influences failed to "bring about any fundamental changes in any part of Indonesian social and political order." Instead, what one finds is that such outside influences form a "thin, easily flaking glaze; underneath it, the whole of the old indigenous forms has continued to exist." That is, Indonesians (and I would extend this to the rest of Southeast Asia and thus the Philippines) took on *forms*, not *ideas*. The process of taking something foreign and making it indigenous has been called domestication, indigenization, localization, and so forth. H.G.Q. Wales used the phrase *local genius* to express how Southeast Asians retained indigenous ideas while absorbing aspects of the cultures of others. Foreign cultures often provided concrete expression for indigenous beliefs. John Leddy Phelan, in his classic work *Hispanization of the Philippines: Spanish Aims and Filipino Responses*, noted:

> The Filipinos were no mere passive recipients of the cultural stimulus created by the Spanish conquest. Circumstances gave them considerable freedom in selecting their responses to Hispanization. Their responses varied all the way from acceptance to indifference and rejection. The capacity of the Filipinos for creative social adjustment is attested in the manner in which they adapted many Hispanic features to their own indigenous culture.

As a Latin American historian, Phelan failed to understand or appreciate the process of *domestication* as practiced in Southeast Asia.

As a result, one must make a distinction between *core values* and *surface values* or *expressions* otherwise, if one is not careful, the visual, the concrete will be mistaken for what is truly indigenous, that is, *core values*. As a result of the length of time Filipinos were under colonial powers, the distinctions between core values and surface values have been blurred, adding to the potential for confusion on the part of those outside Philippine society. For example, although the Philippines is the only Christian nation in Asia (with a Muslim minority in the south), Philippine scholars refer to Filipinos not as Christians but as Christianized animists, or *anitists* (from the word *anito*, spirit). Both Catholicism and Islam, religions brought in by outside forces, retain aspects of the traditional indigenous religion. Outsiders have failed to realize this, much to their frustration, because they cannot reconcile the differences.

But it is even more complicated than simply *core values* versus *surface values*. Societies are not static; they are always changing. In addition, populations tend not to be uniform. Philippine scholars have noted "The Great Cultural Divide" one finds in Philippine society. It exists between a thin layer of the economic and political elite (as well as much of the middle class) who have embraced "foreign" ways and the majority who continue within the indigenous culture. The project of growing as a nation and a people, the creation of a national discourse, requires some type of accommodation. The outsider, however, usually sees only that thin veneer of the familiar, but then is confused by apparent differences in what is behind and beyond the veneer.

This book examines that place in the world known as the Philippines—its history, geography, people, languages, and customs—and seeks to present it in an accurate manner. Although I will not attempt to demystify what makes the Philippines the nation and the people that it is, I will try to help the reader reconcile some of the paradoxes and come to a better understanding of the Philippines. The purpose of this book is to inform those who are unfamiliar with the Philippines and prepare them if they should choose to visit the Philippines. I hope that I have succeeded in my task.

In my life, I have incurred many debts (*utang na loob*). I cannot mention all those who have helped me on my journey. To my family, who has shared parts of the journey with me, it would not have been the same without you. To my friends on Melrose, particularly Dan Nable, thank you for your friendship, support, and loyalty.

This book is possible only because of the invaluable support and encouragement of those involved with its production. Lucien Ellington has very patiently guided me, made helpful suggestions, and has kept me going through this process. Without Lucien, the book would not have been written.

Alicia Merritt of ABC-CLIO has been equally patient and encouraging. Again, without Alicia, this book would not be possible. Ellen Rasmussen has done an outstanding job of finding photographs to go along with the text. Peter Westwick has helped to bring the project to a successful conclusion.

My colleagues at California State University, Long Beach, have provided the academic environment helpful to completing this book. I want to thank Arnold Kaminsky, who brought me to Long Beach, and John Tsuchida, the chair of my department. Three colleagues have stood by me and been friends throughout this entire process: Linda Maram, Barbara Kim, and Feng-ying Ming. Thank you for your support. I want to thank Elizabeth Pastores-Pallfy for her help on the economic aspects of the American period. Presented during a conference, her work on the time period and its economic impact has been invaluable.

During my time at UC Irvine, Steve Topik and Marc Kanda were a constant source of encouragement. Although she was once my student, Lily Ann Villaraza has become a colleague and a real help in both my research and writing. Then there are the many students who have over the years listened and added to my courses on the Philippines. *Maraming salamat sa inyong lahat.*

My brother, though my junior by several years, has preceded me in many ways, including this project, having written the book on Vietnam for this same series. Shelton and I attended UCLA together and both received our Ph.D.s there— he a year ahead of me. I thank him for his help and example; he is a tough act to follow.

Although, as I have already mentioned, I grew up in the Philippines and have a doctoral degree in Southeast Asian history with an emphasis on the Philippines, in many ways I have learned more about the culture, customs, and people of that land from my wife. Because we both grew up in the Philippines, we have been able to share endless stories of common childhood experiences, such as eating forbidden food from street vendors. However, for all my familiarity with things and ability to understand the language, I was still an outsider, and the meanings and nuances of many of those experiences had escaped me and only now are better understood with her insights and explanations. Guia Silverio Woods has not only filled in the gaps of my knowledge of the Philippines, she has been and remains a source of inspiration to continue my research and writing on the Philippines.

—*Damon L. Woods*

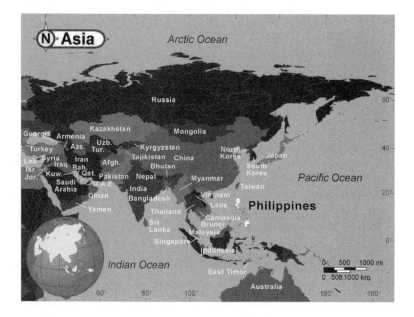

PART ONE
NARRATIVE SECTION

CHAPTER ONE

History and Geography

During the past 150 years, the Philippines has been under the control of three empires. The last half of the nineteenth century found the Spanish Empire, which had ruled the Philippines for more than three centuries, in serious decline. The rise of Filipino resistance and the emergence of a nation seeking a place on the international stage, the United States, led to the end of Spanish rule, and for the next forty years, the Philippines belonged to the United States as its only colony; but the designs of the Japanese Empire, with its Greater East Asia Co-Prosperity Sphere, temporarily ended American rule. For a brief but brutal three years, the Philippines belonged to the Japanese Empire. With liberation in 1945 and independence in 1946, the Philippines had to face the challenge of becoming a nation.

PHYSICAL GEOGRAPHY

The Philippines is an archipelago consisting of 7,107 islands, of which only 500 or so are larger than 1 square kilometer and almost one-third of which remain unnamed. Spread out over half a million square miles (1.3 million square kilometers), it is located between latitudes 21E N and latitude 5E N off the coast of mainland Asia. It is surrounded by water: To the north is the Bashi Channel; to the south is the Celebes Sea; to the east is the Pacific Ocean; and to the west is the South China Sea. The archipelago stretches 1,854 kilometers from north to south and at its widest is 1,104 kilometers. The northernmost island, Y'ami, in the Batanes group, is less than 250 kilometers from Taiwan, and the southernmost island, Salaug, of the Tawi-Tawi group, is less than 50 miles from Borneo.

1

An aerial view of the mountain landscape of the island of Bohol.
(Yann Arthus-Bertrand/Corbis)

The total land area of the archipelago is 300,780 square kilometers, 96 percent of which is made up by eleven islands. Less than 10 percent of the more than 7,000 islands are inhabited. Two islands, Luzon (105,708 square kilometers) and Mindano (92,586 square kilometers), make up 65 percent of the total land area and are occupied by 60 percent of the population. A comparison of the land mass taken as a whole makes it about the size of Italy, slightly smaller than Japan, and slightly larger than the British Isles.

The archipelago can be divided into three major island groups: Luzon, the Bisayas, and Mindanao. These three groups are represented by the three stars on the Philippine flag. Farthest north is Luzon, the largest island, and the location of Manila, the capital and seat of the government. The islands of Mindoro and Marinduque are often grouped with Luzon. To the south is Mindanao, the second largest island; included with it, as a region, are islands that reach down to

Mayon Volcano, located on the southern portion of the island of Luzon, is known for its distinctive shape. (Paul A. Souders/Corbis)

Borneo. In between the two large islands is the region known as the Bisayas, consisting of more than 6,000 islands. The eight major islands in this group are Panay, Negros, Cebu, Bohol, Leyte, Samar, Masbate, and Palawan. The province of Palawan, off to the west, includes the large island of Palawan and more than 1,700 surrounding islands.

The Republic of the Philippines is organized into sixteen regions, which include seventy-nine provinces, 113 cities, and 1,496 municipalities.

Located at the edge of the Asiatic continental platform, the Philippines rises out of the ocean, in part, as the result of volcanic activity as well as the shifting of tectonic plates. One of the deepest areas of the Pacific Ocean is found off the coast of Mindanao, in the Mindanao Trough, which reaches a depth of more than 10,000 meters. The Philippines is located on the so-called Belt of Fire, which runs from Indonesia through the Philippines and reaches to Japan; and the Belt of Fire is a part of the Chain of Fire, which runs from the Aleutians down through the Americas, up through New Zealand, and then joins the Belt of Fire in Asia.

As a result, the highest points in the Philippines are volcanic peaks. Twenty-one active and some two hundred dormant volcanoes are scattered throughout the archipelago. Among the active volcanoes are Ragang on Mindanao; Canlaon on Negros; and Mayon, Taal, and Pinatubo on Luzon. Dormant for longer than six hundred years, Mount Pinatubo erupted on June 9, 1991, with an eruption ten times larger than that of Mount St. Helens in 1980. A giant ash cloud rose 35 kilometers into the atmosphere, and ash two inches or deeper reached an area of 4,000 square kilometers surrounding Pinatubo. Nine billion tons of ash covered 200,000 acres. The economic impact was devastating: More than a million people were left homeless. But its effects were not limited to the Philippines; the average temperature worldwide was lowered for several years because Pinatubo's ash blocked out sunlight, and sunsets worldwide were colored with "Pinatubo pink" for months afterwards.

Being a part of the Ring of Fire also brings with it the constant threat of earthquakes. The archipelago experiences on average five earthquakes a day, of varying intensity, the strongest recorded marking 7.9 on the Richter scale.

Because the Philippines is an archipelago, water dominates many aspects of its existence, including climate and weather patterns. The territorial waters cover more than 600,000 square miles (1.5 million square kilometers) and provide a rich resource for fishing.

Fifty-nine lakes and 132 major rivers serve as freshwater sources. The three largest lakes are Laguna de Bay (922 square kilometers) and Lake Taal (266 square kilometers) on Luzon, and Lake Lanao (347 square kilometers) on Mindanao. The ground water storage is estimated to contain more than 260,000 cubic meters.

The Philippines is a tropical land, having an average temperature of 27°C and a high average humidity. The Philippines has two seasons—wet and dry. These seasons are determined by two patterns. The Southwest Monsoon blows through for five to six months each year, usually from June to October or November. This wind—known locally as the *habagat*—brings rain for most of its cycle. The Northeast Monsoon—known as *amihan*—generally signals the end of rainy season. In addition to the monsoons, three other air streams affect the archipelago: the North Pacific trades, the Middle Latitude westerlies, and the South Pacific trades. The Southwest Monsoon is the major factor affecting the climate and, consequently, the economic life of the local population. The average rainfall is 80 inches annually, while the coastal plains receive an even higher amount. Because the Philippines is located in the middle of the most active typhoon belt, the rainy season is punctuated by on average twenty typhoons a year. These typhoons bring with them heavy rain and strong winds (up to 200 kilometers per hour), which can do great damage to life and property.

One of the consequences of the water-dominated weather patterns is that the soil is leached of much of its nutrients. Roughly 35 percent of the land area is cultivated. Rice, maize, coconut, and sugar cane make up the bulk of the agricultural production.

The Philippines is rich in mineral resources, including copper, gold, nickel, and iron. The Philippines is the sixth largest producer of gold and has the world's largest deposits of chromite. In addition, there are abundant reserves of non-metallic minerals.

Another of the Philippines' great natural resources is timber, particularly the hardwoods—mahogany, narra, and ironwood. Unfortunately, harvesting this wealth has resulted in the deforestation of much of the country. In 1960, 60 percent of the country was forested; by 2000, only 10 percent remained so. This has had significant consequences, not the least of which are environmental.

The Philippines is a land of spectacular natural beauty that enjoys a wide variety of flora—some eight hundred species of orchids and eighty-five hundred species of flowering plants. Its fauna includes five hundred varieties of birds and at least one hundred of lizards; there is a menagerie of wildlife, including pygmy deer, monkeys, and wild pigs.

THE PEOPLE OF THE PHILIPPINES

The greatest resource of the Philippines is its people. With a population that reached 84 million in 2004 and limited available space, the population density averages 255 persons per square kilometer. The National Capital Region, the destination of many seeking work and better economic opportunities, has about 15,600 persons per square kilometer. In 1995, the age breakdown of the population was:

Ages 0–15—38 percent
Ages 15–65—58 percent
Ages 65 and above—4 percent (IBON, National Profile, 16)

The diversity of the Philippines is displayed in its people, who are called Filipinos, a term that has been used in various ways in the past. The term *Filipino* has not been used consistently. Although several early Spanish chroniclers referred to the natives of the Philippines as "Filipinos," the Spaniards designated the local population *indios,* as they did in the Americas. *Filipino* referred to a full-blooded Spaniard born in the Philippines, in contrast to a *peninsular,* one born in Spain, and *criollo,* one born in the Americas. During the push for freedom from Spain, the term *indio* was rejected and *Filipino* taken as a name that rightfully belonged to the local population.

As others set the boundaries for what would be included in "the Philippines," who should be considered a Filipino has resulted in a "plural society." As an independent Philippines embarked on the task of nation building and creating a national consciousness, a sense of unity was critical. The New Society, inaugurated by President Ferdinand Marcos during the martial law era, used the slogan *Isang lahi, isang bansa, isang tadhana* (One race, one nation, one destiny). Marked by regionalism, the goal of unity has been difficult to achieve. It has been through struggles against foreign intruders that a sense of common cause has emerged from time to time and slowly evolved. In their struggles against the Spaniards, prior to and during the Revolution, Filipinos saw themselves as having some things in common, including the possibility that they were one people. The American presence divided that consensus. The Japanese invasion and occupation, which affected almost all Filipinos, served to create a shared identity. Yet, even after independence and up to the present day, Filipinos are marked by divisions, including ethnic differences.

Filipinos are a blend of ethnicities, the result of migrations to the archipelago; some are recent, others occurred in the distant and unrecorded past. No one knows when prehistoric migrations took place, though theories have been put forward. How these migrants came to the archipelago is another issue; the best explanation is that some of the migrants took advantage of land bridges—Palawan to Borneo, Mindanao to Sulawesi, and Luzon to Taiwan—while others used seagoing vessels, known to have traveled between Mindanao and southern Vietnam as early as the third century CE. These speculations bring with them difficulties, including the bothersome notion that each wave of migrants brought with them a superior culture and technology. Such a view continues to the present, the new and foreign still being seen as superior to that which is already present. We do know that when the Spaniards arrived, the population was primarily Malay. Into this population were added Spanish, Chinese, and later American aspects, along with other ethnicities.

Ethnic Minorities

Many believe that a group known as the Negritos—including the Aetas and Mamanwas—represented the aboriginal population of the Philippines. Dark-skinned pygmies with kinky hair, they can still be found in coastal areas, rainforests, and mountainous regions. They have been viewed as the first group to populate various parts of the Philippines, but who were later driven into the interior by the arrival of other ethnic groups, specifically later waves of migration from other parts of Southeast Asia. The main problem with this view is that there is no evidence to support it. Archaeological research has failed to demonstrate the Negrito, now considered a cultural and ethnic minority, as the original, or even an earlier group to live in the archipelago.

The notion of ethnic and cultural minorities resulted in the formation of PANAMIN (Presidential Assistance on National Minorities) in 1967. With more than three dozen major ethnic minorities scattered across the Philippines, almost 10 percent of the population is designated as belonging to cultural minorities. PANAMIN has dealt with these minorities in different ways, from providing direct aid and seeking to integrate them into mainstream society to sheltering others to help preserve their culture. The various ethnic minorities did not seem to fit into the project of creating a national consciousness based on a shared heritage; a special place had to be made for them. The differences between the minorities and the rest of Filipinos have almost resulted in their being regarded as non-Filipino. The question must be asked: What makes one group a cultural/ethnic minority?

Minorities in the Philippines are peoples who successfully resisted assimilation into the Spanish and then American cultures. As a result, they maintained their own cultures, relatively untainted by foreign contact. They kept their epics, songs, dances, and way of dressing, whereas their fellow Filipinos assimilated into a new way of life and lost much of their culture. The culture of the assimilated Filipinos became a hybrid of indigenous and foreign elements. For many, the minorities are seen as quaint, yet backward. If they were driven into the interior by succeeding waves of migration, each wave being more advanced than the previous, the earlier a particular group arrived on the archipelago, the more primitive it is believed to be. But some Filipinos now realize that such minority groups are links to their own past. Although no group has remained untouched by foreign incursions into the archipelago, those affected less still retain aspects of their culture from pre-Hispanic times. From them, we may learn more about the cultural practices, nature of society, religious beliefs, and more of the ancestors of those Filipinos assimilated into a new way of life.

That minorities are those who resisted assimilation is demonstrated by the fact that 60 percent of the ethnic/cultural minorities in the Philippines are Muslim. Their resistance is all the more impressive in light of the Spanish desire and efforts to rid the archipelago of Islam, as they had done on the Iberian Peninsula. Five major groups make up this Muslim minority: Tausug, Maranao, Maguindanao, Samal, and Badjao. Found on Mindanao and the Sulu Archipelago, they have successfully maintained a sense of identity and continue to claim parts of the region as their own. Manila has recognized this and established an autonomous region for self-rule. But not all the minorities found in Mindanao are Muslim. The hill tribes or highlanders of Mindanao include the Tiruray, T'boli, Bagobos, Subanon, Bukidnon, Mandayas, Manobos, and B'laans. As with other minorities in the Philippines, they are known for their colorful dress.

The autonomous region of the Cordilleras includes five major ethnic groups. These highlanders, or Igorots, as they are known, include the Benguet, Bontoc, Ifugao, Kalinga, and Apayao. Unconquered, they have maintained their culture, but were still in contact with Hispanized lowland people. Some of the Igorots were nomadic, but most are now

Wearing the traditional clothing of the Cordilleras, this man belongs to the Ifugaos, as indicated by the fabric's designs and colors. (Paul A. Souders/Corbis)

sedentary. One of the most impressive artifacts is the Ifugao rice terraces located in Banawe. Built between 2,000 and 3,000 years ago, these terraces on the side of mountains cover one hundred square miles (260 square kilometers).

The Hispanized

Filipino lowlanders, those who assimilated, share a common lifestyle and culture, with geography and language dividing them. There are as many as a hundred languages spoken throughout the archipelago, but nine are used by 90 percent of Filipinos. These languages are Tagalog, Cebuano, Ilokano, Hiligaynon, Bicol, Waray, Kapampangan, Pangasinanse, and Maranao. The culture they share is based on a combination of indigenous ways (from pre-Hispanic times), and has been subjected to Catholic, Spanish, American, and Chinese influence. But Filipinos are regional in their thinking and maintain

the stereotypes of other ethno-linguistic groups; their thinking was heightened by a colonial presence that sought to keep
them divided lest they unite and drive out the intruders.
Some such stereotypes are discussed in Teodoro A.
Agoncillo's *History of the Filipino People,* which has served as
an official textbook in schools in the Philippines. Beginning in
the north with the Ilocanos, Agoncillo notes: "[Ilocano] fru-
gality is proverbial and compares favorably with that of the
Scot." He continues south by remarking that a Tagalog "is at
once a lover, a born poet and a musician," and "the Visayan
is a spendthrift" yet "more self-reliant than the Tagalog."
These widely held stereotypes mask a basic truth: Lowland
Filipinos have more in common than they may realize. Kinship, not a sense of shared heritage, is the basis of connection
for Filipinos.

The Chinese

Although the Chinese had been trading in the Philippines for
centuries before the arrival of the Spaniards, they did not
begin to settle and mix with the local population until Manila
was taken by Legazpi in 1571. Known as Sangleys, they were
craftsmen and merchants. Providing labor for the Spanish in
Manila, they also were the keys to internal and external trade.
The Manila Galleon was the economic mainstay of the Spanish community and required intermediaries with Chinese
merchants who sailed into Manila every March to trade goods
from Mexico. Most of the Chinese who lived in the Philippines
were required to live in ghettos known as *parian.* They were
subject to discrimination and periodic massacres, to which
the Spaniards usually turned a blind eye.

But the Chinese persevered, creating trading networks
across the archipelago that served as the buffer between the
Spaniards and the local population. The rise of a *mestizo* class,
the *ilustrados,* was a result of the relationships between Chinese men and Filipinas. Versed in the cultures of both parents,

mestizos sought to embrace aspects of the Spanish culture. In the nineteenth century, changes in Spanish policies allowed the economic strength and reach of the Chinese community to expand. The Chinese thus came to dominate internal trade, causing resentment. The Spaniards represented a political imperialism, the Chinese an economic domination.

The economic strength of the Chinese, far out of proportion to their numbers, continued to expand during the twentieth century. The Americans sought to limit through immigration policies the economic power of the Chinese community, but to no avail, the true number of Chinese in the Philippines always being underestimated.

The rise of nationalism in China has changed the dynamic of the Chinese presence in the Philippines. A significant segment of the Chinese community has failed to become emotionally involved with life in the Philippines. Chinese schools, newspapers, and lifestyles have separated and marked as "different" Chinese immigrants from Filipinos. Seeking to hold on to their identity as Chinese while making their fortunes in the Philippines has created acrimony.

In 1990, ethnic Chinese made up less than 1 percent of the population. But intermarriage with Filipinos has made it difficult to define who is Chinese. Illegal immigration also has made it difficult to keep an accurate count of Chinese in the country. They are the least accepted ethnic group because they are perceived as controlling much of the commerce in the Philippines.

Filipinos of the Diaspora

It is estimated that within two decades, one-third of all Filipinos will live outside the archipelago. The diaspora of Filipinos has generally been in response to economic difficulties. As a result, new generations of Filipinos identify themselves by their country of birth or childhood as well as by their parents' country of origin. One hears of Filipinó Americans (or

Fil-Ams), Filipinó British (or Fil-Brits), and so on, terms used to describe the children of Filipinos raised abroad, as well as *mestizos* and *mestizas*. There are still strong ties to the homeland, even if the culture appears foreign to them.

HISTORY

When one studies the history of the Philippines, several factors should be taken into account, beginning with the tremendous diversity within the archipelago. This diversity includes language, culture, and geography; but it also includes historical experience. Thus, when one speaks of Philippine history, at best, one is looking at different aspects of that history. One should recognize and remember that the experiences in a particular place at a particular time may have been unique to the people of that place and time. Also to be considered are the geographical context, the sources used for writing Philippine history, and the colonial experiences of the people of the Philippines. It is said that it is possible to mark or delineate a people's time by the abuses they have endured. In addition to what they have suffered, people who have been under a colonial power also find that either their story is told through the lenses of their colonial masters or their story is not told at all. For much of the Spanish period, the focus of the various accounts was the Spanish presence—its activities and accomplishments. But it was not that way in the beginning.

The Southeast Asian Context

One of the more common errors made about the Philippines is to assume or even assert that the archipelago and its inhabitants are not a part of Southeast Asia. Thus, it is argued that the Filipino people and their history should be studied within the context of other Pacific island groups, or even Latin America. Much of this confusion stems from the fact that from 1565 to 1898, Spain ruled the Philippines. Thus, the dominant religion is Catholicism, which is unlike any other country in Southeast Asia. With Catholicism as the predominant religion, social customs have been affected. One hears Spanish surnames and observes the annual fiestas, which are centered around the local patron saint's day and scheduled according to the Catholic Church's calendar. One can have a sense of being in Latin America rather than in Southeast Asia.

Despite being named by outsiders after a European prince, the Philippines was and is a vital part of Southeast Asia, historically, linguistically, and culturally. In its core culture, the Philippines is a part of Southeast Asia, particularly insular Southeast Asia. Understanding that the Philippines was and is a part of the region allows one to fill in certain gaps when material about the Philippines is unavailable but is available for other parts of Southeast Asia.

It is important to understand that Southeast Asia was not a cultural *cul-de-sac,* a region catching cultural strains from India and China. Growing evidence demonstrates that instead of being the recipient of cultural influence from other areas, Southeast Asia was a source of different aspects of culture, particularly material and linguistic. D.G.E. Hall in his *History of Southeast Asia* noted a Southeast Asian core culture that included material, social, and religious components. The Philippines shared and continues to share various aspects of that culture. Perhaps the most obvious examples would be the place of rice in daily life—culinary, economic, and political; the egalitarian view of women; and the role of animism as the core value that informs almost all others in Southeast Asia.

The difference between core values and surface values must be recognized. Confusing the two may give one an incorrect perspective of Southeast Asian culture. Like much of Southeast Asia, the Philippines has been influenced by outside forces and cultures. Rather than simply taking on new cultural forms or practices, the people instead "domesticated" them and made them their own. The result is often that the visible and tangible aspects of culture (surface values) appear to have been borrowed, but the thinking behind what is seen is indigenous (core values). Much of Southeast Asia "domesticated" Indian influence, including various aspects of Hinduism, Buddhism, and Islam. And although there was some Indian influence on the Philippines, the real domestication of a foreign culture and religion took place when Filipinos encountered and dealt with the Spaniards.

Thus, it is still common to think of the Philippines in terms of the Spanish presence, and to refer to the Philippines prior to 1521 as the pre-Spanish Philippines. This includes the prehistory and early recorded history of the archipelago.

Pre-Spanish Philippines

The written materials about the pre-Spanish Philippines are not only scarce but also written almost exclusively by outsiders. Prehistory, a period when no written sources are available, is generally viewed as being a time when the population had not developed politically to the point of keeping records. As hunters and gatherers on the move, they had no need for writing. We know of no kingdoms, empires, or political realities in the Philippines of that time that kept records. It is also assumed that the inhabitants of the Philippines had no system of writing. In reality, the local population found record keeping in written form unimportant because they relied on oral tradition. A system of writing was available, but they did not employ it for writing a history. In fact, they did not keep a history, even in oral form, because their animism focused more on the present than the past.

As a result, reconstructions about pre-Hispanic society are based on archaeological evidence, the few written materials, and traces of foreign cultures. The existing evidence has been interpreted and arranged differently by different groups; thus, there is a lack of agreement about how things were.

Chinese Records

The Sung dynasty received much of its economic support from tariffs on overseas trade, and it is during this time that the first mention is made of an area believed to be the Philippines. In official Sung documents dated 972, mention is made of a place called Ma-i. Ten years later, traders from Ma-i brought goods to China. The first recorded Philippine tribute mission reached China in 1001. From the region of Butuan on Mindanao, the mission sought equal status with Champa, a kingdom in southeast Vietnam, a request that was denied because Butuan was under the authority of Champa.

Chao Ju Kua, the superintendent of maritime trade in the province of Fukien, wrote a book on the various peoples with whom the Chinese traded. Completed in 1225, it mentions Ma-i and other islands in the archipelago and locates them north of Borneo. The natives of Ma-i, according to Chao Ju Kua, lived in large villages of more than 1,000 houses. In 1349, Wang Ta-Yuan wrote an account of the places he had visited after twenty years of traveling overseas. He gave greater detail about Ma-i, and also mentioned Sulu, Mindanao, and Manila. When the Spaniards arrived, the name of the island Ma-i was changed to Mindoro because of the gold found there, *min de oro.*

When the Ming Dynasty sent emissaries in 1368 to announce its coming to power, different political entities in Luzon responded in 1373. In 1405, Feng-chia-hsi-lan (Pangasinan) in central Luzon responded to the announcement of a new emperor. Sulu, near Mindanao, sent a tribute mission to Beijing in 1417, with three leaders seeking primacy. The emperor chose Paduka Batara of the east country; however, he died in China and was buried with Chinese trappings of royalty.

Portuguese Reports

When the Portuguese came to Southeast Asia in 1511, they found individuals from Luzon in Malacca, including a colony of some five hundred Tagalogs on the west coast of the Malay peninsula. Tome Pires, who was in Malacca in 1512–1515, in his *Summa Oriental* called the people from Luzon *Luções* (Luzones) and noted that they included a number of prominent business people who ran their own shops in Malacca. The Portuguese governor appointed one of them, Regimo Diraja, police magistrate. The Portuguese Bras Bayao stated that the Luzones were good navigators and discoverers. In addition, Luzones had the reputation of being fighters, participating in various battles in the region, including the 1525 battle to retake Malacca; the siege of Acheh in 1529; and the defense of Ayutthia in 1547. Pirate crews were also known to include Luzones.

Archaeology and Reconstructions

Archaeology presents a most helpful tool when dealing with the prehistory of the Philippines. The data can be (and has been) interpreted in different ways, resulting in different reconstructions of prehistoric Philippine societies. Three aspects should be noted as significant. First is the dating of human settlements with dates earlier than previously believed. Among the oldest sites found is the Tabon Cave, on the island of Palawan, in which human fossils, dating between 24,000 and 22,000 BCE, were discovered. This discovery alone has challenged many of the assumptions made about the date of the populating of the archipelago. In another cave, the Manunggul Cave, a burial jar dating between 900 and 775 BCE was found. On the jar cover is a carving of two men rowing a *banca,* an outrigger boat, presumably to reflect a belief in the journey between the land of the living and the afterlife. Archaeological sites in other parts of the Philippines also demonstrate earlier-than-expected dates for the populating of the islands.

The second aspect of archaeological work is the presence of Chinese trade ceramics. Excavations throughout the Philippines point to extensive trading. This trading had two dimensions. First, there was trade with the outside world; that is, Chinese traders would come to various locations along the coasts of the islands and barter Chinese porcelain for local products. These products came either from the sea—tortoise shell, pearls, coral—or forests—cotton, betelnut, rattan. The second dimension is that of extensive internal trade networks, which brought goods from the interior in exchange for goods from foreign merchants, thus explaining the discovery of Chinese porcelain throughout the Philippines.

But a series of discoveries indicate a third aspect: Filipinos were not at the mercy of those who could travel the oceans because they, too, were sailors. Discoveries in the last quarter of the twentieth century of eight boats near Butuan City on Mindanao have demonstrated this. The boats were dated from the third to the fourteenth centuries CE. Their average length is fifteen meters, three meters across the beam. Their size suggests that they were capable of making long voyages, and artifacts found nearby confirm this.

The Laguna Copperplate Inscription

For all the guesswork about the prehistory of the Philippines, based on archaeological finds, accounts from outsiders, and reconstructions based on both, a recent find provides tremendous insight into the state of society, or at least some societies, in the Philippines as early as the ninth century CE. The Laguna Copperplate Inscription (LCI) was accidentally discovered in 1986 when the delta of the Pagsanjan River, near the town of Lumbang in the province of Laguna, was being dredged for sand. Originally rolled up, it measured about 7 by 12 inches when unrolled. It was not until 1990 that the artifact came to the attention of the National Museum in Manila. Antoon Postma was approached by the museum to examine and decipher what appeared to be an inscription on this piece of copper.

The results revealed a document written on the fourth day of the waning moon of the month of *Waisakha* in the *Shaka*

*The Laguna Copperplate Inscription, the oldest known document
found in the Philippines, dates from the ninth century.
(Hector Santos, "The Laguna Copperplate Inscription" in
A Philippine Leaf, at http://www.bibingka.com/dahon/lci/lci.htm)*

year 822 (April 21, 900 CE by the Western calendar). It was
not only the earliest document discovered in the Philippines
but the only pre-Spanish document discovered thus far. The
LCI was a *suddhapattra,* a legal document of pardon created
by the parties involved and then engraved on copper, a non-
perishable material. This document stated that the debt of gold
(one *kati* and eight *swarna*—the equivalent of 865 grams)
owed by Namwaran was cancelled and the document given to
his daughter Angkatan, and to Bukah, possibly her brother.
The authority to cancel the debt was exercised by Jayadewa,
ruler of Pailah, with Sumuran, the ruler of Puliran, as witness.
Also mentioned are rulers of Binwagan, Dewata, and Medang.

Written in a language unknown at this point, it contains
elements of Old Javanese, Old Malay, Old Tagalog, and Sanskrit. The LCI demonstrates significant points about the pre-
Spanish Philippines. Contrary to conventional wisdom, the
Philippines did not exist in almost total isolation from the rest
of Southeast Asia, or Asia in general. The Chinese records

indicate this, but not the complexities revealed in the LCI. Political connections between rulers in the Manila area (Paila, Puliran, and Binwagan), in Mindanao (Dewata), and Java (Medang) are demonstrated. A common or accepted system of weights and measures defined the amount of the indebtedness being cancelled. It is worth noting that within the Southeast Asian context, the *suddhapattra* was intended for a woman, Angkatan, the daughter of the debtor.

Sanskrit was used for the technical terms, specifically the dating of the documents and the political titles of the individuals involved. Although it is the farthest Southeast Asian country from India, the Philippines was affected by the process known as Indianization. The method or methods of transmitting this influence are unknown, but the results are evident, particularly in terms of language. Juan R. Francisco has identified 150 separate Sanskrit words that are the origin of Philippine terms. More than half of these are in Tagalog, the language used in the Manila Bay area, and the other two major languages, Bisayan and Ilokano, were also affected.

Perhaps one of the most fascinating revelations of the LCI is that place names used in the document still remain, more than eleven centuries later. Tundun for modern-day Tondo; Puliran for Pulilan in Bulacan on the Angat River; Paila for farther up the Angat River at the Ipo Dam site; and Binwangan at the mouth of the Bulacan River, near Obando. Chao Ju Kua mentions Tondo in 1225; when the Spanish arrived in Manila in 1570, they recorded that Tondo was located across the river from Manila.

The results paint a picture that is different from what was previously suggested. The archipelago was not an isolated outpost but an active and interactive part of the region, and a recognized location.

THE SPANISH PERIOD

The Spaniards stumbled on to the Philippines while seeking a new route to the Moluccas, which were also known as the

The Lapu-Lapu Monument marks the site where Lapu-Lapu, a local leader, killed Ferdinand Magellan on Mactan Island. (Jan Butchofsky-Houser/Corbis)

Spice Islands. The Portuguese navigator, Ferdinand Magellan, had been to the Spice Islands and believed that they could be reached by sailing west around South America rather than east around Africa. He convinced Charles V of Spain to fund the expedition. Equipped with five aging vessels and 235 men, Magellan left San Lucar, Spain, on September 20, 1519. Only one ship, the *Victoria,* would return with eighteen of the original 235 men, as well as three captives who were probably Filipinos (the first to arrive in the West), on September 6, 1522—the first European vessel to circumnavigate the globe.

The voyage was brutally difficult. The expedition lost one ship in Argentina and another while rounding the southern tip of South America. The men were reduced to eating rats, leather, and sawdust. On March 16, 1521, they sighted land south of the island of Samar. Locals advised them to go to Cebu for food, and on April 7 they arrived on the island. The local leader was named Humabon, whom Magellan convinced to convert to the Catholic faith and then placed in charge of the other local leadership. This move was resisted by some of those leaders, including Lapu-lapu, a leader from the nearby island of Mactan. A battle ensued, and Magellan was killed and his men forced to leave the archipelago. The survivors reached Tidore and were able to buy spice to bring to Spain.

After the return of the single vessel, Spain sent other expeditions, not to return to the Philippines but to reach the Spice Islands. In 1527, the first expedition in the Pacific was launched from the Americas. The expedition led by Ruy Lopez de Villalobos and launched from Acapulco in 1542 with six ships and 370 men reached the Philippines without incident. Villalobos named the part of the archipelago he encountered *Islas Felipinas* in honor of Prince Philip of Spain, who would later as king be responsible for a permanent Spanish presence in the Philippines.

In 1564, Miguel Lopez de Legazpi left Mexico with four ships and 380 men. Andres de Urdaneta, an Augustinian friar and survivor of an earlier expedition, served as navigator. He joined the expedition believing that the Spice Islands, not the Philippines, were their goal. After arriving in the Philippines, Urdaneta led a return voyage by what is now known as the Urdaneta Passage, thus marking the first such journey on a route that was used by the galleons until the nineteenth century. The arrival of this group marked the beginning of a permanent Spanish presence in the Philippines. Their first fort was built in Cebu, and the second on the nearby island of Panay. Finding sufficient food was the most significant problem during the first three decades of the Spanish presence in the Philippines. The local agricultural system was subsistence, not surplus, meaning there was not enough food for the Spaniards. Reinforcements and supplies arrived from Mexico in 1566, 1567, and 1571 and enabled the Spaniards to prepare to take Manila, the trading center of the islands and an outpost of Muslim Brunei. On May 19, 1571, Legazpi took Manila without bloodshed, and on June 3, he proclaimed it the capital of the Spanish presence. From Manila, expeditions were sent out to explore and conquer the rest of Luzon.

One thing that should be kept in mind about the colonial powers that came to the Philippines is that the Philippines was not their primary goal: Magellan was looking for the Spice Islands. The United States kept the Philippines as a location near China for trade. The Japanese wanted to eliminate the American presence and threat to Japanese activities in the region.

For the civil authorities, the Manila Galleon was the economic lifeline of the colony. Because foreigners were not allowed to enter China, the Philippines provided a neutral location where Spaniards could trade with Chinese merchants. A ship owned by the Spanish Crown would leave Acapulco in February or March loaded with goods from Mexico— primarily silver and chocolate—and with passengers such as government officials and their families, soldiers, and priests. Thirty to forty Chinese junks would arrive in Manila in March with various goods, primarily silk and porcelain. Transactions would take place in Manila. To encourage immigration to this isolated outpost of the Spanish Empire, the Spanish residents all shared in the profits of the trade.

Although the Chinese had been trading with Filipinos for centuries, they did not establish significant communities in the Philippines until the Spaniards settled in Manila. The Spanish authorities looked to the Chinese for skilled labor and economic matters. Because of the small number of Spaniards in the Philippines, the Chinese became the economic buffer between the Philippine economy, which had a strong barter component (though not exclusively so), and the Spanish market, which was monetary in nature. Although the Chinese had been trading in the islands for centuries, the coming of the Spaniards and the need for such a buffer marked the beginning of Chinese communities and intermarriage with Filipinas, resulting in *mestizos,* the basis of a new class in Philippine society.

The Friars

It has been said that "the Spanish history of the Philippines begins and ends with the friar" (León Ma. Guerrero). Indeed, the one constant of the Spanish presence in the islands was the friars, members of various mendicant orders. Beginning with the arrival of six Augustinians with Legazpi in 1565, the friars came as *doctrineros,* or teachers; today, they would be called missionaries. The Philippines presented a double opportunity for the various Orders: to regain what they had lost in the Americas and a place from which to launch missionary activity in China. As an archipelago, the Philippines presented problems as well as opportunities. Faced with the absence of a common language, Spanish authorities decided, contrary to Crown policy in the Americas, to divide the Philippines according to linguistic groups and to assign them to the Orders. The intent was that each Order could concentrate its linguistic and teaching efforts on the specific groups to which they had been assigned. The exception to this policy was the Tagalog region, including Manila and the provinces surrounding it. Here, every Order was given the freedom to work.

The Orders became extremely powerful. Being the only Spaniards outside of Manila most of the time and the only Spaniards who spoke local dialects, they acted as the conduit through which civil authority had to work in the areas outside Manila. Without their cooperation, which they withheld from time to time, little could be communicated to the local population. Their financial support came from the *Patronato Real,* the Royal Patronage, which meant that they had a certain amount of legal authority. Filipinos seeking to deal with the Spanish authorities in Manila would have to go through the Spanish friars in their home districts. Finally, the Orders remained powerful by virtue of being Orders; individual members might leave or die, but the Orders remained. Over the years, through legal and suspect means, the Orders acquired vast *haciendas,* also a source of support and power. Thus, their power was disproportionate to their numbers. In addition, no Filipino could join the Orders because the policy of *limpieza de sangre,* purity of blood, required racial purity— in Spanish terms.

During the early decades of the Spanish presence, Spanish officials and friars took an interest in the customs and religious practices of the Filipinos. The reasons for this interest varied from a desire to know how to control the local population—either for political or religious purposes—to a natural curiosity. It is from the written accounts and reports as well as the policies and actions of the officials and friars of those early years that we learn the most about Philippine society and culture. Three areas of Philippine society and culture surprised the Spaniards and, in some ways, are still surprising them today.

Because the friars had come to convert, they explored and wrote about the religion and religious practices of the locals, whom the Spaniards considered pagans. In reality, the Filipinos were animists at the time of the Spanish intrusion, and in a real sense remain animistic in their core beliefs and values. Animism, or what some call primitive religion, is a basic belief that a force or power animates the universe. There are some important implications of this belief system, the first being the central place of power in the thinking and worldview of Filipinos. As Benedict Anderson has wonderfully detailed in his essay, "The Idea of Power in Javanese Culture," the definition of power in the lives of the Javanese (and by extension, in the lives of Southeast Asians generally) is radically different from that of the West. Perhaps the most significant difference is that the cultures of the West focus on the exercise of power, but those of Southeast Asia, including the Philippines, focus on the accumulation of power. Believing that the amount of power in the universe is constant, the distribution of power is the issue. If one accumulates power, someone or something else must lose power. If the individual accumulates power, he will experience a loss in another area of life (the principle of compensation). For example, if one abstains from food, sleep, or sex, one can gain power. Again, in the West, these forms of abstinence are seen as secular or religious asceticism; but in the Philippines and Southeast Asia, they are a means to an end. Along with this asceticism came rituals and objects that were also means to that end. Rituals that contained ascetic aspects were important. One finds an obsession with ceremonies in the Philippines, particularly those introduced by the friars. However, these ceremonies were assigned animistic significance—a means of accumulating power. The possession of certain objects that were believed to have power was another path to the gaining of power. The friars brought with them religious images and, later, relics, which were viewed in a different light by their new converts.

But the friars failed to understand the disconnect between the new faith they were bringing and how their new converts understood and embraced the practices of that new religion. As John Phelan noted, Filipinos were "no mere passive recipients of the cultural stimulus created by the Spanish conquest." Phelan devoted an entire chapter to what he called the Philippinization of Catholicism in which he described those practices of Catholicism embraced by the Filipinos, including fiestas and the ritual of confession. The friars, and Phelan as well, failed to recognize that the thinking of Filipinos was different from that of the friars who had brought them a new religion.

The weakness of any animistic system is the absence of a true ethical system; morality is often not the issue, but rather how one can gain power. In what could be viewed as the quest for a holy life or a more righteous way of life, the individual abstains from certain practices while engaging in others. In reality, the individual might be seeking to gain some benefit, favor, or power. This is illustrated by the practice of some Filipinos who, during Holy Week, flagellate themselves or submit to being crucified, although only for a short time. The person crucified either is seeking a favor or is paying a debt to God for a favor received. Those watching the event might try to collect drops of the crucified individual's blood on pieces of cloth; they then bury the bloodied cloths in their fields to obtain a better harvest. The core value is animistic, but the surface value, the observable, is Catholic.

In their reports, the friars focused on the religious personages of the Filipino cosmology. Thus, they wrote of *Bathala Maikapal,* the creator deity, which they saw as matching the Christian God. Although pre-Spanish Filipinos might have believed in a creator, such a being was seen as distant and not interested in the affairs of humanity. In reality, spirits, or *anito* (a word found from one end of the archipelago to the other), were the ones to be reckoned with in daily matters. Problems, disease, and other difficulties were believed to be caused by such spirits, and therefore the anitos had to be appeased. The religious system, if it could be called that, revolved around dealing with these spirits. The Spanish friars viewed such practices as pagan and disturbing; but one other aspect of these practices also disturbed them—women as leaders.

Women in Philippine Society

The second surprise to greet the Spanish intruders was a society that had no subordinate position for women. Such an egalitarian view of women ran counter to the Spanish vision of society. One's ancestry was reckoned bilaterally; that is, from both the father's and the mother's side. Particularly offensive was the sexual freedom women enjoyed. Premarital sex was approved of, and women could initiate divorce proceedings as easily as men. Women as religious leaders created the most problems for the Spaniards. In the local religion, "priests," or those who served as intermediaries with the spirits, were usually women known as *babaylans* or *katalonans.* Men who served in this capacity dressed as women. The intrusion of the Spaniards was resisted by the spiritual leaders (women) but not the political leaders (men). Spanish accounts tell how *babaylans* led men into battle in attempts to withstand the Spanish efforts at conquest.

Seeking to neutralize or blunt the force and authority of women leaders, the Spaniards appropriated a local myth involving the *aswang*. The *aswang* in local folklore was a shapeshifter—an animal that could change its shape and appearance. This myth was changed, and the new *aswang* was a Filipina, specifically, one who was a *babaylan*. One of the earliest accounts by a Spanish Franciscan flatly affirmed that the *babaylans* were *aswangs*. Among the changes made in the local myth of the *aswang* was the belief that this shape-shifter was a viscera-sucker who preyed on people at night, particularly on the unborn children of pregnant women. It was said that such women would go through a self-segmenting process in which the lower part of the body—the reproductive half—is left behind, and the upper half takes part in killing. The *aswang* was said to have a penchant for human fetuses, internal organs, and bodily discharges. Its tongue could be elongated until it was as thin as thread and could be stuck through thatched roofs to take those things they desired. In addition, the *aswang* could use her long fingernails to cut open a pregnant woman's stomach and steal the child.

One might wonder how the Spaniards came up with such an elaborate mythology, but it should be kept in mind that the image that emerged was a reversal of roles for the *babaylan*. The woman who had been a healer and midwife in the community was now cast as the killer of unborn children. And the *aswang* was portrayed as one with no sense of family solidarity, no sense of kinship. To become an *aswang*, one had to cannibalize a member of her family; that is, the basic unit in society was rejected. So, in seeking to force a change in the Philippine view of women, the Spaniards created a myth to destroy the most important role for women, that of *babaylan*. It is worth noting that the *aswang* remains one of the monster stories in Philippine society. As recently as 2004, two persons in the Metro-Manila area were decapitated by their neighbors because they were believed to be *aswangs.*

Ironically, although the formal leadership position of women as leaders in religious matters was taken away, Filipinas became and remained the most devout Catholics. And the dominant figures in Philippine Catholicism are the Virgin Mary and her son, the Santo Niño. It was the motherhood of Mary, her function as mediator and her ability to intercede with God on behalf of others, traits similar to those of the *babaylan,* that have allowed her to have such a dominant place in Philippine Catholicism.

The Literate Filipino

The third surprise was the existence of a literate society. Early accounts from civil and ecclesiastical authorities record that the majority of the population in certain parts, such as Manila and its surrounding region, were literate. Although modern scholars have struggled with these reports—and there are many such reports—the evidence of widespread literacy is persuasive. The Tagalogs (among others) had a system of writing known as *baybayin.* (It is common today to refer to the system as *alibata.* This incorrect name was the invention of Dean Paul Versoza of the University of Manila, who coined the term *alibata* in 1914. It was his claim that *alibata* was based on the first three letters, *alif, ba, ta,* of the Maguindanao arrangement of Arabic letters.) The system of writing was not alphabetic but rather a syllabary, sharing the Sanskrit characteristic of a consonant being pronounced with the vowel following it, with diacritical marks being added to express other vowels.

The greatest proof of such literacy is the printing program created by the Spaniards to reach this literate population. The Spanish friars, or *doctrineros,* came to the Philippines to evangelize and to disciple the local population. This required learning the language and then communicating the Catholic faith to Filipinos, but there were difficulties. Rituals, such as baptism, were often performed with little explanation, but they were embraced by Filipinos as potentially new means of acquiring power. After being in the Manila area for two decades, several of the friars emerged as experts in local languages and could effectively translate important aspects of the Catholic religion into Tagalog. But their skills were not shared by every friar. The reality of a literate population presented another means of indoctrinating Filipinos—through printing.

The Spaniards did not come to the Philippines prepared to engage in a printing ministry, and thus brought no presses with them. But there were individuals in the Philippines familiar with the technology of printing: Chinese who had converted to Catholicism. They were employed to construct the first printing press in the Philippines. The press used xylography, in which the letters or characters were hand-carved into blocks of wood; the block was then inked and pressed against paper. (Although the technology was Chinese and not practiced among Filipinos, there was an indigenous word for the process—*limbag*.) In 1593, the first book, *Doctrina Christiana*, was printed. It contained various prayers and other religious materials, such as the Lord's Prayer, Hail Mary, the Ten Commandments, and a brief catechism. The book was written in Spanish and Tagalog in Romanized letters and then in *baybayin*. It is clear that the book was intended for the local population and not the friars. It is also clear that the Spaniards were attempting to encourage Tagalogs to make the transition from Tagalog written in *baybayin* to Tagalog written in Romanized letters. Between 1593 and 1610, the Spanish friars published various works in Tagalog for the local population. The most significant figure in this process was the Dominican friar Francisco Blancas de San José. Of the first six books printed by the Spaniards in Tagalog for the Tagalogs, only the first, the Doctrina Christiana, was not written by Blancas de San José.

In 1604, the Dominicans began to use moveable type. This signaled the end of the use of *baybayin* in printing. In 1608, the press was moved to the town of Abucay, in Bataan. This move brought about significant changes and events, for example, printing was now exclusively done with Romanized letters. It was also in Abucay that Filipinos replaced the Chinese as printers. One of these Filipinos was a Tagalog named Tomas Pinpin. Not only did he print Blancas de San José's Tagalog grammar for a Spanish audience, but a Filipino named Diego Talaghay published Pinpin's own work, *Librong pagaaralan nang manga Tagalog nang uicang Castila* (a book designed to teach Tagalogs the Spanish language). Pinpin's stated goals were to help Tagalogs learn Spanish in order to become better Christians and to create bi-lingual *Tagalogs-ladinos,* as he called them. Ladinos would be able to speak, read, and write in Tagalog (with Romanized letters) and in Spanish. His true purpose was subversive: He wanted to help his people survive in a world and a marketplace dominated and controlled by the Spanish intruders.

The attitude of the friars towards the local population changed over time. Phelan has noted that the Christianization of the Philippines (from 1565 to 1700) can be divided into three periods: (1) preparatory and exploratory; (2) the golden age of missionary work; and (3) acute disappointment. The period after 1700 could be categorized as one of cynicism towards Filipinos and conflict with the civil government.

REVOLTS

After this time of exploration and reporting to Spain about various aspects of the Philippines, the Spaniards, both civil and ecclesiastical, settled down to the business of running the colony. And, as stated above, their reports back to Spain focused less and less on the local population—unless there were problems. Between 1569 and 1898, there were at least eighty-five significant revolts, some political, some religious, and some in response to social and economic dislocation. These are the times when the local population shows up in Spanish reports.

The Spaniards responded harshly to such resistance to their rule. It is important to note that this presentation is not intended to view the story of Filipinos in terms of their responses to intrusion and oppression, but to challenge the notion of passive acceptance, as well as to chart in part changes in Philippine society.

Revolts in the Seventeenth Century

In 1621–1622, an outlawed *babaylan* named Tamblot, from the island of Bohol, began to lead his people away from Catholicism toward a return to the old ways. He guaranteed that the spirits of their ancestors and other spirits would support them and bring back to life anyone killed in battle by the Spaniards. Two thousand joined his movement, but Spanish authorities, with the help of Cebuano auxiliaries, easily crushed it. Tamblot's actions triggered another revolt on the nearby island of Leyte, led by Bankaw, the *datu* of Limasawa, and the *babaylan* Pagali. Bankaw had welcomed Legazpi in 1565 and had been baptized as a young man. This revolt marked a desire to return to the old ways. Bankaw was captured and decapitated, his head put on a stake and publicly displayed as a warning against rebelling against the Spanish presence.

The appropriation of the new language of Catholicism was demonstrated in a revolt in 1663. A Christianized *babaylan* named Tapar, in the province of Iloilo, proclaimed himself God Almighty. Dressing as a woman, as most *babaylanes* in the Bisayas were women, he used Catholic terminology to establish a new religion, combining aspects from the old religion with Catholicism. He rejected the need for Spanish priests and argued that his people had their own priests, bishops, and popes. After his followers killed a Spanish friar and burned his house and church, they escaped to the mountains. Through the use of spies and Cebuano mercenaries, the Spaniards captured most of the leaders of this revolt.

The most significant revolt of the century, in that it posed a direct threat to the continued Spanish presence in Manila, occurred from 1660 through 1661. In response to the oppressive draft labor system *(polo)*, 1,000 men revolted under the leadership of Francisco Manyago. What began among the Kapampangans (people from the province of Pampanga) spread to the northern provinces, including Pangasinan and Ilocos. The Spaniards and Kapampangans were quick to reach a settlement because Manila needed the food and materiel, as well as soldiers, provided by Pampanga, and Pampanga needed military protection against their neighbors in Zambales. The Ilocanos and those from Pangasinan continued the bloody revolt, killing friars and looting and desecrating churches. Although their forces included more than 9,000 men, these Filipinos were ultimately defeated by Spanish forces and their leaders executed.

Revolts in the Eighteenth Century

Where earlier revolts had resisted Spanish authority, policies, and religion, the revolt of 1745, the first among the Tagalogs, was in response to the acquisition of land by the various Orders through fraud. The issue was the ownership of certain lands, the conflict being between communities, the towns versus the haciendas owned by the various Orders. An investigation by Pedro Calderón, an *oidor* assigned to the task, revealed the Orders to be in the wrong. The Spanish Crown accepted and acknowledged Calderon's findings, but little was done to correct the situation. The Philippine revolution, which would occur 150 years later, had its roots in this revolt.

In 1762, Diego Silang, an Ilocano from Pangasinan, along with leaders from the Ilocos region, Abra, and Cagayan, led a revolt in Northern Luzon; tribute and draft labor were the issues that sparked this uprising. Silang proclaimed Vigan the capital of Free Ilocos. At about the same time, the British attacked and took the Philippines from Spain, and recognized

Silang as the legitimate head of the Ilocos government. Bishop Bernardo Ustariz, the bishop of Vigan, proclaimed himself the provincial head, excommunicated Silang, and then arranged to have Silang assassinated. Gabriela Silang, Silang's widow, continued the revolt. She was captured and executed by the Spanish authorities.

Revolts in the Nineteenth Century

Leading up to the Philippine Revolution in 1896, a series of millenarian movements and subsequent revolts took place, the two most significant having their origins in the *cofradias,* or Catholic organizations/brotherhoods.

The first such movement was led by a devout peasant named Apolinario de la Cruz. He left his home for Manila to join the priesthood, only to discover that the various religious orders did not accept *indios,* the name by which Spaniards referred to Filipinos. While appealing the decision, he continued his studies and established in 1832, along with other men from his home province, a *cofradia* whose membership would be open only to Filipinos. Named *Hermandad de la Archi-Cofradia del Glorioso Señor San Jose y de la Virgen del Rosario* (Brotherhood of the Great Sodality of the Glorious Lord Saint Joseph and of the Virgin of the Rosary), it was known as the *Cofradía de San José.* The small group remained unnoticed by Spanish authorities from 1832 to 1840. After de la Cruz's final appeal to enter the priesthood was rejected in 1840, the movement left Manila and returned to the province, where it experienced an explosion of growth. Persecution by fearful Spanish religious authorities served to radicalize the group and resulted in two major battles. The *cofradia* was successful in the first but devastated in the second. De la Cruz was captured and executed on November 4, 1841.

Another *cofradia,* established in Manila at the Santo Domingo convent in 1872 by church officials, was the *Guardia de Honor de Maria* (Mary's Honor Guard). Minimal requirements and the colorful scapularies worn by members led to an explosion of growth, both in the Manila area and in the provinces. The shortage of priests to oversee the *cofradia* resulted in the movement embracing indigenous practices along with Catholic rituals. Julian Baltazar, from the town of Urdaneta, became the unofficial leader. When the Church withdrew recognition, the severing of ties was complete. Persecution and conflict resulted in a militarized group that became a significant force during the Philippine Revolution.

THE IMPACT OF THE SPANISH PRESENCE

Although there is more to tell about the Spanish time in the Philippines, identifying and discussing the impact of the Spanish presence on the Philippines will help finish the story and explain the paradoxes found in the Philippines.

Spain *unified* the archipelago; that is, the Spanish intruders set the boundaries for the territory they called the Philippines. This geographical definition of the Philippines remains to the present. At the same time, Spain *divided* the peoples of the archipelago because their policies exploited the differences between the various ethnic groups. For example, the Spanish government divided up the archipelago along ethno-linguistic lines to assign fields of mission work to the Orders. The friars learned the languages of their regions and became the conduit of communication between civil authorities and the local population. Thus, interaction between the different linguistic groups declined under this Spanish arrangement. In addition, whenever one ethno-linguistic group revolted, the Spaniards sent soldiers from other groups to subdue them. As a result, the differences between the various groups of the Philippines were emphasized. Such differences have been retained in the minds of many Filipinos and have resulted in the absence of real national unity. Unfortunately, written records do not exist, but archaeological records demonstrate significant interaction between various ethnic groups prior to the Spanish intrusion.

Perhaps the most visible impact of the Spanish colonial presence was the importation of Catholicism. Although transformed by what Phelan has called the Philippinization of Catholicism, in which "the Filipinos endowed certain aspects of the new religion with a ceremonial and emotional content" (Phelan 1959:72), the Roman Catholic Church remains a lasting reminder of the Spanish presence. Its importance or significance in the rest of the story of Spanish colonialism is seen in several areas. First, the language and symbols of the Church were co-opted by Filipinos, including those opposing Spanish religious leadership, as seen in the millenarian revolts of the nineteenth century. Second, it was the conflict between Filipino priests and the Spanish friars that ultimately led to the revolution of 1896.

But the most important impact of the Spanish presence was the changing of the face of Philippine society. The Spanish presence and their policies, knowingly or unknowingly, restructured the societies of those Filipinos under their rule, particularly in the creation of social classes. Philippine societies prior to the coming of the Spaniards did not have classes as such, although the Spaniards thought they did and acted on that belief. The place of animism and their view of power allowed for great fluidity in social structure, a fluidity the Spaniards either did not understand or refused to accept. Thus, indigenous leadership positions were made hereditary by the Spaniards, for example, enabling the rise of an elite class. Those Filipinos who became bilingual, in Spanish and their own language, were known as *ladinos*. The offspring of unions between Spaniards and Filipinas, and well as those between Chinese and Filipinas, produced *mestizos*. In addition, those Filipinos chosen to manage the haciendas of the Orders gained economic affluence and came to be known in the nineteenth century as *ilustrados*. These groups together formed an elite class that gravitated toward the Spanish world and its culture rather than that of the indigenous population. The result was a cultural divide that remains to this day. Even though they fought against the Spaniards in the revolution, they did so for different reasons.

Two additional consequences of the Spanish presence should be mentioned. In the face of the Spanish presence and all it entailed, such as oppression and marginalization, Filipinos developed coping mechanisms that were survival values more than surface values. Unfortunately, these values have been mistaken as indigenous rather than reactive. The process of responding to the presence of foreigners and their culture, which had been adopted as much as allowed by the new elite, resulted in what is known as the colonial mentality, a sense of cultural and, ultimately, racial inferiority. Thus, anything foreign was considered superior to anything Filipino. Pride in one's culture and language was replaced with a desire to adopt foreign ways.

The Road to Revolution

The year 1872 saw a pivotal event in Philippine history. After a brief flirtation with allowing Filipinos (those Hispanized and in the Manila area) certain freedoms, political changes in Spain resulted in a return to repressive policies. This conservative shift was due in no small part to the influence of the friars who believed the *indios* were unqualified to participate in civic matters.

Early in the morning of January 20, 1872, the Filipino workers at the Cavite Arsenal discovered, to their surprise and anger, a new deduction in their already meager wages. In response, they "revolted" in what was a labor dispute, or strike. Several Spanish soldiers were killed, leading the governor of Cavite to telegraph Manila about a "rebellion." Military units were sent and the "rebellion" was put down; the leaders and some participants were arrested and executed. However, the Spanish authorities used this event as an excuse to arrest Filipinos they believed to be a threat to the regime, accusing them of complicity with the strike.

Although some Filipino civilians and priests were exiled to Guam, three priests, Fr. Mariano Gomes (aged eighty-four) of Bacoor, Cavite; Fr. Jose Burgos (aged thirty-five); and Fr. Jacinto Zamora (aged thirty-seven), all of the Manila Cathedral, were found guilty of treason and sentenced to death. Their real crime was their work as leading advocates of equality for Filipino priests with Spanish friars. On February 17, 1872, the three priests were executed by garrote at Bagumbayan. The Spaniards had relative peace for the next twenty years. But Filipinos, including the elite, realized that being Filipino, to any degree, would always make them suspect and second class in the eyes of the Spanish authorities. Fr. Jose Burgos, who had a doctorate in canon law, was the son of a Spanish father and a Spanish *mestiza* mother, but the fact that he had Filipino blood condemned him. The priests are considered martyrs and are collectively referred to as *Gomburza,* a name formed from the first syllables of their last names.

Filipino responses to the Spanish presence and Spanish oppression, particularly as seen in the activities of the friars, developed on two fronts. In fact, it has become popular to think of the struggles of the nineteenth century in terms of two different aspects of Philippine society. Those educated within the Spanish system, particularly those who traveled to Europe to further their education, were influenced by liberal political theories and began to agitate for equal rights for the Philippines. On the other hand, the peasantry thought simply in terms of liberation or freedom. So while the *ilustrados* thought in terms of reform, others thought in terms of revolution. The controversy carried over after the revolution when it was asked who the national hero should be—Jose Rizal, from the bourgeois class, who rejected the use of violence, or Andres Bonifacio, who had pushed for revolution.

After the execution of the three priests, the situation in the Philippines remained relatively quiet for more than a decade. It was among the sons of wealthy Filipino families who traveled to Europe, primarily Spain, that discussions began about changes in the Philippines. Because these sons enjoyed the freedoms in Spain not available to their countrymen, their discussions focused on what could be done in Spain for change in the Philippines. Experience had proved that attempts to work for change in the Philippines would result in more difficulties for Filipinos. This movement was called the Reform Movement because it advocated political, social, and religious reforms in the Philippines, reflecting conditions in Spain. The goal was reform, not revolution; assimilation, not separation. This group was also known as the Propaganda Movement because its members wrote and published essays and articles in Spain to inform Spaniards of conditions in the archipelago and to express their ideas regarding possible reforms. In 1889, the Propaganda Movement began to publish *La Solidaridad* (Solidarity), a newspaper in which members wrote of their hopes for change in the Philippines.

Although brilliant and gifted individuals were a part of this movement, little change was seen. Divisions within the movement affected what little impact it might have had. Three individuals, each from a different background, stand out as pillars of this movement: Graciano Lopez Jaena, Marcelo H. del Pilar, and Jose Rizal.

Graciano Lopez Jaena was from the central part of the Philippines. He studied in a seminary but, because of a story he had written about a certain friar, he had to move to Manila and then to Spain. There, he studied medicine, first in Valencia and later in Madrid. Of the members of the movement, he was the great public speaker and had the ability to move crowds with his speeches. In time, he became an embarrassment to the Filipino community for his eccentricities. It is said that he wore ragged clothing and spent most of his waking hours sitting in a café, drinking wine. However, when *La Solidaridad* was founded, he was made the first editor. Fearing that he would not do the required work, his friends paid his living expenses in return for work he did for the paper. But his life began to spiral downward. He contracted tuberculosis and died on January 20, 1896.

Marcelo H. del Pilar was the political analyst of the movement. After attending the University of Santo Tomas for his law degree, del Pilar traveled and campaigned against the abuses of the friars. He also sought to encourage Filipinos to embrace work, self-respect, and dignity. He founded a newspaper, *Diariong Tagalog* (Tagalog Newspaper) in 1882, but had to leave the country in 1888 because of things he had written in that newspaper. Two aspects of his work with the newspaper should be noted. First, he wrote in Tagalog. (Other members of the Reform Movement wrote in Spanish because they wrote their articles in Spain.) Del Pilar would write in Spanish eventually, but when in the Philippines, he preferred his native tongue. Second, he used satire and parody when writing about the friars, one of the reasons he had to leave in 1888. In Spain, he became editor of *La Solidaridad,* replacing Jaena. The aims of *La Solidaridad* were expanded under his leadership: He wrote in favor of assimilation, demanding that the Philippines be Hispanized. However, before his death, he became disillusioned and, in a break with Rizal and others, switched from supporting assimilation to revolution. On July 4, 1896, del Pilar died in Spain of malnutrition.

Jose Rizal is the best-known of those in the Reform Movement. The seventh of eleven children, he showed intellectual prowess. At the age of twelve, he was sent to Manila to study, first at the Ateneo de Manila, a school run by the Jesuits. The Jesuits had a strong influence on Rizal, and when he left them he was a devout Catholic. He then enrolled at the University of Santo Tomas, a school run by the Dominicans. It was here that Rizal underwent significant changes. During his years at the university, his parents were treated unjustly, and his mother was imprisoned for one year. Rizal also experienced injustice. When he was eighteen, he entered a literary contest and won first prize; but the prize was withdrawn when it was

*A memorial found at the Luneta, location of the execution of the
national hero Jose Rizal. (Leslie Laddaran)*

discovered that he was a Filipino. These events convinced
Rizal that Filipinos would not be given justice in their own
country. On the advice of his older brother, Paciano, Rizal left
the Philippines to continue his medical training in Spain. His
achievements are staggering: He was a poet, a painter, a sculptor (having won medals for his work), a novelist, a historian
(having annotated Antonio de Morga's 1609 *Sucesos de los
Islas Filipinas*), a physician, an ophthalmologist, a surgeon,
and a philologist. He spoke Spanish, Latin, French, Italian,
English, German, Japanese, Dutch, Catalan, Tagalog, Visayan,
Ilocano, Cebuano, Subano, and Malayan. He could translate
Greek, Hebrew, Arabic, Sanskrit, and Chinese. He could read
Russian, Swedish, and Portuguese.

But his best known accomplishments are the two novels he
wrote. It was his first novel, *Noli Me Tangere,* that brought
him to the attention of the Spanish friars and thus the Spanish authorities in the Philippines. Written when Rizal was
twenty-six, and although a novel, it was an accurate descrip-
tion of life in the Philippines under the tyrannical rule of the

friars. The title can be translated as *Do Not Touch Me,* and Rizal is said to have taken it from the Gospel of St. John, in which the resurrected Jesus tells Mary, "Do not touch me." He chose the title because he wrote of things that were considered so sensitive they were untouchable. Written in Spanish, it was printed in Germany, and only 2,000 copies were printed. Its impact was immediate and profound, with friars condemning it and punishing anyone caught reading it. The book scathingly exposed the corruption and cruelty of the friars, which was all too familiar to most Filipinos.

A sequel, *El Filibusterismo,* dedicated to the memory of Gomez, Burgos, and Zamora, was published in 1891. In the dedication, Rizal wrote of the three priests:

> The church, by refusing to degrade you, has placed in doubt the crime that has been imputed to you; the government, by surrounding your trials with mystery and shadows, causes the belief that there was some error, committed in fatal moments, and the entire Philippines, by worshipping your memory and calling you martyrs, in some sense recognizes your culpability.
>
> In so far, therefore, as your complicity in the Cavite mutiny is not clearly proved, as you may or may not have been patriots, and as you may or may not have cherished sentiments for justice and for liberty, I have the right to dedicate my work to you as victims of the evil which I undertake to combat. And while we await that Spain some day shall restore your good name and shall cease to be a party to your death, let these pages serve as a tardy wreath of dried leaves over your unknown tombs, and any one who, without clear proofs, attacks your memory, stains his hands in your blood.

The novel was political and dealt in part with the real possibility of violence as a means to ending Spanish rule. The dichotomy in Philippine society between the elite and peasants was vividly illustrated in both novels, the central question being how Filipinos should respond to Spanish injustice in allowing the friars free rein—self-improvement or violence?

Rizal returned to the Philippines in 1892. On July 3, he founded *La Liga Filipina* (the Philippine League), a civic organization seeking reform and the improvement of conditions for all Filipinos. Some of the aims of the organization were to unite the archipelago; to provide mutual protection for its members, as well as defense against violence and injustice; to encourage education, agriculture, and commerce; and to study and bring about reforms. Rizal was arrested three days later and exiled to the town of Dapitan, in northwestern Mindanao. His arrest and exile ended all hopes for achieving the goals of the Reform Movement.

In its place came a new organization. The day after Rizal was exiled, July 7, 1892, a secret organization was founded. Its name was *Kataastaasan Kagalang-galang na Katipunan nang mga Anak nang Bayan,* or the Highest and Most Respectable Association of the Sons of the Land. It came to be known as the *Katipunan,* or Association, for short. Its aims were threefold: political, moral, and civic. The political goal was separation from Spain while seeking to educate Filipinos and instill in them the principle of self-help and defense of those in need.

Influenced by contacts with Masonic lodges established in the Philippines by *ilustrados* who had joined the Masonic orders in Spain, the *Katipunan* employed secret rituals for those joining. When an individual wished to join, he was asked three questions: What was the condition of the Philippines in early times? What is its condition today? What will be its condition in the future? If the applicant answered the questions correctly, and because he had been provided the answers beforehand, he was asked whether he wanted to continue and whether he had the courage to continue. If he answered affirmatively, he was taken into another room, where his courage was tested. If he passed this physical test, he was brought to yet another room, where the final rites took place. An incision was made in his left forearm, and he signed the oath of membership with his own blood. (Some of these documents have survived to the present and can be viewed at the Philippine National Library in Manila.) But there were significant differences between the *Katipunan* and the *Liga*. Their names alone give indications of this. The *Liga* had a Spanish name, the *Katipunan* a Tagalog name. The *Liga* was a Philippine organization, the *Katipunan* was, at least in the early stages, a Tagalog organization. The *Katipunan* was a secret organization, the *Liga* had been established in the open. Perhaps most significantly, the *Liga* sought reform, but the *Katipunan* was aiming for revolution.

After Rizal was exiled to Dapitan on Mindanao, both the *Liga* and *Katipunan* struggled, the *Liga* finally dying out. But beginning in 1895, events in the Philippines started to move at a dizzying pace. The catalyst was Andres Bonifacio. He had been present at the founding of both the *Liga* and *Katipunan,* but eventually realized that neither one was having a real impact. In 1895, Bonifacio took control of the *Katipunan* and made significant changes. In January 1896, the *Katipunan* had about 300 members. Within six months, the membership had exploded to 30,000. At least two factors were responsible for this. Bonifacio changed the method of recruiting members, and the *Katipunan* published a newspaper with the name *Kalayaan* (Tagalog for "freedom"). Edited by Emilio Jacinto, the newspaper published 2,000 copies of its first and only edition. Spanish authorities captured the printing press just as the second edition was to be published.

It has been argued that although the *ilustrados* had political theory, they had no movement; on the other hand, peasants had movements without political theory. Bonifacio provided the synergy to bring the two components together, but not without difficulties. Perhaps the most frustrating hurdle he faced was recruiting *ilustrados* to join the movement. Even Rizal, who had been the most significant figure in the push to gain freedom, refused to embrace the aims and the spirit of the *Katipunan.* Bonifacio had commissioned Dr. Pio Valenzuela to travel to Dapitan in June 1896 to consult with

Rizal. To avoid suspicion, Valenzuela brought a blind patient with him for Rizal to examine. In private, Valenzuela told Rizal of the *Katipunan* and its goals. Rizal rejected the notion of an armed revolution, much to Bonifacio's anger when he heard the report from Valenzuela. In addition, Rizal refused to allow the *Katipunan* to rescue him because he had given his word to the Spanish authorities that he would not attempt to escape.

Bonifacio was convinced that he needed wealthy Filipinos to join the struggle for freedom, and when they did not join, he tried unsuccessfully to radicalize such individuals by putting their names on documents, implicating them in subversion against Spanish authority. In the process, some prominent Filipinos who knew nothing about the *Katipunan* were arrested and executed.

Although one might keep the existence of a secret society of 300 members hidden from the authorities, a group with 30,000 members was another matter altogether. When Spanish authorities discovered the existence of the *Katipunan* on August 19, 1896, Andres Bonifacio summoned the leaders to meet at Balintawak. Five hundred members of the *Katipunan* attended. Although the exact details of the next few days are in dispute, when members were asked whether they would fight the Spanish to the death, all agreed to do so. Bonifacio had them tear up their *cedulas* (personal identity papers) and shout, "Long live the Philippines" *(Mabuhay Filipinas)*. On August 25, 1896, the first battle took place between the *Katipunan* and Spanish soldiers. This marked the beginning of the Philippine Revolution. The revolt against the Spaniards spread; soon, when Filipinos throughout the archipelago joined the fight, it became more than a matter of the *Katipunan* against Spanish authority.

The year 1896 saw not only the beginning of the Philippine Revolution but also marked the deaths of three of the pillars of the Reform Movement. On January 30, Graciano Lopez Jaena, the great orator of the movement, died in Spain of tuberculosis. Marcelo H. del Pilar, the editor of *La Soli-daridad,* died in Barcelona of malnutrition on July 4. Then Jose Rizal, after a trial in which he was found guilty of rebellion and sedition, was executed on December 30 by firing squad at Bagumbayan Field, where the three priests, Gomes, Burgos, and Zamora, had been garroted more than two decades earlier.

Even before the outbreak of hostilities, the *Katipunan* in Cavite had two major factions—the *Magdiwang* (led by Baldomero Aguinaldo) and Bonifacio's faction, the *Magdalo* (led by Mariano Alvarez). The friction between the two factions led to reverses on the battlefield. It was decided that the two groups should meet and seek to resolve the differences. On March 22, 1897, the two factions met at Tejeros, in the hacienda recently captured by the revolutionaries. One of the main sticking points between the two groups was whether a new organization or structure should be established to replace the *Katipunan.* While one side argued that the *Katipunan* had the necessary structure and had led the way in the revolution, the other side countered that the *Katipunan* as a secret organization was not what was needed. The meeting was heated and the two sides almost came to blows. After a recess to cool off, the meeting resumed and Bonifacio, as the chairman, agreed that a new government should be established to take the place of the *Katipunan.* That new organization was the Republic of the Philippines, the first republic in Asia. Emilio Aguinaldo (of the *Magdalo*) was elected president; the other officers—vice president, captain general, director of war, and director of the interior— were from the *Magdiwang* faction. But this historic meeting ended badly when Bonifacio's credentials for director of the interior were questioned because he was not a lawyer. Bonifacio was insulted and proclaimed the actions of that meeting were annulled. The next day, Bonifacio and forty-five of his followers met again at Tejeros and again rejected the decisions of the previous day. With his followers, Bonifacio tried to establish a rival republic. This split was disastrous for the movement and resulted in the arrest and eventual execution of Andres Bonifacio and his brother, Procopio, by firing squad on May 10, 1897.

The fortunes of the revolution continued to deteriorate throughout the rest of 1897. Emilio Aguinaldo continued as the new standard bearer, but was forced to move from Cavite, southeast of Manila, to Bulakan, north of Manila. From this new location, Aguinaldo issued a proclamation, titled "To the Brave Sons of the Philippines," in which he listed the demands of the revolution. The most significant of these were the expulsion of the friars and returns to Filipinos of the hacienda lands and representation in the Spanish Cortes. The demands demonstrated the ambivalence of some who were fighting the Spaniards. On November 1, a constitution was signed; this came to be known as the Biyak-na-Bato Constitution and was based on the Cuban Constitution of Jimaguayu. Yet, within a week, the truce of Biyak-na-Bato was signed. The truce provided that Aguinaldo and others would go into voluntary exile abroad with 400,000 pesos in hand and 400,000 to be paid in the future when certain conditions had been met.

When Aguinaldo left for Hong Kong on December 27, the door was opened for events that would change the direction of events in the Philippines. First in Hong Kong, then in Singapore, contacts between Aguinaldo and representatives of the United States took place. Spanish-American relations were at an all time low, primarily over events in Cuba. Open conflict was anticipated between Spain, whose imperial days were coming to an end, and the United States, which had ambitions to be an imperial power. If war resulted, the Philippines would be one of the places of conflict. The American consul in Singapore, E. Spencer Pratt, conferred with Aguinaldo and persuaded him to cooperate with Admiral George Dewey, commander of the American Asiatic Squadron, in fighting the Spaniards. Pratt assured Aguinaldo that the Americans had no designs on the Philippines.

THE AMERICAN PERIOD

When war was declared, Dewey received orders to sail to Manila. On May 1, 1898, Dewey confronted the Spanish fleet in Manila Bay. Although outnumbered, the Americans enjoyed superior firepower and destroyed the Spanish fleet in short order; all this under the watchful gaze of the German fleet, which was also in Manila Bay. Aguinaldo returned on May 19 with weapons purchased from and supplied by the Americans. Filipino forces began to win battle after battle and take territory. Within a month, most of the island of Luzon was under their control.

On June 12, 1898, Aguinaldo proclaimed Philippine independence in his hometown of Kawit, in Cavite. Ninety-eight individuals, including an American army officer, signed the document declaring independece. However, relations between Filipinos and Americans were beginning to sour. The Filipinos had believed that the Americans would leave after the defeat of the Spanish forces: After all, Dewey gave these assurances in his meeting with Aguinaldo. But nothing was recorded of that meeting and no agreement signed. Dewey later denied giving Aguinaldo a guarantee regarding American intentions. Instead, the Americans secretly negotiated terms of surrender that stipulated Spanish forces would surrender to the Americans and not to the Filipinos. After a mock battle on August 13, the Spaniards capitulated to the American forces, with negotiations culminating with the Treaty of Paris.

The years of 1898 and 1899 presented various challenges for both Filipinos and Americans. Aguinaldo returned to the Philippines to find the split between *ilustrados* and peasants again a factor in decisions regarding the structure of an independent Philippines. With the guidance of Apolinario Mabini, known as the "Brains of the Revolution," Aguinaldo promoted a style of government featuring a strong executive branch. But those (primarily *ilustrados*) writing what came to be known as the Malolos Constitution advocated a legislature more powerful than the executive and judiciary branches. Their position reflected several hopes: that a republican form of government would make it easier to gain international diplomatic recognition and, among some, that the United States would annex the archipelago. Thus, the split between Aguinaldo and his opponents was a disagreement over the future direction of the Philippines. Aguinaldo eventually surrendered power to the *ilustrado* faction in order to gain their support.

The Americans, on the other hand, were trying to decide what to do with the Philippines. President William McKinley was caught between two opposing points of view: those who advocated retaining the Philippines as a colony and the anti-imperialist group. Those who wanted to keep the Philippines as a colonial possession had diverse motivations: the desire to be a world power, the lure of the China market, missionary zeal, racism, and altruism. Those who were opposed believed that to acquire a colony was contrary to the historical and political tradition of the United States. President McKinley, surprised by the opposition to keeping the Philippines and needing to win support for the Treaty of Paris, which included a provision giving Spain $20 million for "improvements" made in the Philippines, issued his Benevolent Proclamation on December 21, 1898. His contention was that the United States intended to assume control over the Philippines, but was doing so for altruistic reasons. As McKinley told a visiting delegation of Methodist church leaders:

> The truth is I didn't want the Philippines, and when they came to us, as a gift from the gods, I did not know what to do with them. . . . When I next realized that the Philippines had dropped into our laps I confess I did not know what to do with them . . . and I am not ashamed to tell you, gentlemen, that I went down on my knees and prayed Almighty God for light and guidance more than one night. And one night late it came to me this way—I don't know how it was, but it came: (1) That we could not give them back to Spain—that would

be cowardly and dishonorable; (2) that we could not turn them over to France and Germany—our commercial rivals in the Orient—that would be bad business and discreditable; (3) that we could not leave them to themselves—they were unfit for self-government—and they would soon have anarchy and misrule over there worse than Spain's was; and (4) that there was nothing left for us to do but to take them all, and to educate the Filipinos, and uplift and civilize and Christianize them, and by God's grace do the very best we could by them, as our fellow-men for whom Christ also died. (Schirmer, 1987: 22–23)

On the night of February 4, 1899, fighting broke out between the American soldiers and Filipinos. On February 6, the United States Senate voted to keep the Philippines; the margin of victory was one vote. Having fewer soldiers but superior weapons, the Americans expected to defeat the Filipino forces easily. Filipinos adopted guerilla tactics and, by June, the Americans were no farther than 30 miles from Manila. As the conflict dragged on, Americans began to use more drastic and inhumane measures against the civilian population they believed were supporting the guerillas. As one American general declared, "It may be necessary to kill half the Filipinos in order that the remaining half may be advanced to a higher plane of life than their present semi-barbarous state affords." In certain provinces, the local population was rounded up and placed in concentration camps with the hope that this would isolate those fighting the Americans.

In 1899, the Schurmann Commission, led by Jacob Schurmann, was sent to the Philippines to investigate the situation. The Commission reported that all Filipinos wanted complete independence, but doubted that they had the capacity for self-rule. Schurmann promised that the United States would help fulfill the aspirations of educated Filipinos (the *ilustrados*) in creating a new government. Schurmann stated, "The destiny of the Philippine Islands was not to be a State or a territory . . . but a daughter republic of ours—a new birth of liberty on the other side of the Pacific . . . a beacon of hope to all the oppressed and benighted millions [of Asia]."

The *ilustrados* were the key to American success. Each side needed the other. The Americans needed them to break the resistance against American rule, to end the war, and to demonstrate to the world America's altruism. The *ilustrados* needed the Americans to achieve political dominance in the vacuum created when the Spaniards left, to realize social ascendancy, and to acquire economic security. Thus, American success in the Philippines was based on a contradiction: To end nationalist resistance to the American presence and rule, the United States had to promise to work in line with the goals of the *ilustrados*.

By 1908, at least one American, William Howard Taft, the governor general of the Philippines, realized that in securing the collaboration of the *ilustrados,* the United States had set the stage for an oligarchy, not a democracy as promised and intended. Education, which the Americans brought with missionary zeal, was thought to be the key to bringing out a more equitable situation in Philippine society. As Taft stated: "[The] work of instruction in individual rights will require many years before the country is rid of the feudal relation of dependence which so many of the common people now feel toward their wealthy or educated leaders."

Unfortunately, time was a luxury that the Americans did not have. As early as 1900, the *ilustrados* were encouraged to form a political party, the Federalista Party, which advocated working with the Americans and eventual statehood. Factions split off quickly and established separate power bases, some advocating eventual independence (the Americans had prohibited public or open mention of independence). In 1907, the first national elections were held for the National Assembly, the lower house of the legislative branch (the Philippine Commission serving as the upper house, its nine members appointed by Washington), and some candidates campaigned as *Immediatistas* and *Urgentistas*. Merging as a single party, the *Union Nacionalista* won fifty-nine of the eighty seats in the house. From this group came young leaders who would dominate Philippine politics for the next three decades, including Sergio Osmeña and Manuel Quezon.

The key issue was the timing of independence with a delicate dance resulting that would affect Philippine politics up through independence. Knowing that advocating independence played well with the masses, politicians played that card publicly, but privately they wanted the Americans to stay because the United States provided security—economically and politically—for the nation and these politicians. This hypocrisy would continue for most of the twentieth century, well beyond independence. Manuel Quezon represented this position.

On the American side, generally, the Republicans opposed the granting of independence, but Democrats favored it. When the Democrats took the White House and controlled the Congress in 1912, the official position was to speed up the process of decolonization. President Woodrow Wilson appointed Francis Burton Harrison as governor general. During his tenure, Harrison increased Filipino representation in the bureaucracy from 71 percent to 96 percent. In 1916, the Democrats passed the Jones Act, which promised independence in the Philippines as soon as a stable government could be established. The Clarke Amendment, which passed in the Senate but failed in the House, specified that independence would be granted within four years.

Beginning in 1919, independence missions from the Philippines would visit Washington, D.C., to make an appeal to the U. S. Congress for independence. The first mission was led by Manuel Quezon, who was willing to accept a twenty-five-year Commonwealth; this would give the benefits of self-government without the liabilities of having complete authority. The Americans would be in charge of defense, currency, trade, and foreign policy; the local elite would have political, social, and economic power. But Quezon did not have the opportunity to go public with his plan because in 1920 the Republicans won the White House.

The Harding administration sent Leonard Wood and William Forbes to investigate the situation in the Philippines. Their mission concluded that independence should be postponed: The Philippines was not prepared sufficiently for self-government because political power rested in the hands of a tiny elite. Leonard Wood, authoritarian and a magnet for Filipino hostility, presented an opportunity for Quezon to use that hostility as a means of establishing himself as the most important political figure in the Philippines. Splitting the major political party, the *Nacionalista* Party, Quezon managed to take center stage.

Other independence missions were sent to Washington in 1922, 1923, 1924, 1925, 1927, 1928, 1930, 1931, and 1933. The push for independence received a boost in the 1930s from two sectors. The first was the familiar support of the Democrats, who regained control of the Congress in 1930 and the White House in 1932. The other was the unexpected support from economic interest groups who, in the midst of the Great Depression, wanted the Philippines to be given independence; thereby, as a foreign nation rather than an American colony, it would lose the easy access to American markets that its cheap labor and products such as sugar, tobacco, and coconut oil had given it. The Oriental Exclusion Act of 1924 did not apply to Filipinos as long as the Philippines remained an American colony. Independence would change that and the equivalent of free trade would be lost to products from the Philippines.

The independence mission of 1931 persuaded Representative Butler B. Hare, along with Senators Harry Hawes and Bronson Cutting, to sponsor a Philippine independence bill. Passed on December 30, 1932, and sent to President Herbert Hoover, the bill was vetoed and returned to Congress, which overrode the veto. But Quezon rejected the Hare-Hawes-Cutting Law and persuaded the Legislature to do so as well, leading to a major split in national political leadership. Quezon led the next independence mission in 1933 and obtained an almost identical bill known as the Tydings-McDuffie law, which was passed by the Democratic-controlled Congress and then signed by President Franklin Delano Roosevelt on March 24, 1934. Quezon returned to Manila in triumph and the Legislature accepted it.

The Tydings-McDuffie Act provided for the creation of the Commonwealth of the Philippines, with full independence to be granted in ten years. It authorized the Legislature to call for a constitutional convention to draft a constitution. Foreign relations, tariffs, and coinage were to be under United States control during the transition, with quotas for Philippine imports of sugar and coconut oil, as well as an export tax on all items shipped into the United States.

A constitution was drafted and approved by the convention on February 8, 1935, then by President Roosevelt on March 23, and ratified by a plebiscite on May 14. The Commonwealth of the Philippines was inaugurated on November 15, 1935, with Manuel Quezon as president and Sergio Osmeña as vice president.

World War II interrupted the transition period of the Commonwealth. Although the first law passed by the National Assembly had been the National Defense Act, requiring compulsory military service and the organizing of the Philippine military, and in spite of Quezon's choice of Douglas MacArthur as military advisor, along with Dwight D. Eisenhower as one of his assistants, the Philippines was not prepared for Japanese aggression.

The Japanese Occupation

On July 26, 1941, escalating tensions with Japan made it necessary for General Douglas MacArthur to be called back to active service by President Roosevelt and appointed commander of the United States Armed Forces in the Far East

(USAFFE). Included in the USAFFE were Philippine reserve and regular forces. MacArthur was given the impossible task of preparing the Philippines for war with Japan. At the time the Japanese were attacking Pearl Harbor, the date in the Philippines was December 8 because it was across the international dateline. On December 8, the Japanese bombed various locations in the Philippines, including Clark Field, Davao, Aparri, and Baguio City. Having destroyed the few American military planes in the Philippines, the Japanese were able to land troops two days later on Northern Luzon at Aparri and Vigan; two days later, more landings took place in Southern Luzon, and they met no resistance. On December 22, USAFFE forces failed to prevent more major landings.

On December 29, President Roosevelt sent a message to the Filipino people: "I give the people of the Philippines my solemn pledge that their freedom will be redeemed and their independence established and protected." In the meantime, the Filipinos were on their own. On January 2, 1942, the Japanese entered Manila, which had been declared an open city by General MacArthur. On February 20, President Quezon left by submarine, and, on March 11, MacArthur left by PT boat, ordered to do so by President Roosevelt. Now the soldiers in the field, both American and Filipino, were on their own. With troops coming from Northern Luzon and Southern Luzon, the Japanese were able to reach Manila on January 2, 1942. They had faced little opposition.

General MacArthur had a plan to hold off the Japanese until reinforcements and supplies could be sent from the United States. (The plan would have been brilliant if reinforcements and supplies had been sent.) The plan called for all USAFFE troops on Luzon to retreat to the peninsula of Bataan, on the west side of Manila Bay. MacArthur outmaneuvered the Japanese commander, General Masaharu Homma, and got his troops relatively intact to Bataan. The Japanese launched several offensives against the troops of Bataan, only to be forced to retreat with heavy losses. The

The start of the Bataan Death March. (Library of Congress)

stubborn resistance of the fighting men of Bataan was not only heroic but slowed down the Japanese timetable for taking Asia. Japanese army and navy troops, supported by bombers, tried again and again to take Bataan, but to no avail. They tried to persuade Filipino troops to surrender and leave the Americans to fight alone, but the strategy did not succeed. Meanwhile, the USAFFE troops on Bataan were being worn down. It became apparent that no reinforcements were coming and that the supplies they had were rapidly dwindling. By mid-March 1942, supplies were almost gone and malnutrition resulted from the lack of rations. Malaria, dysentery, and other physical ailments were creating more casualties than the Japanese.

On April 9, 1942, General Edward P. King, commander of the forces on Bataan, surrendered to the Japanese. Some

78,000 men were included in this surrender. These troops were then forced to march from the peninsula to the central plain of Luzon. This march of death has come to be known as the Bataan Death March. On May 6, the island fortress of Corregidor fell, marking the surrender of the last American forces in the Philippines. The Philippines now belonged to the Empire of Japan.

The Japanese had a plan for a puppet government composed of Filipinos. On January 8, 1942, they ordered Jose B. Vargas, the mayor of Manila, to organize a civil government. Before his departure, President Quezon had given instructions to the political leaders left behind: They were to protect the local population from the Japanese. The United States could offer no protection; the Philippines had to comply with Japanese orders. For the "maintenance of peace and order and the promotion of the well-being of [the Philippine] people," Vargas and others agreed to work with the Japanese. The Philippine Executive Commission was established; there were six commissioners and Vargas was chairman. On June 19, 1943, a convention was held for the drafting of a constitution and in September, a legislature was elected. They, in turn, selected Jose P. Laurel as president of the Republic of the Philippines.

But many Filipinos chose not to work with the Japanese. Along with soldiers who had escaped the Japanese, civilians formed guerrilla bands. Civilians by day and guerrilla fighters by night, they performed various important functions, including ambushing and attacking Japanese troops whenever possible. Although many had limited success against the Japanese presence, they managed to relay intelligence to Allied forces, keep the local population informed about the progress of the war, and, above all, keep alive the dream of a free Philippines.

Keeping alive the dream of a free Philippines was done in several ways, particularly by keeping the people informed of the progress of the war. Under the Japanese occupation, it was practically impossible to receive accurate news reports. Filipinos could try to read between the lines of Japanese news broadcasts. They could try to tune in to Radio San Francisco, a transgression punishable by death. Or they could read the "newspapers" produced by local guerrilla groups. Colonel Guillermo Nakar, part of a group operating in Northern Luzon, published *Matang Lawin* (The Hawk's Eye). Beyond conveying news and information, it gave a sense that the people were being watched over. One of the most widely circulated underground newspapers was *The Liberator,* put out by Leon O. Ty of the Philippine Free Press.

Guerrillas sought to present an alternative to the Japanese. One of the most visible ways they did this was by issuing currency. There were different currencies, some almost primitive, throughout the Philippines, and the promise was made that they would be redeemed after the war. Indeed, after the war, the U.S. Congress voted $25 million to redeem the various currencies issued by guerrilla groups.

One of the difficult issues during and after the Japanese occupation was the matter of collaboration. President Quezon had told his subordinates that they had to stay behind, even though he was taken out by submarine to safety. When Jose P. Laurel, the acting chief justice, asked to go along, Quezon reportedly told him that he would have to stay behind and protect the Filipino people. Quezon told the high officials of the Commonwealth that they were to "do the best they could. Bargains would have to be made to protect the people from the brutality of the Japanese." MacArthur told them that they could cooperate with the Japanese but not take the oath of allegiance. However, the United States could provide no protection. The Filipino people were on their own. What some called collaboration others believed to be service to their country and to their countrymen. Without Filipinos in public service positions, society would have suffered greatly. But to serve, they had to work with the Japanese occupiers. Families and communities were divided

General Douglas MacArthur wading ashore at the island of Leyte as the retaking of the Philippines began. (National Archives)

when some worked with the Japanese and others fought against them alongside the guerrillas.

Professor Teodoro Agoncillo argued that World War II was a time when Filipinos lost their social and moral balance. Seeing themselves as abandoned and having to survive by their own wits, the local population participated in activities they would have condemned in better times. Some collaborated; others called themselves guerrillas, yet were little more than bandits; and thousands died at Bataan because doctors sold their medicine on the black market. Many broke into graves to steal the gold out of the teeth of the dead to use to buy food. In this light, the promise "I shall return" had an almost biblical resonance to it.

And MacArthur did return. The retaking of the Philippines began on the island of Leyte, with 650 ships and four army divisions. Landings commenced on October 20, 1944. On January 9, 1945, the Americans landed at Lingayen Gulf on the western coast of Northern Luzon. Finding themselves surrounded in Manila, the Japanese troops went on a killing spree, and 100,000 Filipino civilians were murdered.

The resulting damage of the war was extensive, the economic infrastructure being devastated. Roads, bridges, mills, farms, and business buildings had been destroyed. Manila suffered greater devastation than any Allied city, second only to Warsaw. Farms operated at less than 60 percent of prewar levels, and livestock were reduced by 65 percent. Irrigation facilities had been destroyed. Production was at a standstill, with little or no capital to finance the rebuilding of the country. There was an acute shortage of food.

The Philippine Civil Affairs Unit (PCAU) had been created in New Guinea prior to MacArthur's landing at Leyte to provide rapid relief to people in areas when they were liberated. Distribution centers were set up and food was rationed out according to the number of members in a family. The PCAU was also to help with civil administration, working with municipal officials and schoolteachers. It provided employment by hiring people to help with the distribution, and this was to begin the process of circulating currency.

Sergio Osmeña was now the president (President Quezon had died in August 1944 in New York). It fell to him to reorganize the government, but he faced a real problem in that many of the politicians in the Commonwealth government had collaborated with the government. Osmeña was afraid that if he reconvened Congress, the collaborators might control the Congress. MacArthur forced the issue, arguing that it was the policy of the United States to restore constitutional government as soon as possible. On June 9, 1945, Osmeña called a special session of Congress. Manuel A. Roxas, who wanted to be president and was MacArthur's choice for the position, immediately spoke for the collaborators, arguing that those employed during the Japanese occupation had been loyal to the Commonwealth. This won him many supporters in the Congress. When Osmeña convened Congress, one of their first acts was to vote themselves three years back pay, claiming that they had been working for the Common-wealth all along. Government workers wanted the same arrangement, but Osmeña could not promise to pay them because there was no money. But Roxas made the promise that, if he was elected, he would recommend that they receive back pay.

President Roosevelt had stated that those who collaborated with the enemy should be removed "from authority and influence over the political and economic life of the country." Two bills were presented to the Philippine Congress to establish a court to try collaborators, but Osmeña thought them insufficient. He presented an administrative measure providing for a court whose judges were not identified with the collaborators. Roxas fought this, but the Osmeña bill passed when Harold Ickes, the U.S. secretary of the interior, sent a cablegram hinting that U.S. aid would be withdrawn.

Roxas, who had been a member of the Laurel government under the Japanese, solved the collaborator issue when he was elected president in 1946 by proclaiming amnesty for all collaborators. One of those accused as a collaborator refused to accept amnesty and insisted on having his day in court. Claro M. Recto fought his case in court and won. In his book, *Three Years of Enemy Occupation,* he argued that he and others were serving their country and not collaborating.

American financial aid to the Philippines was intended for rebuilding the country. This aid included more than $1 billion in army surplus. However, strings were attached to the aid. Representative C. Jasper Bell of Missouri introduced a bill providing for free trade between the United States and the Philippines for a period of twenty years. It was opposed and reduced to eight years, and required that Americans have parity rights in terms of doing business, something that the Philippine Constitution did not allow. When the U.S. Congress passed the Tydings Rehabilitation Act, which provided that $620 million be given to those who had suffered damage during the war, the condition was attached that no more than

$500 million could be given unless and until an agreement was reached between the presidents of the Philippines and the United States regarding trade relations.

Philippine Independence

On July 4, 1946, a date chosen by the Americans, the Philippines was granted independence. Manuel Roxas became president, Elpidio Quirino vice president. The election that brought Roxas to power also meant a return to power of those who had been in control prior to the Japanese occupation. It also signaled a backlash against such individuals. The Democratic Alliance had six candidates elected to Congress. Led by Luis Taruc of Tarlac, they opposed collaborators and parity rights for Americans, something that required a three-fourth's majority to amend the Philippine constitution. They were able to block this move. Roxas had them removed from Congress by resolution, claiming electoral fraud in their election. When the Congress presented the issue to the Filipinos in a plebiscite in 1947, it passed.

In the early American period, labor and peasant leaders sought to unite peasants and laborers into unions. Their complaint was against the elite, who controlled much of the nation's wealth. In 1922, peasants banded together in the *Confederacion de Aparceros y Obreros Agricolas de Filipinas,* or the Philippine Confederation of Tenants and Agricultural Workers. In 1924, it was renamed *Katipunang Pambansa ng mga Magbubukid sa Filipinas,* or the National Farmers Association of the Philippines. The Socialist Party was founded in 1929 and, one year later, the *Partido Comunista,* or the Communist Party. The Socialists worked for reform and were not outlawed; the Communist leaders were imprisoned in 1932 and then pardoned in 1938. The two movements merged in 1938, aligning those who did not identify themselves as Communists with the Communist organization.

Luis Taruc, military leader of the Huks during World War II and later a major figure in the Communist insurgency, is pictured here with members of the movement. (AFP/Getty Images)

When war broke out, peasant leaders met and decided on a united front. They would be "anti-Japanese above all." In March 1942, the *Hukbalahap* was formed. Short for *Hukbó ng Bayan Laban sa Hapón,* or the Group of the Land Fighting the Japanese, its members were known as the Huks. To carry out their policy of working for a free Philippines, the peasant leaders adopted a three-point platform: economic, political, and military. Luis Taruc was selected as chairman of the military committee. The Huks were disciplined and successful in their struggle against the Japanese. But when the Americans returned, the Huks were shunned; the Americans replaced those elected to office with other guerrilla leaders. The American Counterintelligence Corps arrested the members of the Huk General Headquarters, including Luis Taruc.

Roxas sought to win Taruc's support, but was unsuccessful. The Huk movement was not only anti-Japanese, it was also anti-collaborator, and was becoming anti-American. Roxas forced Taruc and his allies from Congress, and issued a proclamation declaring the Hukbalahap to be an illegal association, organized for the purpose of overthrowing the government. Shortly after this proclamation, Roxas died unexpectedly, and his vice president, Elpidio Quirino, finished his term, but he also inherited the Huk problem. Quirino took a different tack, which appeared to be conciliatory. He sent his brother, Antonio Quirino, a judge, to meet with Taruc. Quirino agreed to the terms of the Huks, proclaiming a fifty-day amnesty period for the Huks to surrender their weapons. Three hours after the end of the amnesty, Philippine troops attacked the Huks. Taruc accused President Quirino of bad faith and pointed to the agreement he had signed with Judge Quirino. The agreement contained provisions, such as an agreement with the United States stipulating no military bases, which were not likely to be accepted, the Quirino approach seemed a ploy to destroy the Huk movement.

An ambush on April 28, 1949, near Bongabon, Nueva Ecija, cost the Huks popular support. Among the dozen victims were Aurora Quezon, the widow of the late President Quezon, and her daughter. Although the Huks denied any participation, Taruc admitted for the first time that the goal of the movement was the overthrow of the government. In late 1950, the Philippine armed forces and Manila police were able to capture major figures in the leadership of the Huks.

The next president, Ramon Magsaysay, was more successful in dealing with the Communist insurgency. Although he was elected in 1953 with the help of Col. Edward Lansdale of the Central Intelligence Agency, who came up with the slogan, "Magsaysay, he's our guy," Magsaysay was seen as a man of the people, in contrast to previous political leaders. He had come to national prominence as the secretary of national defense during the administration of Quirino. Magsaysay had practiced a policy of seeking to win over the dissidents and convincing them that their future would be better if they worked for peace. Many did leave the Huk movement as a result of Magsaysay's work. As president, he continued his approach to the problem of the insurgency. Early in 1954, he sent a secret emissary to Taruc, a journalist named Benigno Aquino, Jr. (Ninoy), the son of a prominent politician. After four months of negotiations, Taruc surrendered, recognizing the sovereignty of the Republic of the Philippines. He was then sentenced to twelve years in prison.

Magsaysay, having been identified with the common man, sought to improve the lot of the rural poor. His approach included three aspects: improving the land-tenure system, with land resettlement as part of the answer; easy-term credit as well as providing education and infrastructure to improve their chances of not only better crops but also getting their products to markets; and community development with self-help as the critical component. In 1954, he pushed through Congress the Agricultural Tenancy Act, which provided greater protection for tenants and granted them the freedom to choose the system of tenancy under which they would work. Because the government did not have the money to purchase the large estates, public lands were given to qualified settlers. In the first year of Magsaysay's presidency, 241,000 hectares were distributed among settlers, and the amount of land distributed grew every year. Magsaysay also worked to construct roads to link communities and to make it easier to get products to markets. In the first year of his presidency, 252 kilometers of new roads were built, and more than twice that amount the following year. Irrigation projects were also expanded, and experts were sent into rural areas to teach farmers better methods of agriculture.

Magsaysay actively cultivated his image as a man of the common people. He took time to listen to them and their grievances. He ate with them, slept in their homes, and was photographed wearing clothes found among the rural people. He opened the presidential palace, claiming that it belonged to them. The presidential guard could not keep track of the numbers that came. The grounds were used for picnics, and people wandered through the palace. In the process, the palace and its grounds were damaged by those who littered and loitered. It was argued that Magsaysay spoiled the people; indeed, the price for the programs he instituted was more than the government could afford, as his successor discovered.

Tragically, on March 16, 1957, while President Magsaysay was returning from Cebu, his plane crashed, killing all but one aboard. For the second time in a little over a decade, a vice president had to complete the presidential term. Carlos Garcia completed the last eight months of Magsaysay's term. The election in November 1957 was the noisiest, most expensive, and most acrimonious the country had seen. It also marked the emergence of the Catholic Church as a major player in the political arena.

Garcia was elected, but his running mate for vice president, Jose Laurel, Jr., was defeated. Instead, Diosdado Macapagal, the vice-presidential candidate of the Liberal Party, was elected. Although Magsaysay was popular, the government was in trouble economically. Garcia sought to institute programs of restraint in government spending. He also believed that in the private sector, free enterprise would serve only to preserve foreign (that is, American) domination of the national economy. Garcia sought to bring about Philippine economic independence through the Filipino First policy; that is, he encouraged Filipinos, when there was a choice between products made in the Philippines and other countries, to buy Filipino goods. Although Magsaysay had focused on the agricultural aspect of the economy, Garcia wanted a more balanced economy with equal support for agriculture and industry. And he wanted to eradicate, if possible, corruption.

In spite of Garcia's program of austerity in government spending, the economy continued to deteriorate. In the process, he had alienated many, at home and abroad, by his policies. Cuts in government spending and increased support for industry left some feeling that he had turned his back on Magsaysay's legacy. Foreign businessmen were not happy with his "Filipino First" policy. The idea that the Philippines could achieve economic independence as well as be dealt with as an equal also did not go over well. But what marked his legacy was the corruption that was seen as rampant during his administration. Having campaigned to get rid of corruption, his administration was seen as the most corrupt ever. In the meantime, the plight of the poor continued to worsen. In the next presidential election, Garcia was defeated by his vice president, Diosdado Macapagal.

Although the Liberal Party was Macapagal's political party, it was in the minority. But Garcia's administration was voted out because it was seen as wasteful and corrupt, and so Macapagal was handed the presidency. His presidency is remembered for a number of things: his attempts at land reform through the Agricultural Land Reform Code; the changing of the national independence day from July 4 (chosen by the United States) to June 12, chosen by Aguinaldo in 1896; the Stonehill scandal; and his commitment to support the U.S. efforts in Vietnam with combat troops. Although he promised to strengthen the moral fiber of the country and to set an example of honest and simple living, promises that caught the imagination of the Filipino people, he nonetheless lived extravagantly.

Ferdinand E. Marcos

The election of 1965 signaled another change in leadership. With rampant graft and corruption, plus the problem of peace and order, people came to see the Macapagal administration as inept, even though Macapagal was a man of personal integrity. Ferdinand E. Marcos, president of the Senate and a member of the Liberal Party, had called on Macapagal to honor a promise to support him and not run for reelection. Macapagal refused. Marcos switched to the Nacionalista Party and became their candidate, but the campaign was expensive and vicious. The *Iglesia Ni Cristo* entered the political arena and has been a major player ever since. Marcos won the election.

At least three things marked the early years of Marcos's first term in office and shaped events to come: the continuing deterioration of law and order tied in with the plight of rural Filipinos, as seen in two separate massacres in 1966 and 1967; Marcos's position regarding the conflict in Vietnam; and the rise of student activism against Marcos, who came to be viewed as a puppet of the United States.

The first massacre occurred in Culatingan, a barrio of the town of Concepcion in the province of Tarlac, in central Luzon. On June 13, 1966, three Philippine Constabulary agents shot seven farmers of that barrio in the back. The Philippine Constabulary justified the killings by arguing that the farmers were Huks and that a battle had taken place. Two of the seven, however, survived, and challenged the government's account of what had happened. On the recommendation of national defense officials, Marcos promoted the three Philippine Constabulary agents. The second massacre involved members of a millenarian sect led by Valentin de los Santos. Known as *Lapiang Malaya,* or the Free Party, they were marching on the presidential palace, Malacañang, to demand that Marcos resign. Early in the morning of May 21, 1967, thirty-two members of the sect were killed by the Philippine Constabulary near the border of Manila and Pasay City. Although the cult members were a curiosity (they claimed the breastplates they were wearing would stop bullets), this massacre, along with the Culatingan affair, demonstrated the failure or the refusal of the national government in Manila to understand and connect with the majority of Filipinos, who lived in rural areas.

When he was president of the Senate, Marcos had opposed Macapagal's plan to send combat troops in a show of support for the U.S. efforts in Vietnam. In 1954, the Philippines had lent support to U.S. efforts with Operation Brotherhood, a

President and Mrs. Ferdinand Marcos during their first state visit to Washington, here with President and Mrs. Lyndon Johnson, 1966. (Library of Congress)

project in which doctors and nurses were sent to Vietnam. In 1955, a military unit of guerrillas from World War II was reformed into the Freedom Company of the Philippines. Working with the CIA, they were to carry out secret operations throughout French Indochina. This was viewed as a failure. In 1964, Secretary of State Dean Rusk initiated the More Flags Program to garner international support for the fight against the Communists in Vietnam. Of the twenty-one countries contacted, only eleven agreed to participate; the Philippines under Macapagal was one of that group. But the Senate, willing to send medical personnel and engineers, refused to send combat troops. PHILCON I (the Philippine Contingent) consisted of forty people, sixteen being advisors in psychological warfare. Macapagal negotiated with Washington to send the Philippine Civic Action Group (PHILCAG), which consisted of 2,000 combat troops.

After Marcos won the election on a platform opposing PHILCAG, he agreed to send PHILCAG as an engineering and civic unit, not a military unit. When PHILCAG arrived in South Vietnam in 1966, it consisted of dental, medical, engineering, and security units. In turn, the United States gave $35 million to finance PHILCAG, as well as support to the Military Assistance Program, which allowed Marcos to modernize and increase the size of the Philippine military. Marcos's support did not meet U.S. expectations; President Lyndon Johnson had hoped for a more visible token of military support in exchange for the millions he had given Marcos. It could be argued that Marcos got what he wanted from the United States, but it cost him dearly on the local front.

The view of Marcos as a puppet of the United States was reinforced in the minds of many Filipinos by events surrounding the Manila Summit of 1966. In the first year of his term in office, on his way back to the Philippines after a visit to Washington, D.C., Marcos called for a summit to deal with the Vietnam problem and to find a possible solution to end the war in Vietnam. Because only countries that supported the United States were invited, the summit was thought to be engineered by Lyndon Johnson to show that the United States was not alone in trying to defeat communism in Vietnam. Marcos's six-point agenda was conciliatory; it included a review of the proposals for peace talks, an evaluation of strategy in the event North Vietnam rejected the proposals, and a discussion of the political problems in South Vietnam. Leaks from the summit revealed that President Johnson was in charge. When a communiqué was written, Marcos refused to sign it, viewing it as an ultimatum, not a peace proposal. Some changes were made, but the tone was still belligerent.

It was during this summit that student activism in the Philippines came into its own. Led by students from the University of the Philippines and the Lyceum of the Philippines, demonstrations were held in opposition to the summit. Three thousand members of the *Kabataan Makabayan,* or Nationalist Youth, demonstrated in front of the American embassy. The police were accused of overreacting and beating students.

This marked the beginning of student involvement in political activities, as well as the beginning of what many considered to be a campaign against Communist elements in the movement. There was a growing belief that the government, particularly the president, had sold out to the United States. In 1969, Marcos withdrew PHILCAG from South Vietnam. But his close ties to the United States remained an issue.

In 1947, President Roxas had signed an agreement granting the United States twenty-two base sites, with a ninety-nine-year lease and the right of extraterritoriality for American personnel. Clark Air Base (157,000 acres) and Subic Bay Naval Base were two of the largest U.S. bases overseas. Subic could store 1 million tons of cargo, 40 million gallons of oil, and 200,000 tons of ammunition; it was homeport for 175 ships, 700 aircraft, and 75,000 men in the Seventh Fleet. These bases provided logistical support for the war in Vietnam. By 1967, the bases accounted for 9.5 percent of the GNP of the Philippines. On one side, resentment was building because the presence of the bases implied that the Philippines was tied to U.S. interests, including supporting U.S. efforts in Vietnam, even though Philippine combat troops were not in South Vietnam. On the other side, Marcos used the bases as leverage with the United States.

Martial Law

In 1969, Marcos became the first president to be reelected. Shortly after the election, the nation was rocked by violent student demonstrations. Believing that democracy was corrupt and paralyzing, Marcos embraced an ideology of "constitutional authoritarianism" to replace the oligarchy that had emerged early in the twentieth century. While a constitutional convention worked to write a new constitution, Marcos issued Proclamation 1081, and on September 22, 1972, declared martial law "to protect the Republic of the Philippines and our democracy." Using the threat of a Communist takeover and the chaos created by student activism as justification for his actions, Marcos suppressed all forms of dissent and opposition. The media, in all forms, was shut down. No student demonstrations, labor strikes, or public meetings were allowed. Thousands were arrested and habeas corpus was suspended. The private armies of the oligarchs were disbanded and some 500,000 privately held weapons were confiscated. With a powerful military behind him, Marcos was in control. He tripled the size of the military and expanded its role in society, thereby politicizing the military.

In spite of the harsh and repressive measures taken, the declaration of martial law won strong support from the business community and from President Richard Nixon. In the first three years, tourism and government revenues tripled, and the economy grew at an annual rate of 7 percent. One billion pesos came into the treasury in response to an amnesty for back taxes. The money was used to build roads, bridges, irrigation facilities, airfields, schools, tenement houses for the poor, hospitals, homes for lepers, and public buildings, and to improve Manila's drainage system. In the early years of martial law, Marcos was compared to Singapore's Lee Kuan Yew, a dictator who did what he believed necessary for his country. Marcos established a new political party, *Kilusang Bagong Lipunan,* or the New Society Movement (KBL). But his victims were generally ignored and forgotten by the world.

In the international arena, Marcos began to make foreign-policy decisions demonstrating that the Philippines would pursue its own agenda and not that of the United States. These policies included closer ties with members of ASEAN, the establishment of closer relations with China and the Soviet Union, support for Arab countries in their quest for a peaceful settlement in the Middle East, and the seeking of a new basis for continued relations with the United States. This last area meant a renegotiation of the bases agreement. Marcos wanted payment for the use of the land, a Filipino commander for the bases, and the flying of the Filipino flag at the bases.

By 1975, the ideological fervor began to wane. The New Society inaugurated by Marcos appeared to be little more than a vehicle on which the Marcos family and their friends could become wealthy. Imelda Marcos, the president's wife, came to symbolize this corruption. As the governor of Metro-Manila (the National Capital Region), she chaired no less than twenty-three government councils, agencies, and corporations, controlling hundreds of millions of dollars annually through their budgets. She oversaw the building of eleven five-star hotels, the Manila Cultural Center, the 5,000-seat International Convention Center, a $21 million Film Center, and a sprawling terminal at the airport.

While the Marcoses and their friends were getting richer, others in society were becoming dissatisfied. To the south, an organized insurgency in Mindanao known as the *Moro National Liberation Front* (MNLF) had a stated goal of full independence. There were more than 50,000 guerrillas in the early 1970s, but Marcos was able to neutralize their effectiveness by making concessions and buying off some of the leadership. Their numbers had dropped to 10,000 by 1981. The insurgency that would not go away was the New People's Army (NPA), the radical guerrilla arm of the reorganized Communist Party of the Philippines, which was tied to Beijing. In 1974, the *Partido Komunista ng Pilipinas* (PKP), the Moscow-oriented group, agreed to cooperate with Marcos. Seen by many as the successor to the Huk movement, the NPA grew as Marcos's repression and corruption became more evident. The brutality of the military pushed many in the countryside to support the insurgency. Marcos used the NPA to justify the continued use of martial law, and the NPA used the Marcos dictatorship as its reason for the struggle.

In response to international criticism, Marcos lifted martial law in 1981 and held an "election" to prove that he still had popular support. So confident was he of that support that he allowed opposition news to be broadcast and printed. Radio Veritas, the radio system run by the Roman Catholic Church, was allowed on the air again. Benigno Aquino, Jr. (Ninoy), Marcos's strongest political rival, had been arrested the day after the declaration of Martial Law and had been in prison since, but now he was allowed to leave the country for medical reasons. Marcos's health was also deteriorating and the maneuvering for power was beginning.

In August 1983, Aquino decided to return to the Philippines, but he was assassinated as he was exiting the plane. This event would ultimately lead to the downfall of the Marcos dictatorship. After the assassination, the economy was in free fall, with the peso dropping from a rate of six pesos to the dollar to twenty to one. Those who had money sent it abroad; those who could leave the country did so. With the brain drain, the flight of capital, loss of confidence in the government (Marcos), and $27 billion in foreign debt, the Philippines was essentially bankrupt.

Marcos called for Assembly elections in February 1984, hoping to legitimize his continued control of the country, as well as to neutralize the opposition. That opposition was divided about what course to take. Even with a divided opposition and less-than-fair elections, one-third of the new legislature belonged to the opposition. In many ways, this set the stage for an election that would come two years later.

In the meantime, the United States began to have doubts about its continued support of Marcos. The instability of the political situation was seen as a major threat to the continued presence of the U.S. bases in the Philippines, as well as their security. If the Communists won, U.S. interests would be seriously damaged. With external as well as internal pressure increasing, Marcos announced in November 1985 that a "snap election" would take place in February 1986. Discussion centered around who would run against Marcos. A divided opposition would make it possible for Marcos to continue. Corazon "Cory" Aquino, the widow of Ninoy Aquino, was a popular choice. A quiet and devout woman from one of the wealthiest mestizo families of central Luzon, she had no experience in political office. But with the acquittal of General Fabian Ver and others of the assassination of her husband, as well as strong encouragement from Cardinal Jaime Sin, she declared that she would run against Marcos.

THE EDSA REVOLUTION AND A NEW BEGINNING

The opposition united behind Corazon Aquino. The election was held on February 7, 1986, and Marcos and Aquino claimed victory and planned competing inaugurations. The United States, international funding agencies, and the world community watched with alarm as the society appeared poised to drift into anarchy. The NPA appeared to be the big winner; they had supported Marcos in the hope that the chaos that followed would open the door for them to seize power.

At this point, the military became a major player. A secret organization of mid-level military officers, known as the Reform the Armed Forces Movement (RAM), made plans to overthrow Marcos. General Ver moved to arrest RAM and their political sponsor, Juan Ponce Enrile, the minister of defense. Joined by General Fidel Ramos, a West Point-trained officer and vice-chief of the armed forces, on February 22, they occupied two military installations in Quezon City, Camp Aguinaldo and Camp Cramé.

Enrile admitted that there was massive cheating in the elections and asked Cardinal Sin for help. Using Radio Veritas, Cardinal Sin summoned the people into the streets to protect the soldiers at Camp Aguinaldo and Cramé. The faithful responded by the thousands. Interestingly, Aquino was not a central player during this uprising, nor did she make appearances, although Sin used her as a rallying point. These events have come to be known as People Power and the EDSA Revolution.

On February 25, Cory Aquino was sworn in as president, and, within hours, after also being sworn in, Marcos left the

Philippines and went into exile in Hawaii, where he would die some three and a half years later. The Marcos dictatorship was over. But the future was in doubt. Freedom had been restored, but in the absence of an ideological basis by which social and political structure could be changed, power returned to those who had held it before Marcos took over.

President Aquino had inherited an economic disaster. The bottom 20 percent of the nation earned about 5.5 percent of the income; the top 2 percent earned 53 percent. Politically, things were uncertain. Aquino released political prisoners, offered amnesty to the NPA, and sought to enter into dialogue with all sides, including the military. Her cabinet consisted of those from the left and the right. She had to walk carefully among the various factions.

On March 25, 1986, one month after assuming office, President Aquino issued a Presidential Proclamation basing her political legitimacy on the EDSA Revolution instead of the election. She proclaimed an interim "Freedom Constitution," thereby rejecting the 1973 "Marcos Constitution." She assumed powers rivaling those claimed by Marcos to gain control. On May 25, she created a constitutional commission and appointed its delegates—all educated, upper class, mostly lawyers, and with direct or indirect ties to the Roman Catholic Church. The constitution they created reaffirmed the traditional, elite realities that had been the mark of Philippine politics since Rizal. In essence, it was a return to the 1935 Commonwealth Constitution.

President Aquino's six years in office were marked by a series of natural disasters, including the eruption of Mount Pinatubo, major earthquakes, and floods. These seemed almost symbolic of the almost endless difficulties that faced the Aquino presidency. They not only exposed the weaknesses of the nation's infrastructure but also created an overwhelming burden on an economy already in crisis. Halfway through Aquino's presidency, the economy dropped significantly. The inflation rate was more than 10 percent, and unemployment was more than 17 percent. The GDP per person fell from $870 in 1986, when Aquino took office, to $720 in 1991. The country was falling further into poverty, ironically at the same time neighbors such as Indonesia, Malaysia, and Thailand were experiencing economic growth.

Although many were optimistic because of the results of People Power and Corazon Aquino's rise to power, this optimism soon faded. Although some would view her presidency as a failure, Aquino did accomplish the goal she had specified so often: She restored democracy, including free speech and democratic succession. On May 11, 1992, every political office in the Philippines was up for election. This included twenty-four Senate seats, two hundred seats in the House of Representatives, seventy-three governorships, sixty-two mayoral seats, and 1,543 municipal mayoral positions, along with thousands of other local offices. A total of 82,450 candidates ran for the 17,205 offices available.

As David Steinberg has astutely observed, four realities were demonstrated and confirmed by this election. First, there was a peaceful transition of power. After People Power ended the Marcos dictatorship, the question was whether there would be a peaceful and legal transfer of power as the result of democratically held elections. Second, it was clear that Filipinos took their new democratic obligations seriously. Nearly 80 percent of registered voters (60 percent of them under forty) went to the polls. Third, for the first time since the beginning of the century, the influence of the United States was minimal and, above all, irrelevant. Fourth, the traditional party system was no longer of any consequence. Those candidates who did best were those without party affiliation or those whose parties had no real meaning in the traditional sense. Certain traditional aspects of Philippine politics remained: patron-client relations, regionalism, and personalities. But the system of traditional political parties had collapsed. However, the oligarchy remained the controlling power. As Steinberg writes, "Alliances shifted, but the players remained the same" (2000, 187). Yet, one could argue that democracy was the real winner.

One significant aspect of this presidential election was that money did not determine the outcome. A lot of money was spent, but it did not decide who won. For example, it was reported that the $135 million that disappeared when the Marcoses fled the country was used for Imelda's run for the presidency. But she won only 10 percent of the vote. A determinant in the election was where the candidate was born and what language he or she spoke. Filipinos pragmatically voted their own self-interests. This meant that many did not listen, for example, to Cardinal Sin when he urged the public not to vote for non-Catholics. Two of the seven presidential candidates were Protestant, and Ramos, a Protestant, won. And the *Iglesia Ni Cristo* favored a Catholic over the Protestant choices. However, in the election of senatorial seats, name recognition and past political experience mattered. Although there were some new faces elected to Congress, most members were part of a traditional power base at the local and national levels.

Seven candidates ran for the office of president to replace President Aquino; the constitution did not allow for a second term. Among those running were familiar names, including Imelda Marcos, the widow of Ferdinand Marcos, as well as other *"trapos,"* traditional politicians from traditional political parties. But the victor was Fidel Ramos, a major figure in the events of the EDSA revolution and the defense minister in the Aquino administration. He formed a coalition party, but it was his loyalty to Aquino during the many coups against her administration and her active support on his behalf that helped him win. In fact, she supported Ramos and not the candidate put forward by her own political party. Ramos won the presidency with 23.5 percent of the vote.

Fidel "Eddie" V. Ramos assumed the presidency on June 30, 1992. He faced many problems: poverty, unemployment, a widening gap between the rich and the poor, and exclusion from the economic boom much of Southeast Asia was experiencing. Like Aquino, Ramos had to make hard economic decisions, required by the International Monetary Fund, so that the Philippines could secure new foreign credits. So although Ramos needed to spend funds on public works and to prime the economy, the IMF demanded cuts in public spending.

The Ramos administration emphasized and concentrated on "the four D's": devolution, decentralization, deregulation, and democratization. This meant that the power that had been assumed by the central government in Manila was to be returned to local control at the municipal and provincial levels. Economic progress was decentralized and efforts were made to rebuild regional economies. Deregulation sought to reduce governmental control, which had the dual effect of suppressing entrepreneurial investing and encouraging corruption. Democratization was seen as not only a political tool but an economic one as well to increase competition in the marketplace.

The Ramos administration enjoyed various economic successes. The first was the reworking of the tax code to encourage payment of taxes. It had been estimated that between $1.5 and $2.5 billion in owed taxes were not collected. With the support of the House of Representatives, Ramos was able to push a new tax bill through the Congress in 1996. This bill increased exemptions, lowered the maximum rate, and simplified the filing process. The second success was in the area of banking reform. Like the telecommunications industry and shipping, banking was controlled by a few families. When Ramos became president, there were only twenty-six Filipino-owned commercial banks; the four foreign banks in the Philippines had been licensed to operate during the days of the Commonwealth. Unlike the rest of Asia, where the difference between rates to borrow and to lend was about 2 percent, the gap in the Philippines was about 6 percent. This allowed banks to make huge profits, but also discouraged entrepreneurs. Many Filipinos put their money in banks outside the country, which did not help the Philippine economy. The new banking laws and regulations introduced during the Ramos years helped to encourage economic growth.

Perhaps the greatest success attributed to Ramos was in the area of energy. The shortage of energy had begun during the Aquino years and continued into Ramos's administration. It was a source of embarrassment that Metro-Manila, the symbol of modernity, experienced "brownouts" caused by the shortage of energy. Rationing meant that some areas were without electricity for up to ten hours a day. This not only affected existing industry and business, it also discouraged foreign businesses from investing in the Philippines. A significant part of the problem was that Manila had simply outgrown the power available. Ramos was given emergency power to award power-plant projects without the long and expensive process normally required. Soon, "brownouts" became a thing of the past. The success that Ramos achieved in this area not only encouraged economic growth, it also opened the way to deregulating other utilities, including telecommunications, and to the privatization of the Metropolitan Water Works and Sewage System in Manila.

Another significant success was the transformation of the former naval facilities at Subic Bay. The U.S. Navy had left behind a facility valued at least at $3 billion. This facility included, in part, a 9,000-foot jet runway, golf courses, and electric power plants. Richard Gordon, the mayor of Olongapo, the town outside the former Subic Naval Base, was put in charge of the Subic Bay Metropolitan Authority (SBMA). It was important to bring in foreign investors and to build up the economy of an area that had suffered as the result of the departure of the U.S. Navy. By 1996, about two hundred companies announced their intentions to invest over $1.2 billion in Subic. The biggest names were the Taiwanese computer giant, Acer, and Federal Express, which made Subic a regional hub for the airfreight business. Gordon had his critics, but the economic success was undeniable.

Crime remained a constant threat. Ramos established a commission and designated the vice president, Joseph Estrada, to deal with the problem. Estrada had not been Ramos's running mate—as in the past the new Philippine electoral system allowed one to vote for candidates for president and vice president from different parties—and Ramos was not sure what to do with him. Estrada, a former movie star, used his position to enhance his own political ambitions. Ramos eventually dismissed Estrada from the position because of the many unexplained deaths of alleged criminals while they were in police custody.

Although the decision to end the agreement with the United States on their bases was reached before Ramos became president, he had to deal with the new international diplomatic realities that resulted. The Philippines now had to provide for its own defense and military supplies and training. The superpower was no longer around to provide a safety net. The Philippines had only one or two F-5 jets capable of combat. The radar system that the Americans had built was gone. The Philippine navy did not have the necessary equipment to prevent smuggling and illegal fishing. When the Philippines claimed the Spratly Islands, which were thought to have significant undersea oil fields, the military had no power to enforce that claim. Equally important, it appeared that the United States no longer cared what happened to the Philippines. The Philippines was not critical or strategic to America's goals in the region. American politicians who had supported Philippine interests in the U.S. Congress either were no longer in power or no longer possessed the necessary political influence. Ramos reached out to Filipino Americans living in the United States as a potentially important factor in the post-bases era.

The election of 1995 is worth noting because it saw a return to political power of names from the past: Juan Ponce Enrile, Gregorio B. Honasan—one of the founders of RAM and the leader of at least one military coup attempt against President Aquino—Ferdinand Marcos, Jr., Imelda Marcos, and Gloria Macapagal-Arroyo, daughter of President Macapagal. The success of Ramos's presidency led many to suggest that the constitution be changed to allow him to run for a second term. This movement—Change the Charter or Cha-Cha for short—was met with immediate opposition. Corazon Aquino, who had supported Ramos's run for the presidency, began to speak out against his reelection. Yellow, which had been the color of her candidacy and presidency, was revived as she and others not only opposed the Cha-Cha but raised the specter of another dictatorship. Rumors circulated that Ramos would declare martial law in order to stay in power. Cardinal Sin, who had opposed Ramos's candidacy, stated that Ramos would "lead [the Philippines] back into the dark ages of pre-Martial Law, political dynasties, war lordism, corruption, sham democracy and debilitating democracy." Sin was wrong in 1992 and again in 1998. Ramos was committed to democracy and allowed the Filipino people to elect his successor.

The presidential election of 1998 was won by Vice President Joseph Ejercito Estrada. Widely known as "Erap"—*pare,* or "friend," spelled backwards—this former movie star (Estrada being his stage name) identified with the common people. In many ways, Estrada was similar to Ramon Magsaysay, and he caught the imagination of the masses. Where Magsaysay had dealt with the Communist insurgency, Estrada had dealt with the problem of crime. To the educated urbanites, he was an anomaly, a walking joke. His mangling of English was the source of much amusement. But the common people saw him as one of their own. His campaign slogan, *"Erap para sa mahirap,"* or "Erap (friend) for those who have a hard life," symbolized that connection. His poor English made him the butt of jokes but also endeared him all the more to the common people. His own campaign printed a collection of jokes about his misuse of English titled: "ERAPtions: How to Speak English Without Really Trial." One such story of Erap's mangling of English is found in Steinberg's book: "At first he was embarrassed by his English malapropisms. He threatened, 'I'll stop speaking in English. From now on, I will just speak in the binocular'" (Steinberg 2000, 211).

Estrada began his political career as a mayor during the martial law era, and then became a senator after the EDSA Revolution. He decided to run as an independent candidate for vice president and won easily. He had a paunch and a slicked-back pompadour hairstyle. A heavy smoker and drinker, he was also a known womanizer who kept several mistresses, the mothers of his illegitimate children. However, he also cared for his mistresses and children, taking the time to visit the children, and even to discipline them when necessary. His directness was considered refreshing. He offered a breath of fresh air into the political process and arena. Gloria Macapagal-Arroyo was elected vice president in 1998, although she was not Estrada's running mate.

But several missteps prevented his presidency from gaining momentum. Shortly before taking office, he agreed to allow the Marcos family to bring the body of President Marcos from his hometown, where it lay in state in a glass case, and to bury him in the *Libingan ng mga Bayani* (the National Heroes Cemetery). This brought out the old alliances from the EDSA Revolution days, and Mrs. Aquino wore her familiar yellow dresses. The specter of a return to the days of Marcos would be thrown up time and time again. In fact, Estrada allowed Marcos supporters to return to their positions of economic strength. In addition, Estrada was willing to permit General Fabian Ver to return to the Philippines after being in exile for twelve years.

Although he had voted against the American bases agreement when he was a senator, Estrada changed his position vis-à-vis the United States and arranged for the U.S. military to pay calls to the Philippines. His administration was able to negotiate a Visiting Forces Agreement (VFA) with the United States, which allowed the U.S. Navy to visit Subic. One of the main reasons for this change of heart was the problem involving the Spratly Islands. Claiming the islands as their own, even though 1,000 miles from the mainland, China began constructing a fort on a reef near the islands. The value of these islands is in the undersea oil reserves believed to be there. In the face of Chinese aggression, the Philippines was powerless to do anything. But although the United States did sign the VFA, it has yet to take a position as to who has territorial rights to the Spratlys.

Two years into his presidency, on October 16, 2000, Estrada was accused by a close associate of receiving protection money from illegal gambling as well as kickbacks from various enterprises. Calls for his resignation began the next day. Within weeks, the House of Representatives began the process of impeaching Estrada on the grounds of bribery, graft and corruption, betrayal of the public trust, and violation of the constitution. Among the various accusations made against him was that he used the money he had taken to build mansions for his mistresses. Although his womanizing had almost been a point of pride, the taint of corruption changed this. The impeachment trial started on December 7, 2000, with the chief justice of the Supreme Court presiding and the members of the Senate acting as judges. Evidence was presented pointing to corruption and betrayal of the public trust, and former colleagues came forward to confirm the violations. One particular piece of evidence began a series of events that led to Estrada's removal from office. On January 16, 2001, a brown envelope that had been given by a bank was presented. The prosecutors were convinced that the evidence contained in the envelope would show that Estrada had bank accounts valued at more than 3 billion pesos. However, the majority of the senators (eleven out of twenty-one) voted to bar the opening of the envelope. The prosecutors walked out, believing that the truth would not come out and that Estrada would be acquitted by this group of senators.

The way was now open for a repetition of the events of 1986, with thousands of Filipinos, representing different parts of the political spectrum, going to EDSA to protest and to demand the removal of Estrada. Cardinal Sin, who had been pivotal in the original EDSA revolution but had been marginalized since then, once again called on Filipinos to go and stay at EDSA until Estrada resigned. Thus, what is now known as EDSA II began. The next day, January 17, there were 100,000 people at the EDSA shrine. The following day, the number had increased to 300,000. It was on the third day that high-ranking military and police officials withdrew their support for Estrada and joined the protest. More than half the cabinet resigned and joined the protest as well. By the end of day three (January 19) there were nearly two million people at EDSA demanding that Estrada resign. Estrada stated on national television that he would not resign. The trial was to go forward, the brown envelope could be opened, and he would await a verdict. About an hour later, Estrada was again on national television, this time proposing that rather than resign, he would call for early elections in May.

On January 20, in the face of Estrada's refusal to resign, the Supreme Court reached a unanimous decision that the position of president was vacant; thereby the vice president must fill the vacancy. At noon, Gloria Macapagal-Arroyo (GMA) took the oath of office in front of the thousands gathered at the EDSA Shrine. As had happened almost fifteen years earlier, a president who was believed to be corrupt was forced from office and replaced by a woman. Corazon Aquino was the widow of a national political figure, and Gloria Macapagal-Arroyo was the daughter of President Diosdado Macapagal. Ironically, Macapagal-Arroyo was inaugurated on the same day as was U.S. president George W. Bush, the son of a former president.

Estrada agreed for the good of the country to step down only to change his mind and insist that he did not resign and therefore was still legally the president. It was believed that Estrada took this position to claim immunity from prosecution until the end of his term. In April 2001, Estrada was arrested. His supporters came out in force to the EDSA shrine leading to what is called EDSA III, or *EDSA Tres*. This gathering, which some claimed was larger than that of EDSA II, lasted for four days, but had no real political impact, and in failing to achieve any significant change called into question the true nature of EDSA I and EDSA II. Whereas people believed that it was People Power that drove Marcos from office after more than twenty years in power, and that Estrada was forced from office by a similar phenomenon, reality began set in. The role of the military in both "revolutions" was not insignificant. Had the military not joined the first "revolution," it very well might not have succeeded. And as for EDSA II, some military officials made public statements that Estrada was not removed from office by People Power, but by a military coup.

Many Filipinos did not know about EDSA III, not simply because it took place in Manila but because the new president, Gloria Macapagal-Arroyo, pressured the media to stop their coverage of the event. The urban elite, the wealthy, and the powerful had never liked Estrada and were glad to see him go. When the ordinary Filipino sought to express his or her support for the man they felt understood them and cared about their problems, the elite did not want to hear about it.

It has been noted that GMA attended Georgetown University, where she was a classmate of Bill Clinton, future president of the United States. After two years at Georgetown, she returned to the Philippines to marry Jose Miguel "Mike" Arroyo. She earned a degree in commerce from Assumption College, and a master's (from Ateneo de Manila University) and a doctorate (from the University of the Philippines) in economics. She held teaching positions in each school between 1977 and 1987. She joined the Aquino administration in 1987, as assistant secretary of the Department of Trade and Industry, and was promoted to undersecretary two years later. It was in 1992 that she formally entered into politics and was elected to the Senate. She considered running for the presidency in 1998, but was convinced by then-President Ramos to run as the vice-presidential candidate with Jose De Venecia. He lost to Estrada, but she won with more than twice the number of votes of her closest opponent. Estrada made her a member of his cabinet, assigning her the position of secretary of the Department of Social Welfare and Development.

The manner in which she became president almost guaranteed that her term in office would be plagued continually by questions of legitimacy. Not only did she have to contend with Estrada supporters, but an increasingly restive military and politicians who sought to destabilize her regime. Two events seemed to help her achieve some respite. The first was September 11, 2001. She was among the first world leaders to call President Bush after the terror attack in New York City and to pledge her support in fighting global terror. With a growing Muslim insurgency, the pseudo-Islamic terror group Abu Sayyaf, and the ever-present Communist New People's Army, she needed help from the United States and in turn pledged to work with the Bush administration in fighting terrorism. The second event was her public announcement on December 31, 2002, that she would not run for president in 2004. This gave the impression that she would focus on the problems in the country rather than try to win support for reelection.

But GMA changed her mind and decided to run after all. She was behind in the polls and was running against another former actor, Fernando Poe, Jr., Estrada's best friend. Even more popular than Estrada, Poe had no experience whatsoever in public service. With a popular vice-presidential candidate, Noli De Castro, a former television news anchor, and support from key provinces, GMA and De Castro were both elected. Although there were charges of cheating, GMA was president as the result of an election and not because of a military coup or because thousands of protesters had gathered in one place. On June 30, 2004, she took the oath of office in Cebu, the first time a Philippine president had been inaugurated there. This was done in response to Cebu's support for her in the election.

GMA continues to face the same problems with which her predecessors have struggled, such as a weak economy and corruption in both the private and public sectors. But she has additional challenges, including terrorism and a revival of an Islamic insurgency in the south.

The Philippines has been shaped by outside forces, its boundaries defined by others, its history impacted by intruders, and its cultures affected by contact with those of conquerors. But one should not think of the Philippines or its inhabitants as passive recipients. The modern nation state follows the lead of what was established, but regionalism remains through adaptation.

But some matters were beyond the control of Filipinos. The policies and practices of the Spaniards had brought about a division in Philippine society. This division was later confirmed and entrenched by the Americans. Melba Maggay refers to this as the "Great Cultural Divide": "There exists in the Philippines an invisible yet impermeable dividing line between those who are able to function within the borrowed ethos of power structures transplanted from without."

References

Agoncillo, Teodoro A. *History of the Filipino People.* 8th ed. Quezon City: R. P. Garcia Publishing Co., 1990.

——. *The Fateful Years: Japan's Adventure in the Philippines, 1941–1945.* Vols. 1 and 2. Quezon City: University of the Philippines Press, 1965.

——. *The Revolt of the Masses.* Quezon City: University of the Philippines Press, 1956.

Blair, Emma Helen, and James Robertson, eds. *The Philippine Islands, 1493–1898.* 55 vols. Cleveland, Ohio: Arthur H. Clark, 1903–1909.

Chirino, Pedro. *The Philippines in 1600.* Translated from the Spanish by Ramon Echevarria. Manila: Historical Conservation Society, 1969.

Constantino, Renato. *The Philippines: A Past Revisited.* Quezon City: Tala Publishing House, 1975.

Cushner, Nicholas P. *Spain in the Philippines: From Conquest to Revolution.* Rutland, Vermont: Charles E. Tuttle Co., Inc., 1971.

De la Costa, Horatio. *The Jesuits in the Philippines: 1581–1768.* Cambridge, Mass.: Harvard University Press, 1961.

Enriquez, Virgilio G. *From Colonial to Liberation Psychology.* Manila: De La Salle University Press, 1994.

Francisco, Mariel N., and Fe Maria C. Arriola. *The History of the Burgis.* Quezon City: GCF Books, 1987.

IBON Philippine Profile. Manila: IBON Books, 2002.

Ileto, Reynaldo C. *Pasyon and Revolution: Popular Movements in the Philippines, 1840–1910.* Quezon City: Ateneo de Manila University Press, 1979.

—. *Filipinos and their Revolution: Event, Discourse and Historiography.* Quezon City: Ateneo de Manila University Press, 1998.

Jocano, F. Landa. *Filipino Prehistory: Rediscovering Precolonial Heritage.* Metro Manila: PUNLAD Research House, Inc., 2000.

—. *Filipino Worldview: Ethnography of Local Knowledge.* Metro-Manila: PUNLAD Research House, Inc., 2001.

Karnow, Stanley. *In Our Image: America's Empire in the Philippines.* New York: Ballantine Books, 1989.

McCoy, Alfred W., and Ed. C. de Jesus, eds. *Philippine Social History: Global Trade and Local Transformations.* Quezon City: Ateneo de Manila University Press, 1982.

Mendoza, Susanah Lily L. *Between the Home and the Diaspora: The Politics of Theorizing Filipino and Filipino American Identities.* New York: Routledge, 2001.

Patanñe, E. P. *The Philippines in the 6th to 16th Centuries.* Quezon City: LSA Press, 1996.

Phelan, John Leddy. *Hispanization of the Philippines: Spanish Aims and Filipino Responses, 1565–1700.* Madison, Wisc.: The University of Wisconsin Press, 1959.

Schirmer, Daniel B., and Stephen Rosskamm Shalom, eds. *The Philippines Reader: A History of Colonialism, Neocolonialism, Dictatorship, and Resistance.* Boston: South End Press, 1987.

Schumacher, John N. *The Propaganda Movement 1880–1895.* Quezon City: Ateneo de Manila University Press, 1997.

Scott, William Henry. *Cracks in the Parchment Curtain.* Quezon City: New Day Publishers, 1982.

—. *Prehispanic Source Materials for the Study of Philippine History.* Rev. ed. Quezon City: New Day Publishers, 1989.

—. *Looking for the Prehispanic Filipino.* Quezon City: New Day Publishers, 1992.

—. *Barangay: Sixteenth-Century Philippine Culture and Society.* Quezon City: Ateneo de Manila University Press, 1994.

Steinberg, David Joel. *The Philippines: A Singular and a Plural Place.* 4th ed. Boulder, Colo.: Westview Press, 2000.

CHAPTER TWO

The Philippines' Economy

A recently published book on the problems of the Philippine economy is subtitled *The Political Economy of Permanent Crisis in the Philippines.* This captures the way the Philippine economy has been for some time now. Why is it that the Philippines, which is rich in natural resources and has one of the most educated populations in the world, still has such a high poverty rate and an economy that does not appear to work? This chapter examines the historical background to the economic situation in the Philippines, focusing on those aspects that affected the nature and direction of the Philippine economy, including the problems in today's economy.

PRE-SPANISH TRADE

Much of the evidence for trade within and beyond the islands is based on archaeological finds and historical records from outsiders. From these one can reconstruct a sense of the economic activities that existed prior to the coming of the Spanish. Although no kingdoms or empires arose in the Philippines, that is, political entities based on trade as in the rest of Southeast Asia, networks existed that entailed international trade as well as internal trade.

The Laguna Copperplate Inscription, which dates from 900 CE, is a document that cancels the debts owed by an individual named Namwaran. This artifact demonstrates that a political network existed that stretched from the Manila Bay area to Java. But the network must have had an economic component, because the canceled debt mentioned a specific amount of gold.

The earliest Chinese records of trade with individuals from the Philippines date from 982 CE. Mention is made of men from Ma-i (Mindoro in the Philippines) who traveled to Canton to trade. In 1225, Chao Ju Kua, the superintendent of maritime trade in the province of Fukien, wrote a book describing the various peoples with whom the Chinese traded. More than a century later, Wang Ta-Yuan, after twenty years of traveling and trading outside China, wrote of the places he had visited. Both accounts mention Ma-i and Wang Ta-Yuan also refers to areas now known as Manila, Sulu, and Mindanao. The products the Chinese sought to trade for in the Philippines were either from the sea or from forests. Such goods included bees wax, abaca (hemp), copra (dried coconut), betel nut, rattan, animal hides, coral, pearls, giant clams, and tortoise shell. In exchange for these goods, the Chinese traded porcelain. The discovery of porcelain artifacts throughout the Philippines indicates extensive trade—first with the Chinese and then between the coastal peoples, who met with the Chinese merchants, and the peoples of the interior, who were the source of products from forests.

The people of the archipelago did not trade only with those who could travel the seas to meet with them in the islands. In the past few decades, archaeologists have discovered seagoing vessels that date from the third to the fourteenth centuries CE near Butuan City on Mindanao. Not only does their size suggest the capacity to travel long distances, but artifacts found nearby demonstrate they had traveled outside the archipelago.

When the Portuguese came to Southeast Asia, they found individuals from Luzon in Malacca, including a colony of some five hundred Tagalogs on the west coast of the Malay peninsula. These people were from Luzon, and were known as *Luções*, or Luzones. Tome Pires, the Portuguese historian, noted that they had their own shops in Malacca and included a number of prominent business people.

With the coming of the West to Southeast Asia, Islam began to spread quickly throughout insular Southeast Asia. Islam was the common denominator among the kingdoms in the region, but trade was the driving force that kept them going and in power. One such kingdom, Brunei, had spread its influence all the way to the Manila Bay area. When the Spaniards finally took Manila, they had to defeat local leaders loyal to Brunei, along with some officials from Brunei sent to defend against the Spanish intrusion. When Magellan arrived in the Philippines and went to Cebu in search of food, the local ruler, Humabon, insisted that the travelers pay tribute because the vessel had left only four days before from what is modern Thailand. These incidents demonstrate that the Philippines was not isolated from the rest of Asia, and in fact was an active participant in the trade of the region.

The Philippines generally has not been the target of foreign intruders. The Spaniards were looking for a new route to the Spice Islands. The Americans wanted a bigger share in the trade with China. The Japanese wanted a clear path to the oil of Indonesia. As a result, they all ended up in the Philippines, participating in and controlling the economic structures of the archipelago.

THE SPANISH ERA

The Spanish intrusion had several effects on the economies of various Philippine societies. These changes began when the spread of Islam was halted north of Mindanao. No longer would the Philippines, particularly the Manila Bay area, be a part of the Muslim trade system that stretched from China to Alexandria, Egypt. In addition, the Philippines was cut off, one might even say sealed off, from the rest of Southeast Asia, and Asia in general. The Spaniards were in charge of all foreign trade, the centerpiece being the Manila Galleon.

The Spanish intrusion had a profound impact on the economic patterns among the various Philippine societies. Farming among pre-Hispanic Filipinos was geared to domestic feeding, not to producing surplus for trade. Trade goods, with the exception of cotton, were not produced as crops. The sudden influx of the Spaniards meant, for a while, food shortages. Without surplus food, the systems of production had to be shifted.

A part of the shift was a new view of land. Among Filipinos, the focus was land use, but the Spaniards saw land ownership as a sign of personal wealth. Rather than accept the communal ownership of land, as Filipinos did, the Spaniards bought and took land from individuals, people who did not own the land because ownership was communal. This shift was one of the early steps toward creating an elite.

Another step was the presence of the Chinese. Most Spaniards lived in Manila and did not go into the countryside; only the friars did so. But the Spaniards needed a buffer between Manila and the countryside. Chinese merchants became this buffer. Although the Chinese had traveled to the Philippines for centuries to trade, there is no record of their living anywhere in the islands or intermarrying with the local population. This changed with the arrival of the Spaniards. Chinese communities were set up in different provinces and cities throughout the archipelago. At the same time, intermarriage created a new class, Chinese *mestizos.*

Pedro Manuel de Arandía (1754–1759), a generally ineffective governor general, sought to break the economic influence of the Chinese in the archipelago. He expelled non-Christian Chinese, opening the door for the *mestizo* community to emerge from the shadow of the Chinese community. Arandía's goal was for the Spanish community to fill the vacuum created by the expulsion of Chinese merchants. For a variety of reasons, including the invasion and takeover of the Philippines by the British (1762–1764), this did not happen. In 1778, the expulsion was revoked.

The Manila Galleon had been the economic backbone for the Spanish community for two centuries. This system involved trade between Chinese merchants with silk, porcelain, and other goods from China, and Spaniards with silver, chocolate, and other goods from Mexico. Meeting in the Philippines was necessary because no foreigners were allowed in China. The trade was beneficial to all parties involved. The Spaniards in Manila shared in the profits. But the troubles of the last part of the eighteenth century moved various Spanish leaders to push the Philippines in the direction of exporting rather than simply importing. Agriculture could have been a means of producing exports and improving the balance of trade. This strategy was not successful until the nineteenth century.

THE NINETEENTH CENTURY

This century saw significant changes that affected the economic patterns and structure in the Philippines, among them, the end of the Manila Galleon with Mexican independence and the opening of the Philippines to foreign traders. The end of the Galleon was potentially devastating. Changes had to be made involving difficult choices. One of the aspects of the Philippine economy that remained constant was agriculture. Because there was little in the way of manufacturing and mining industries, exports until the end of the Spanish period in 1898 were primarily agricultural. But there were changes in the agricultural sphere. From the beginning of the century to the late 1820s, wealthy Filipinos and Chinese *mestizos* raised cash crops for exports because they had found a new source of support in the British and American trading houses established in the 1820s. The example and success of Paul P. dela Gironiere's pioneering plantation approach to growing crops for export marked a shift in the thinking of rich Filipinos and Chinese *mestizos,* as well as the Chinese who immigrated to the Philippines in the middle of the century. Between 1850 and 1898, the Chinese population in the Philippines increased from 5,000 to 100,000. This opening of the Philippines allowed the Chinese to become a major force in the Philippines, and they remain so to the

Planting rice almost a century ago, as seen in this photograph, is still done the same way today in much of the Philippines. (Library of Congress)

present. Almost 1 million Chinese currently live in the Philippines.

Changes in the world economy created growth in the agricultural aspect of the Philippine economy. Perhaps the most significant aspect of these changes is that they set the stage for the rise of the wealthy families who would dominate the local economy and continue to do so to this day.

THE AMERICAN PERIOD

One aspect of Philippine life strongly impacted by the American presence was the economy. Indeed, one could argue that economic reasons were driving forces in the decision to retain the Philippines as a possession of the United States. (Among the economic reasons why the United States decided to keep the Philippines were the islands as a source of raw materials as well as a captive market for American goods and the Philippines as a jumping-off point for larger markets in China and Japan, among others.) And among the justifications given for keeping the Philippines was the responsibility to improve the economic lot of Filipinos. Yet American policies, although having some positive effects, for the most part structured the post-independent Philippine economy for failure. These policies had the double effect of entrenching an elite as well as failing to provide avenues for capitalization of the economy.

The roots of the economic elite were in the latter part of the Spanish period, particularly with the opening of the archipelago to foreign investment. The possibilities of selling agricultural goods such as Manila hemp, which was used for rope and sugar, provided the impetus for a more commercial approach to agriculture. Certain families were able to profit and expand their holdings during the last decades of the Spanish regime. This elite was unknowingly aided by the presence of the Americans and their policies. Hoping to provide opportunities for Filipinos to own property for farming, the U.S. Congress passed a series of laws to try to accomplish this. One of the programs, spelled out in the Friar Land Act of 1904, was to break up the vast haciendas held by the religious orders and to give the local population the opportunity to buy land. There was one problem: Most Filipinos did not have the capital to buy land. The Filipinos who did have money, the elite, were able to purchase land and increase their already strong economic positions. It should be noted that some of the land laws prohibited the expansion of large estates, but the export economy in essence negated these restrictions. In contrast, many Filipinos lost whatever economic power they had, and consequently the gap between the rich and the poor grew year by year. Between 1918 and 1938, the population in the Philippines grew from 10 million to 16 million. But the number of owner-operated farms fell from 1.52 million to 805,000. The number of tenant-operated farms went from 435,000 to 575,000, and the number of part-owners more than tripled, from 225,000 to 830,000.

The owners of the large landed estates were originally cultivators of crops for export, such as sugar, hemp, coconut, and tobacco. As time went on, they became processors (for example, of sugar), and finally they became directly involved in the export of their products. Those who had been planters were now merchants. As a result, the families who had been plantation owners became involved in shipping, insurance, banking, and the importation of various goods. Wealthy families whose fortunes had been made at the local level began to enjoy national economic power. Intermarriage between these families also helped to cement their positions at the top of the economic heap. As their economic power grew, so did their political power, and not merely at the local level, but at the national level as well. By the end of the American period and the beginning of an independent Philippines, these families controlled the Philippines.

American investment in the Philippines was relatively small compared to other countries, but it was significant when seen within the Philippine context. And not only was the amount large for a country as small as the Philippines, but American investment reached into almost all areas of the Philippine economy and dominated the market up to and beyond independence. It was not simply the strength and dominance of American investment that should be noted but the areas in which the investments ruled. These areas were those in which mechanical equipment and technology, which the Philippines and Filipinos did not own or have access to, were required. As a consequence, American business interests controlled public utilities, including radio, cable, telephone, railway, electricity, and water systems. In addition, Filipinos could not compete with the ability of Americans to make capital investments. Filipinos who did have money (the elite) were busy with their own segments of the market and for the most part did not seek to compete with American investors. Some have argued, however, that American capital was beneficial and that it brought technical know-how to the Philippines. But when independence was granted in 1946, Philippine technology and capitalization lagged in comparison to other Asian nations. This was the result of American domination of the market, which did not allow for Filipinos to compete in terms of investment; in addition, the local population was deprived of technical know-how.

At least two points should be noted about the last decade of the American presence in the Philippines, prior to World War II. Although Independence Missions had been traveling to Washington almost yearly since 1919, the granting of independence was as much economic as political in motivation. The Democrats, from President Wilson on, had supported Philippine independence. But the push for independence began to receive unexpected support from organized labor, as well as the sugar, tobacco, and dairy lobbies. The Depression devastated the American economy, and the Philippines was seen as dangerous to a recovery. Cheap Filipino labor was not impacted by the Oriental Exclusion Act of 1924 because the Philippines was not a foreign country, products from the

Bird's-eye view of waterfront, bridges, and industrial buildings in Manila sometime between 1900 and 1930. (Library of Congress)

Philippines had free entry into the United States and competed with American goods. Granting independence would make the Philippines a foreign entity and its citizens and goods seeking to enter the United States subject to the same laws and tariffs as other countries. As mentioned in chapter 1, the Tydings-McDuffie Act created the Commonwealth of the Philippines, a stage that was to lead to complete independence after ten years.

The other economic factor, which also had international political implications, was the increase of Japanese economic interests in the Philippines. By 1941, Japanese interests in Philippine lumber, hemp, and copra were substantial. In addition, Japanese investments in iron, manganese, and copper were 35 percent of the shares, the maximum allowed by law. Thus, the Japanese had a foothold in the archipelago even before the beginning of their conquest and occupation of the Philippines.

POST-WAR PHILIPPINES

The damage that resulted from the war was extensive. The economic infrastructure—transportation, business, and agricultural—was devastated. Shipping and railways were out of commission; roads and bridges were heavily damaged. Farms could operate only at 60 percent of prewar levels because irrigation systems had been destroyed, 30 percent of farming machinery had been lost, and 65 percent of livestock had been killed. With production at a standstill, there was no capital to finance the task of rebuilding.

Senator Tydings traveled to the Philippines in May 1945 to survey the situation. He recommended that the Philippines be given $100 million for rehabilitation and reconstruction. The United States Congress voted $120 million for rebuilding the infrastructure, $75 million for budgetary purposes, and an additional $25 million to redeem currency created by guerrilla movements during the Japanese Occupation. The U.S. Army also turned over $1 billion in surplus to the Philippine government, and the U.S. Reconstruction and Finance Corporation loaned $60 million to the Philippine government. Representative C. Jasper Bell of Missouri introduced a bill providing for free trade between the United States and the Philippines for twenty years. Opposed by Tydings and others, Bell changed the period to eight years and the bill passed. One of the conditions of the bill was that Americans would have the same rights as Filipinos to do business in the Philippines. This condition required that the Philippine Constitution be amended. The United States then passed the Tydings Rehabilitation Act, which provided $620 million for those who suffered loss during the war. But a condition was attached. No more than $500 million could be released until an agreement could be reached between the two countries regarding trade.

The Philippine Congress was reconvened in 1945, and one of its first actions, motivated by self-interest, was to vote its members three years' back pay—three years being the length of the Japanese Occupation. When a small group was able to block efforts to amend the constitution to allow Americans parity rights, President Roxas, a former leader in the Congress, expelled those standing in the way of changing the constitution. The issue was presented to the Filipino people in a plebiscite in 1947. It passed. But for all the American money given, the Philippines made little progress.

Ramon Magsaysay, a charismatic figure who was seen as a man of the people, won the presidential election in 1953. He focused on the rural population, pushing through Congress the Agricultural Tenancy Act in 1954. This act provided for greater protection of tenants who worked on the large estates of the wealthy elite. Magsaysay wanted to break up these estates, but the government lacked the financial power to purchase them. Instead, public lands were given to those wishing to settle on them. Road construction was undertaken to both connect the countryside to the national life and to enable people to take their products to market.

Magsaysay's untimely death left Carlos Garcia to serve the remaining eight months of the term as president. Garcia was elected in 1957, and sought to bring about Philippine economic independence. He developed a number of programs that alienated foreign businessmen and the wealthy elite. Corruption, however, became the major issue of his tenure, and it has remained one of the major problems affecting the economy to the present.

MARTIAL LAW

When Ferdinand Marcos took office in the mid-1960s, the Philippines had real potential for economic growth. But problems such as the inequity of the distribution of wealth, an entrenched elite, rampant corruption, and foreign business interests made that growth almost impossible. Chinese merchants held disproportionate control over retail, wholesale, and distribution. United States businesses, such as Proctor &

Marcos announces the imposition of Martial Law on September 24, 1972. (Bettmann)

Gamble, CalTex, AT&T, and Del Monte, prevented local companies from succeeding. United States banks, such as Bank of America, First National City Bank of New York, and Manufacturers Hanover, and other British and American banks were also the major banking powers in the Philippine economy.

Marcos declared martial law in 1972, claiming that the Communists represented a real danger. But this presented Marcos with an opportunity to make fundamental changes in Philippine society. In the first three years of martial law, the economy grew at an annual rate of 7 percent. Amnesty for back taxes was announced and 1 billion pesos came in, allowing the government to build roads, bridges, irrigation facilities, airfields, schools, hospitals, and public buildings. In seeking to rid the elite of their power, Marcos and his friends took what they wanted. The corruption was staggering, with some estimating that Marcos amassed personal assets of as much as

$20 billion, and the economy began to falter. Foreign banks were more than glad to lend the Philippines large amounts, which were not put to use in the economy but siphoned off by Marcos and his cronies. In the meantime, the loans had to be repaid, but the economy was not producing the necessary funds to do so.

Marcos came up with a temporary solution to two problems facing the economy: unemployment and balance of payments. That solution was to export labor. Recorded remittances from overseas workers in 1975 were $103,000. By 1995, that figure had ballooned to $4.88 billion. Although intended to be a short-term solution, it has become a permanent institution, and more than 6 million Filipinos went overseas to work between 1984 and 1995.

After the assassination of Benigno "Ninoy" Aquino in August, 1983, the economy was in free fall. The peso, which had been just been devalued to six pesos to the dollar, would fall to twenty to one. Filipinos who could leave the country did so. Some 300,000 immigrated to the United States. More than 1.5 million Filipinos were in the diaspora.

POST-MARTIAL LAW

President Corazon Aquino faced serious economic problems when she took office. The disparity between the rich and the poor was greater than ever. A number of factors made her task even more difficult: Political stability seemed illusory, with seven attempted coups making it appear that her hold on power was tenuous. In 1990, Mount Pinatubo erupted, devastating much of the farm land in central Luzon. The next year, the United States began the process of closing its military bases in the Philippines. The United States employed the second highest number of Filipinos; only the Philippine government employed more. And the loans made during the Marcos regime had to be repaid. The country continued to fall into deeper poverty, and the elite, which was conservative, continued to be in charge.

The contrast found in Manila—skyscrapers in the background with slums in the foreground. (Albrecht G. Schaefer/Corbis)

President Aquino's successor, Fidel Ramos, focused on banking reform and ending energy shortages. His efforts were marked with some success. But circumstances beyond his control and that of his successors adversely affected the national economy. The Asian currency crisis in the late 1990s and the weather conditions (related to El Niño) sharply impacted the economy. The peso, which traded at 26.20 to the dollar in 1996, fell to an average of 54.20 in 2003. But there was an upside: Exports became much more competitive in foreign markets as a result of the weak peso.

The year 2003 was one marked by instability and market turbulence. During the first part of the year, the stock exchanges fell because of concerns about a growing deficit, the war in Iraq, and possible international sanctions resulting from deficiencies in the Philippine laws regarding money laundering. The peso depreciated 5 percent against the dollar. The government took action to strengthen money-laundering laws. But the second half of the year began with an unsuccessful military mutiny and was followed by a failed attempt to impeach the chief justice and the resignation of the finance secretary. Foreign investment, which had hit a high of $1.8 billion in 2002, dropped to $319 million in 2003. The peso hit new lows in February 2004 as the presidential election in May approached.

The Philippine economy survived the crises of 2003 and saw a growth rate of 4.5 percent. The agricultural sector and remittances from Filipinos working abroad were important factors to the increasing stability. Inflation remains lower than 4 percent, but unemployment remains high.

Following the reforms and programs initiated by the Aquino administration, the Ramos and Estrada administrations worked to remove those entities (including companies operated by the government and monopolies, for example) that have hampered competition and growth. Ramos in particular worked for the privatization of corporations owned and controlled by the government. The programs of privatization encouraged foreign investment and economic growth. The Foreign Investments Act of 1991 along with the Omnibus Investments Code of 1987 established the regulations and conditions under which non-Filipinos may invest and do business in the Philippines.

Starting a business in the Philippines does involve adhering to a large number of governmental regulations. One guide to doing business in the Philippines lists twelve general business start-up requirements. Among these are five forms of registration: with the Security and Exchange Commission, the Bureau of Trade Regulations and Consumer Protection, the Board of Investments, Philippine Export Zone Authority (for those wishing to locate in any of the various export zones), and the Central Bank of the Philippines (Gonzalez 2000, 78). Several things should be kept in mind. First, foreign investment is welcomed and the vast array of regulations are simply a part of doing business. Second, because personal relationships are central to Philippine society, it is important that one doing business in the Philippines develop personal relationships, not only with those in the private sector but with those in government as well.

When martial law ended, changes in regulations permitted foreign-owned companies to operate in the Philippines. These companies include resident foreign corporations and branches of international corporations. Foreign-owned companies are responsible for the following taxes: (1) capital gains tax (5 percent from the sale of real property to individuals, 10 percent on the sale or exchange of stock up to 100,000 pesos, 20 percent for amounts higher than 100,000 pesos); (2) local taxes (these may be levied by provincial governments); overseas communication taxes of 10 percent on international calls and faxes; and property taxes (commercial, industrial, or mineral lands based on 50 percent of fair market value; agricultural lands at 40 percent; timber, forest, and residential lands at 20 percent).

NUMBERS AND THE ECONOMY

Although the economy has experienced steady growth since 1999—2.4 percent in 1999, 4.4 percent in 2000, 3.2 percent in 2001, 4.4 percent in 2002, and 4.2 percent in 2003—problems remain. Several factors need to be taken into consideration.

- It is estimated that approximately 40 percent of the population lives below the poverty line.
- The money remitted by overseas workers, estimated to be anywhere from $6 to $8 billion annually, continues to be a major factor in the economy as a source of foreign currencies.
- Inflation remains low, approximately 3.1 percent in 2004, and unemployment is at 11.4 percent.
- The composition of the economy is 14.5 percent agriculture, 32.3 percent industry, and 53.2 percent services.

- Industries produce electronics, textiles, pharma-
  ceuticals, and wood products; exports include
  electronic equipment, machinery, clothing, and
  coconut products.
- External debt is $57.96 billion.

Japan and the United States are the leading sources of foreign investment in the Philippines. Along with these two
nations, Singapore, Taiwan, and South Korea are the major
trading partners of the Philippines. The Philippines has had a
special relationship with the United States. Beyond their
shared history, these two nations have in common their democratic values, economic interests, and security concerns, as
well as a generally similar view of the world situation. Companies from the United States have been involved in rebuilding the power utilities and communications infrastructure, as
well as developing the electronic sector. American companies
enjoy an advantage by operating in the Philippines because
the country provides an educated, English-speaking work-
force. The United States has provided three types of economic
assistance to the Philippines. These include economic aid,
military aid, and loans and credits. Japan is the largest
investor in the Philippines and, at the same time, the Philippines is a primary market for Japanese goods. Demand for
these goods, including electronic products and heavy equipment, has continued to rise in the past decade. Unlike American economic assistance, Japan has extended economic
loans and grants (known as the Official Development Assistance [ODA]). Grants are used for direct-project, grant, and
technical cooperation programs; loans are for a variety of purposes, including debt rescheduling.

TOURISM

It is difficult to know the full economic impact that tourism
has in the Philippines, but without question it is an important

source of revenue. The problems in the Philippines, such as perceived political instability or the threat of terrorism, have caused a decrease in the number of tourists. In 2003, fewer than 2 million tourists entered the Philippines, down from more than 2.2 million five years earlier. Tourist money remains important to the economy of the Philippines.

In addition to foreign tourists, there are the *balikbayan* (literally, returning to the homeland) Filipinos who have immigrated to other countries and who return to visit families as well as to see the sights. There are also Filipinos born in other countries who wish to connect with the homeland and see the places they have heard so much about. They are just as much tourists and spend as much money as non-Filipinos.

Certain locations are usually mentioned as places to visit in the Philippines. Manila is the cosmopolitan center and has much worth exploring—whether it be the old walled city, Intramuros, the open-air food places along Roxas Boulevard looking out on Manila Bay, the shopping centers throughout the city, or the night life. Baguio City, often called the summer capital, sits at an elevation of 5,000 feet and thus enjoys cooler weather than the tropical lowlands. Built up by the Americans and designed by Daniel Burnham, it still retains some of its past charm as the "City of Pines." From Baguio, one can go farther into the Cordillera mountain range and visit the Banaue rice terraces. Farther north, along the coast, is Vigan, the provincial capital of Ilocos Sur. Known for its Spanish architecture of the nineteenth century and its cobblestone streets, Vigan almost gives one a sense of being in another century.

The beaches are the main attraction for many tourists. The warm waters of the South China Sea and the temperate weather, along with idyllic locations, make different parts of the Philippines the ultimate destination for tourists. Cebu, along with its booming economic sector, has many beach resorts. Nearby Bohol is known for its pristine beaches. Boracay, off the island of Panay, is famous for its white sand beaches and crystal blue waters, and is a favorite for tourists from all over the world. Palawan has more than its share of secluded beach resorts and small islands, which are primarily resorts. Although tourism is important to the economy of Palawan, its people have embraced the concept of ecotourism and have worked to make sure that the environment is not damaged by the tourism industry. All of the above-mentioned locations are worth a visit.

In 1989, a law was passed by the Philippine Congress to encourage overseas Filipinos to visit the Philippines. Known as the Balikbayan Law, it defined *balikbayans* as former Filipino citizens who now hold foreign passports—including spouses and children, Filipinos who have been out of the country for at least one year, and Filipino overseas contract workers. The Congress agreed to provide the following benefits or incentives for *balikbayans* who visit the Philippines: travel tax exemption, visa-free entry into the Philippines for a stay of up to one year (for those holding foreign passports), and duty-free shopping of up to U.S. $2,000 (U.S. $1,000 as a *balikbayan* and U.S. $1,000 as an arriving passenger). There are limits to the duty-free shopping: It must be done within two days of arrival, can be done only once a year, and must be done personally by the *balikbayan.*

Although these benefits are made use of by returning Filipinos and their families, they are not the primary reasons for returning home to the homeland, the *bayan.* In general, there is a desire to connect or reconnect with one's roots. Those who left the country to find a better way of life want to spend time with family and friends, still an important part of their lives. For those born outside the Philippines of Filipino parents, visiting the Philippines allows them to meet family they have heard so much about, to see places their parents have described, and to be in the land of their ancestors. For some, it is an emotional, even life-changing experience. For others, it is a place offering great shopping and great beaches.

Philippine travel agencies have put together packages for *balikbayans* who wish to spend time in the many resorts found throughout the Philippines. However, the rates for *balikbayans* are what they would be for anyone coming from a foreign country. The rates tend to be given in foreign currency and can be expensive unless one purchases a package deal.

Tourism is not the only avenue available to *balikbayans*. Universities in the United States have set up programs for education abroad in which students study in the Philippines and earn credits with their American universities. These programs, which are either summer or year-round programs, are geared to teaching students about the Philippines—history, culture, and so forth, but with an increasing emphasis on language. Many of the children of the Philippine diaspora were not taught Tagalog, or any other Filipino language. Although they might understand the language, they cannot speak it, or they refuse to do so for fear their pronunciation will be off. By spending a summer or more in the Philippines, learning the grammar and structure of Filipino in an academic environment, and then being able to practice it with the locals, the children of the diaspora are reconnecting through language with the homeland.

Other programs are being set up for adults, usually for Filipinos who left the Philippines to find a new life abroad. Such programs might include tours of historic sights as well as brief seminars about different aspects of Philippine life, history, and culture.

An economic incentive drawing some *balikbayans* back is the ability to buy land. Foreigners cannot own property, but *balikbayans* holding foreign passports can. There is a limit—3 hectares or 7.5 acres in rural areas and 5,000 square meters in urban areas. The Philippine Department of Tourism has noticed a continuing rise in the price of real estate caused in part by the money coming in from *balikbayans* investing in land.

The word *balikbayan* is often followed by the word *box*. There is a thriving industry of shipping goods home to the Philippines in boxes—usually 20 by 20 by 20 inches, with no weight limits. Businesses will pick up the box from one's door and deliver it anywhere in the Philippines. Usually sent by ship, the box takes about a month to arrive in the Philippines. When going to the Philippines, it is not at all unusual for *balikbayans* to pack a *balikbayan* box or two with *pasalubong* (gifts) for family and friends.

THE FUTURE

If the Philippines is to have a vigorous economy marked by steady growth, at least four problems will have to be addressed. The first is the perennial problem of corruption. A recent study by the Asian Development Bank (ADB) ranks the Philippines second only to Bangladesh out of 102 countries in corruption. The second is the government, which some would suggest is the same as the first problem. Setting that aside, there are the twin and contradictory problems of over-regulation and the absence of enforcement of existing regulations. As one writer notes, "A state that promotes development and disciplines the elite and the private sector is what is missing in the Philippines." The same study by ADB noted that the top three problems scaring off foreign investors were macroeconomic instability, corruption, and poor infrastructure. The third problem is the continuing brain drain. Close to 10 percent of the population now work or live abroad, and recent surveys show that one in five Filipinos wants to emigrate. A recent study has shown that health care education and the health care system are seriously threatened by the loss of doctors and nurses to foreign markets. This is no longer a brain drain, but a brain hemorrhage, according to a former health minister. When a nurse in the Philippines earns between $75 and $250 a month and can start at between $3,000 and $4,000 a month elsewhere, the pressure to leave is irresistible. Last,

Filipina nurses are ubiquitous in the American medical scene. They demonstrate both the labor export aspect of the Philippine economy and the brain drain it has experienced for decades. (Dan Habib/ The Concord Monitor/Corbis)

there is a need for investment capital. Unfortunately, perceived government instability and the threat of terrorism keep investors from putting capital into the Philippine economic system. Although the government is a major part of the problem, it is most certainly a necessary part of the solution.

An Example to Consider

While the rest of the Philippines has struggled with problems such as terrorism, corruption, and political upheaval, at least one part of the Philippines has enjoyed increasing prosperity. In doing so, the city of Cebu on the island of Cebu offers an example for future prosperity. Cebu is known as the place where Magellan landed. What is generally not known is that Cebu was a trading center before the arrival of the Spaniards. For a brief period, it became the center for Spanish activities until the move to Manila, at which time Cebu's importance was greatly diminished. This changed in the nineteenth century, when Cebu became an important port because of sugar cane. Cebu attracted Chinese entrepreneurs in significant numbers and began to return to its previous position as an important international trading center. Many of today's wealthiest businessmen, including John Gokongwei (owner of Cebu Pacific Airline), Lucio Tan (owner of Philippine Airline), and Henry Sy (owner of the shopping-mall company SM Prime Holdings), are the descendants of some of those Chinese entrepreneurs.

Cebu has worked hard to attract investors and tourists. Their program began in the 1990s by identifying Cebu as "an island in the Pacific" rather than making reference to its being a part of the Philippines. Finding that the new global economy has made it possible for cities and islands to operate apart from the national context, Cebu offers the following benefits: its own international airport (the Mactan International Airport has regular flights from Japan, Singapore, Hong Kong, and Australia, as well as chartered flights from the United States) and an airline (Cebu Pacific); a geographic location that puts it outside the path of typhoons that hit the islands north of Cebu; and a flat tax rate of 5 percent on a company's gross income. These benefits have attracted tourists, businesses, and investors.

The results have been impressive. Cebu has become a significant commercial hub. Timex (which produces most of its watches in Cebu), NEC Technologies, Pentax, semiconductor producers, and export-oriented furniture businesses make Cebu their production base. About 10 percent of the Philippines' GDP and 9 percent of total Philippine exports come from Cebu, even though it has only 4 percent of the national population. The next wave of investors is connected with call centers providing customer support for businesses in the United States.

Cebu must deal with problems such as with the migrant population, which has flooded the city. Failing to find work, many end up in slums in the city. Water and power sources are also a matter of concern, particularly for industries that require significant amounts of either or both.

It is significant that President Gloria Macapagal-Arroyo chose to take the oath of office after her election in 2004 in Cebu, and not in the capital. Cebu has not only achieved some economic independence but is now pushing for political autonomy, particularly in how taxes are spent. Some leaders in Cebu have suggested that Cebu be allowed to have its own central bank and economic policy. The fact that Cebu has done so well, yet is detached from Manila and the national context, points to the problems the Philippines continues to face in terms of its economy.

References

Aguilar, Filomeno V., Jr. *Clash of Spirits: The History of Power and Sugar Planter Hegemony on a Visayan Island.* Quezon City: Ateneo de Manila University Press, 1998.

Balisacan, Arsenio, and Hal Hill, eds. *The Philippine Economy: Development, Policies, and Challenges.* Quezon City: Ateneo de Manila University Press, 2003.

Bello, Walden. *The Anti-Development State: The Political Economy of Permanent Crisis in the Philippines.* Philippines: CORASIA, 2004.

Corpuz, O. D. *An Economic History of the Philippines.* Quezon City: University of the Philippines Press, 1997.

De Dios, Emmanuel S., and Hadi Salehi Esfahani. "Centralization, Political Turnover, and Investment in the Philippines." In *Corruption: The Boom and Bust of East Asia.* Quezon City: Ateneo de Manila University Press, 2001.

Gonzalez, Joaquin L., and Luis R. Calingo. *Succeed in Business: The Essential Guide for Business and Investment: Philippines.* Portland, Or.: Graphic Arts Center Publishing Company, 1998.

Larkin, John A. *Sugar and the Origins of Modern Philippine Society.* Berkeley: University of California Press, 1993.

Owen, Norman G. *Prosperity Without Progress: Manila Hemp and Material Life in the Colonial Philippines.* Berkeley: University of California Press, 1984.

Wickberg, Edgar. *The Chinese in Philippine Life 1850–1898.* Quezon City: Ateneo de Manila University Press, 2002 (reprint).

CHAPTER THREE
Philippine Institutions

Philippine societies prior to the Spanish intrusion were marked by fluidity and a lack of institutional structure. Religion, government, education, and other institutions were vital aspects of society, but lacked any real sense of structure. The institutions that now mark Philippine society are almost entirely the result of the presence of colonial masters—Spain, then the United States. As a result, such institutions are not indigenous in origin, but have modified over time to fit local sensibilities.

THE GREAT CULTURAL DIVIDE

For all the diversity in the Philippines, there is in Philippine society what one cultural anthropologist has called "the Great Cultural Divide." As one would expect, and as one finds in parts of Asia, there is a separation between rural and urban populations. These are seen culturally, economically, and educationally—even linguistically. But the colonial past of the Philippines has resulted in a chasm between the majority of the population and a minority elite that controls the mechanisms of power.

As Filipinos struggle to regain a sense of self-identity, some believe that the answers are found not on the Western side of the divide but on the indigenous side. But this creates problems for those educated in Western ways of thinking. To them, the majority, the rural-based population, although seemingly quaint, are provincial, superstitious, and somewhat backward.

The creation of the "nation" of the Philippines is the result of efforts by Filipinos whose education and political thinking was influenced by Western rather than indigenous movements. Thus, their culture, although maintaining many elements of local practices, tended to be more Western than Filipino. As a result of their education, these Filipinos were able to get higher paying jobs in urban areas, primarily Manila. English rather than Filipino was the language of choice. The structures created by these Filipinos resulted in a system in which the only perceived hope of upward mobility is through education, which is usually acquired in English. A survey in the late 1960s found the following reasons for preferring English to Filipino: to be more proficient in conversation; to demonstrate that one is educated; to get a better job; to be able to travel; and to maintain dignity and self-respect.

Since the EDSA Revolution, there has been a move toward using the Filipino language rather than English. With national pride and a sense of identity behind the move, the reality of seeking employment either at home with multinationals or abroad in countries that use English has created a dilemma for many.

RELIGION

At its heart, Philippine society is deeply spiritual and religious. This is particularly striking to Westerners, who generally hold, in theory and in practice, to a separation of church and state. It is surprising then to find Bible verses scattered throughout daily newspapers and Bible lessons or studies in the op-ed section. It is not unusual to see the president, as well as many other public figures, participating in and embracing religious activities. The prominent role of the Roman Catholic Church in the EDSA Revolution would be highly problematic for most Americans, even those who are Catholics.

Animism, the belief that there is a supernatural energy that animates the universe and that all life is produced by a spiritual force, colors all aspects of Philippine life. The desire to gain some of the power of the universe is the motivation for most religious activity. Animism remains the core value, and institutional religions provide surface value; that is, institutional religion gives concrete expression and provides the language to express that core value. The language, ritual, and symbols generally come from the world religions that have been brought to the archipelago by intruders. As a result, institutional religion is a visible and significant part of Philippine society.

The Roman Catholic Church

The Roman Catholic Church, although an alien institution, has provided avenues for expressing beliefs in the supernatural. With more than 80 percent of the population being members of the Roman Catholic Church, it must be considered a major institution in Philippine society and life. But for most of its four centuries in the archipelago, it has remained an alien institution, largely uninvolved in social welfare, while performing rituals and requiring allegiance in return. It has, on the other hand, provided a world of rituals, symbols, language, and metaphors that Filipinos used and continue to employ, particularly in times of crisis.

John Leddy Phelan coined the phrase "the Philippinization of Catholicism," which conveys the idea that Filipinos enthusiastically embraced certain aspects of Catholicism as they understood them or as they personalized and externalized them. Some have referred to the product of this mixing of a world religion with local beliefs and practices as folk religion. The celebrations of *fiestas* in connection with the local patron saint, baptisms, weddings, and various holy days demonstrate this mixture. As a result, it has been argued that few are genuine Catholics, and a wide gap exists between professing Catholics and orthodox Catholics.

The foreignness of the Roman Catholic Church was exhibited not only in its theology, which differed profoundly from the animism of Filipinos, but also in the segregation of leader-

The Romanesque-style Cathedral of Manila was built in the Intramuros district on the site of the original chapel, which burned in 1957. The octagonal dome and separate belltower are the church's main characteristics. (Paul Almasy/Corbis)

ship. Membership in the various religious orders (Augustinians, Dominicans, Franciscans, etc.) was not open to Filipinos. Not until the eighteenth century, and at the insistence of the Spanish king, were Filipinos trained for the priesthood. In the nineteenth century, conflict arose when returning Spanish friars found Filipino priests in their pulpits. The controversy had widespread implications and eventually gave rise to the revolution. Every movement, whether the *ilustrado* elite (such as the Reform Movement) or the peasants (the *Katipunan*), demanded that the friars be expelled. The Constitution writ-

Adorned with paint, these performers participated in the annual Dinagyang festival, which honors the infant Jesus. Religious festivals are held throughout the archipelago throughout the year. (AFP/Getty Images)

ten in 1898 called for the separation of church and state, thereby allowing civil marriage without the benefit of a church-sanctioned wedding. Once the Americans took over, the Catholic Church, having lost almost 25 percent of its membership and much of its property to the Philippine Independent Church, agreed to the principle of separation of church and state and also agreed to allow Filipinos into the church hierarchy. A decision in 1906 by the Philippine Supreme Court, composed of Americans and *ilustrados,* ruled that all Roman Catholic Church properties taken over by the Philippine Independent Church had to be returned. This insured the continued power of the Roman Catholic Church and the near demise of what was a Philippine Catholic church.

In the political arena, the Roman Catholic Church became a major player in the elections of 1957. However, it was the

Corazon Aquino in her signature clothing color, yellow, standing next to Cardinal Sin, one of her strongest supporters. (Reuters/Corbis)

Marcos dictatorship that galvanized the Church into becoming active politically and socially. In contrast to the first Filipino cardinal, Rufino Cardinal Santos, elevated in 1960, Jaime Cardinal Sin, elevated in 1976 during the Marcos dictatorship, became a political and social activist; this happened partly as a result of the expanded mission of the church as defined by Vatican II as well as social unrest under Marcos. But the response of the church was not uniform. Some of the local priests embraced Liberation Theology and fought against social inequities. Others espoused a more traditional and conservative approach. Still others were caught in the middle.

The assassination of Ninoy Aquino radicalized not only Cardinal Sin, but most of the Roman Catholic Church, priests, nuns, seminarians, and lay leaders. The struggle was now seen in terms of good versus evil. As the Marcos regime lost power, the church became the center of anti-Marcos activity. Radio Veritas, the Catholic radio network, became the source of uncensored news. Cardinal Sin became one of the key players in the snap elections of 1986. He orchestrated the opposition ticket, convincing Corazon Aquino to run as the presidential candidate and Salvador Laurel to accept the position of vice president rather than president. Cardinal Sin called out the faithful to protect the military mutineers at Camps Crame and Aguinaldo. This demonstration of People Power convinced Marcos to leave the country. Corazon Aquino, the widow of the martyr Ninoy Aquino, became president.

The power of the Catholic Church is limited, however. When Fidel Ramos ran for the presidency in 1992, Cardinal Sin opposed his candidacy because he was a Protestant; but Ramos narrowly won the election in a country that is predominantly Roman Catholic.

The Philippine Independent Church

The Philippine Revolution, while focusing on the abuses of the friars, was directed against the Spanish government and the Roman Catholic Church for failing to control the friars, although their misdeeds were well-known. However, it was not until after the Revolution that an independent church emerged. The figure most associated with this new religious movement was Gregorio Aglipay, a Roman Catholic priest who was made Military Vicar General by President Aguinaldo on October 20, 1898, and then was excommunicated by the Roman Catholic Church on May 5, 1899. But Aglipay was not anti-Catholic and sought to have Filipinos appointed by the Vatican to all Church positions instead of reserving them for Spaniards and, later, Americans. In addition, he wanted to prevent religious anarchy during the time of conflict and transition. The American Catholic representative, Placido Chapelle, who arrived on January 2, 1900, did nothing to heal the breach created by the abuses of the Church.

The Philippine Independent Church, *Iglesia Filipina Independiente,* was created during a union meeting *(Union Obrera Democatica)* led by its founder, Isabelo de los Reyes. De los Reyes called for the establishment of a Filipino Church with Aglipay as its leader. The proposal was approved, but Aglipay and other prominent citizens whose names were included as members of the executive committee were not present to give their consent. Aglipay was in negotiations with a Spanish Jesuit to bring back Filipino priests into the Church—negotiations that failed. As a result, he consented to head the new church and was consecrated Supreme Bishop on January 18, 1903.

Within a few years, a quarter of the Filipino Christian population belonged to the Philippine Independent Church, or the Aglipayan Church, as it would later be called by outsiders. Aglipay sought to have this new church recognized by the newly arrived Protestant missionaries and their religious organizations. Only the Episcopal Church of America recognized the baptism of the Philippine Independent Church. To recoup its losses, the Roman Catholic Church, clearly on the defensive, agreed to certain concessions that it hoped would bring Filipinos back. In reality, it was a decision in 1906 by the Philippine Supreme Court, composed of Americans and members of the Philippine elite, that had the greatest impact. It ruled that all the Roman Catholic Church properties, including church buildings, which were being used by the Philippine Independent Church, had to be returned. This led to a serious decline in Aglipayan membership, standing at 13 percent by 1918. Today, the movement can claim only 5 percent of the population.

Protestantism

President McKinley's decision to keep the Philippines included a religious component, the need to evangelize and convert the local population. He gained support for his decision from major denominations in the United States because they saw the Philippines as a new mission field where they would have the freedom to do missionary work. The rejection of Catholicism by many Filipinos because of the abuses of the church made them open to embracing a new religion. The prospects seemed rosy, but it did not turn out as planned.

Several factors affected the efforts and the results of efforts by the various American Protestant groups in the Philippines. One was the shift from traditional Christianity, with its focus on conversion, to the Social Gospel, which focused on institutional rather than individual changes. This resulted in different approaches to the task as missionaries. The emphasis became social change rather than individual conversion. This led to the building of schools, orphanages, hospitals, and other institutions. In addition, the views of race based on Darwinism caused missionaries to consider their converts unready for positions of leadership. On the Filipino side of the equation, having fought a revolution that had both political and religious aspects, various individuals emerged as leaders within the Protestant camp. Initially excited by the possibility of local leaders, missionaries, like the Spanish friars centuries before, came to the conclusion that Filipinos were incapable of ecclesiastical leadership. This resulted in Filipinos leaving and starting their own groups, including the *Iglesia Ni Cristo* (see below). In addition, those who did not leave remained under the authority and close scrutiny of American missionaries. After World War II, there was an influx of fundamentalist missionaries to the islands. Retaining the emphasis on conversion, they focused on building churches and Bible colleges. Today, Protestants make up at least 5 percent of the population, and that number is growing.

Iglesia Ni Cristo

One of the new religious groups, started by a Filipino who broke away from American missionary authority, was the *Igle-*

sia Ni Cristo (INC), the Church of Christ. It remains a dominant institution in the Philippines today, its churches and
chapels with their easily recognizable architecture scattered
throughout the archipelago. It was founded by Felix Manalo,
who after being raised in a devout Roman Catholic home and
having some contact with millenarian groups at Mount Banahaw, declared himself to be a Protestant at the age of sixteen.
He first joined the Methodist Episcopal Church in 1904 and
then the Presbyterian Church the following year, attending
classes for a short time at the Ellinwood Bible School. In 1908,
he joined the Disciples of Christ and served as an evangelist
for a year before leaving, having been accused of domestic violence. In 1912, he joined the Seventh Day Adventists, but was
suspended a year later for alleged adultery. Manalo decided to
start his own church and, on July 27, 1914, he incorporated
Iglesia Ni Cristo. Beginning in Manila, the movement spread
out into the provinces. By the beginning of World War II, there
were churches of this new group in almost every province on
Luzon and in the eastern part of the Visayas.

The doctrines of the church begin with the belief that Felix
Manalo was the fulfillment of Revelation 7:1–3, which speaks
of the angel from the east. Because Manalo had visited the
United States in 1919 and then returned from the east to the
Philippines, he proclaimed in 1921 that he was that angel. In
addition, the church founded in Jerusalem by Jesus of
Nazareth became apostate and did not exist from 70 CE to
1914, but was reborn with the appearance of the angel from
the east. In contrast to its Protestant roots, the movement is
not trinitarian and holds that Jesus was not divine.

The movement's phenomenal growth has been tied to various factors, beginning with the charismatic leadership of its
founder, who dominated the church for forty-nine years. Not
only an eloquent speaker, he was a master organizer who had
absolute control. Only Manalo had authority to interpret the
Bible, and he prepared the sermon outlines for his ministers.
The indigenous nature of the church also made it popular.

The distinctive architectural style of the Iglesia Ni Cristo *churches found throughout the Philippines. (Catherine Karnow/Corbis)*

Founded by a Filipino for Filipinos, Filipinos alone have been responsible for its activities, including the construction of its many buildings. The use of Tagalog and other local dialects, rather than English, in the services, hymns, prayers, and sermons is also important. The INC has has provided a sense of community for many. Congregations are close-knit, self-contained, and separatist in nature. Members help each other find work, and the church makes loans to those starting businesses. Member are well-trained in the tenets of their faith and, in contrast to other Filipinos, are able to defend their doctrines by quoting Bible verses. On the other hand, the fear of excommunication keeps members from straying. One can be cast out of the church for excessive drinking or gambling, disagreement with the policies of the church, apostasy, marriage to someone outside the church, and adultery.

Politically, the INC has become a force to be reckoned with. The head of the church determines which candidates its members will vote for and the word is sent down to the various congregations. Thus, those seeking local and national offices often approach the leadership for their endorsement.

Islam

Muslim traders probably reached the Philippines as early as the tenth or eleventh century. But, as with much of insular Southeast Asia, attempts to convert the local population did not begin until the fifteenth century. Moving north from the islands of what is now Indonesia, in an expansion that was partly religious, economic, and political, Islam reached Mindanao and then the Manila area on Luzon. (It should be noted that some scholars believe that Islam came to the Sulu Islands, off the coast of Mindanao, from Chinese Muslims, not from Muslims in what is now Indonesia.) At the time of the Spanish intrusion, Manila was under the authority of the sultan of Brunei, on Borneo. The coming of the Spaniards halted the advance of Islam and worked to keep Islam isolated on Mindanao. For most of the Spanish period in the Philippines, Muslims, or Moros, as the Spaniards called them, managed to resist Spanish attempts to establish and maintain control of the Mindanao region. Not until the middle of the nineteenth century, with the advent of improved military technologies, were the Spaniards able to gain control of much of the region. This does not mean that all Muslims were brought under Spanish sovereignty. Some moved further inland; others remained seafarers.

The Americans retained control through military means, by economic incentives, and by various treaties with local Muslim leaders. American policy in the Philippines encouraged Christian Filipinos to homestead in Mindanao. This policy was continued and accelerated after Philippine independence, particularly under the leadership of Ramon Magsaysay. These policies either failed to take into account or underestimated the hostility between Muslims and the Christians who were taking their land. Muslims, who had

Maranao women in Marawi, Mindanao. (Reuters/Corbis)

been the dominant presence in the region, were reduced to a minority. The policies of the colonial masters and the independent national government were aimed at the destruction of the Muslim population. Conflicts between Muslims and Christians became common.

The historical and geographical setting of Islam in the Philippines has prevented it from developing the same level of sophistication found elsewhere among Muslims. Not only has Islam been the minority religion in the archipelago (today about 5 percent of the population is Muslim), but it also has been the religion of ethnic minorities, who are themselves fragmented, persecuted, and relatively poor. The Islam found in the Philippines, until fairly recently, has been highly syncretistic, much like millenarian sects found elsewhere in the Philippines. Some Muslims make offerings to spirits, *diwatas,* who, they believe, can affect one's health, family, and crops. Pre-Islamic customs have been retained in ceremonies marking certain rites of passage—birth, marriage, and death. Filipina Muslims enjoy greater freedom than women in other Islamic societies.

With the rise of Muslim nations and nationalism, the Muslims of the Philippines have been the recipients of support, economic as well as educational, from Libya, Saudi Arabia, Malaysia, and other Islamic states. This has led to a revival of sorts among the Muslim population, as well as armed insurgencies and the creation of terrorist cells in contact with others in the Muslim world. No longer limited to Mindanao, Muslims have migrated to other parts of the Philippines, where they have established communities.

Millenarian Groups

There continues to be a vibrant and vigorous tradition that has found its place in various millenarian movements. Using a combination of indigenous beliefs and practices mixed with those of Roman Catholicism, these movements often started as religious in nature and evolved into political resistance to the status quo. Usually founded or led by charismatic figures, the associations have been marked by the use of *anting-anting,* or amulets, along with special rituals and prayers, often in language that sounds like Latin. The movements have appealed to the marginalized in society; because they live in a world in which they believe they do not have a chance for freedom and equality, many choose to look to the spiritual plane. In joining these associations, they hope to find spiritual power that can bring changes to their lives.

The twentieth century saw a proliferation of such movements, many centered around Mount Banahaw on Luzon, believed to be a place of spiritual power, and perhaps known as such prior to the coming of the Spaniards. Political and economic conditions are often the most important factors in the rise and growth of such groups. Although peasants and the uneducated are usually the most likely candidates to join, the disruptions of urbanization and various technologies have pushed even middle-class individuals to find refuge and solace in such groups. Thus, members of both sides of the Great Cultural Divide have joined such religious sects.

By using the language of nationalism and the past while looking for a better future, members of religious sects have found themselves in conflicts with established governmental, religious, and military authorities. An example is the massacre of thirty-two members of the *Lapiang Malaya* (the Free Party) on May 21, 1967, by the Philippine Constabulary. The members of this group were marching on the presidential palace, *Malacanyang,* to demand the resignation of President Marcos. They wore breastplates that were said to have the power to stop bullets, but the breastplates contained dried grass and failed to protect those wearing them.

These groups are fascinating, repelling, and intriguing to Filipinos who are not members. Many Filipinos scoff at their superstitions and practices, yet, on some level, they believe that members are in contact with higher powers. The past, with its beliefs and practices, seems to be alive in many Filipinos. That certain practices and rituals come from Catholicism is evident, but the fundamental beliefs hark back to the times before foreign intruders brought new ways of thinking, believing, and living.

THE GOVERNMENT

Three general observations can be made about government in the Philippines. The first is that the idea of the state and the state as it exists in the Philippines today are imported realities. The government as an institution is a consequence of foreign intrusions and influences on Philippine society. Second, the political system found in the Philippines serves those who are participants, not the general population. Third, Philippine politics is more about personalities than political ideas.

At the time of the Spanish intrusion, political organization in the Philippines varied from place to place, but shared a

loose-knit kinship-based structure. Leadership was not hereditary but based on a recognition of an individual's abilities or
power, as imagined within the animistic worldview. The eld-
ers of a local community were often consulted for advice, and
their authority was not to be ignored. Religious matters,
which included the wishes of the local spirits, might involve
whether or not to go into battle. The position of *babaylan*
held this authority. In short, there was a fluidity to political
realities that was unfamiliar and not accepted by Spanish officials. They needed an efficient organizational system at the
local level so that collecting tribute would be less costly and
involve fewer Spaniards. As a result, they made the position
of *datu,* or chief, hereditary, exempting the *datu* and his first-
born son from labor requirements. This led to the rise over
time of local elites. Spanish policy changes in the late seventeenth and early eighteenth centuries allowed more individuals to reach positions of power at the local level (because the
Spaniards held the power at the national level). By the end of
the Spanish regime in the archipelago, these local elites were
well entrenched. A study of such elites in central Luzon during the period from 1890 to 1910—a period during which the
Spaniards, then Filipino revolutionaries, and finally the
Americans held the reins of power—demonstrated that the
local elites remained in power through each regime.

As Filipinos sought to create a national government during
their struggle for independence from Spain and the United
States, questions arose about what form of government they
would adopt. Apolinario Mabini, known as the "Brains of the
Revolution," advocated what he called "constitutional authoritarianism," in which a strong executive branch would retain
the bulk of power and a legislature and judiciary would be in
subordinate positions. Mabini believed that the *ilustrados*
were natural leaders and should be in positions of authority.
But the local elites and the *ilustrados* were unwilling to cede
so much power to one person, preferring to have a powerful
legislature. It had been suggested that a government with a

The Philippine legislature before the days of the Commonwealth.
(Library of Congress)

powerful legislature would appear democratic to the Americans, but Mabini's approach would seem autocratic, if not dictatorial.

In reality, it mattered little, because the United States annexed the Philippines as its colony, setting up its own governmental structure. The governor general was the executive branch, and the Philippine Commission and the Philippine Assembly were the legislative bodies. The Philippine Commission, established in 1900, served as the upper house of the legislature and consisted of nine members. At the outset, the Commission was made up of six Americans and three Filipinos, all *ilustrados.* In 1908, the numbers shifted to five Americans and four Filipinos, and under President Woodrow Wilson, Filipinos were given the majority with five Filipinos and four Americans. The National Assembly, the lower house, was elected by Filipinos, with the first elections held in 1907.

As early as 1900, the Americans encouraged the *ilustrados* to form a political party that came to be known as the Federalista Party. This party advocated collaboration with the Americans (while other Filipinos continued to fight) and eventual statehood. Factions split off, some advocating eventual independence, a position that could not be publicly embraced during the early years of American occupation. Those who publicly called for independence when campaigning for the National Assembly in 1907 won fifty-nine of the eighty seats. In reality, their position was little more than political rhetoric because although the masses wanted independence, the developing oligarchy needed the Americans to stay.

The political leaders who would take the lead during the Commonwealth period emerged during this time. When it came time to write a constitution for an independent republic, the politicians followed the lead of their American masters. The constitutional convention that met in 1934, in accordance with the Tydings-McDuffie Act, created a governmental structure similar to that of the United States, at least in formal appearance. The differences included a unitary (versus federal) system, compulsory civil or military service, state ownership of public utilities, state authority to regulate all employment relationships, and extraordinary powers for the president. Some issues, such as the separation of church and state, as well as Tagalog as the national language, were found in constitutions that pre-dated the American intrusion. Although the appearance was that of a democracy, some critics saw the structure as an autocracy. This constitution remained in force after independence in 1946.

After taking the Philippines, the Japanese looked to the political leaders to set up a new system. Many of those who had held office under the Americans continued in office to a lesser degree during the Japanese occupation. The initial structure was that of the Philippine Executive Commission, and included cabinet positions. Needing Filipino support, the

Japanese promised independence and allowed a constitutional convention in June 1943. The result was the creation of the Republic of the Philippines, with Jose P. Laurel, who had been the acting chief justice of the Supreme Court, as president.

The constitution of 1935 remained in place until the adoption of the 1973 Philippine Constitution. On March 16, 1967, the Congress passed a joint resolution calling for a constitutional convention to write a new constitution. Three years later, President Marcos signed the Constitutional Convention Act of 1970, and in November 1970, 320 delegates were elected. They began their work in 1971, but in September 1972, Marcos declared martial law. A national plebescite was held in 1973 to approve the new constitution, and it was adopted. In 1975, Amendment 6 was added; it assigned to Marcos the highest position in government, no matter what form or structure would be adopted in the future.

After the EDSA Revolution in 1986, which resulted in the ouster of Marcos, President Cory Aquino selected forty-eight delegates to write a new constitution. It should be noted that these delegates were from the upper class—mostly lawyers—and many had direct or indirect links to the Roman Catholic Church. Their work resulted in a constitution that reflected many features of the constitution of 1935, and marked a return to power of the elites who had been pushed aside during the Marcos dictatorship.

The system of government established by the 1987 constitution is presidential, with a two-house legislature and an independent judiciary. The president, who is elected by popular vote, is limited to a single term of six years. Because the military is always under civilian authority, the president is also the commander in chief. Citizens voting for president need not vote for his/her running mate as vice president. In the 1992 and 1998 elections, the vice presidents were not from the same parties as the president. Working with the president is a cabinet with about thirty-five positions; cabinet

Supporters of Corazon Aquino and her vice-presidential running mate, Salvador Laurel, celebrate the overthrow of the Marcos dictatorship. (Reuters/Corbis)

ministers are appointed by the president with the consent of the Commission of Appointments.

The power to make laws rests with the Congress, which consists of the Senate *(Senado)* and the House of Representatives *(Kapulungan ng mga Kinatawan).* The twenty-four senators who make up the Senate are elected at large. Each term of office is six years, with a two-term limit. The House of Representatives cannot have more than 250 members, 200 of which are to be elected from legislative districts. Approximately fifty seats are non-elective. In addition, provision has been made for autonomous regions in Muslim areas in Mindanao and in the Cordillera region of Northern Luzon. The term of office is three years, with a limit of three consecutive terms.

The judicial branch is headed by the Supreme Court. The Supreme Court consists of the chief justice and fourteen associate justices who serve for four years. Members of the Supreme Court are appointed by the president on the recommendation of the Judicial and Bar Council. Likewise, lower courts are appointed by the president according to a list of nominees drawn up by a council headed by the chief justice. Unlike the procedure followed in the United States, appointments to the courts do not require congressional approval. The Supreme Court is the final authority on the constitutionality of actions taken by the executive and legislative branches. At the same time, the Supreme Court has administrative supervision over all courts and their personnel.

In addition to the three major branches of government, there are three independent commissions: the Civil Service Commission (CSC), the Commission on Elections (COMELEC), and the Commission on Audit (COA). These commissions have fiscal as well as personnel autonomy. The CSC and the COA have three members each, and the COMELEC has seven, all appointed by the president for specific terms of office.

In 1991, the Local Government Code, in a move to decentralize governmental authority, took many of the administrative and fiscal functions from the national government and passed them to local government units (LGU), which have four levels: provincial, municipal, city, and *barangay*. Now, not only do LGUs have a larger share of revenue, they also have greater responsibility and authority, including the prerogative to impose local taxes and fees.

THE MILITARY

Rule by colonial powers prevented Philippine society from developing a military tradition. Emilio Aguinaldo set up *Academia Militar* in October of 1898, but its operations ceased within three months because of the new conflict with the United States. After the American takeover, all military matters were in American hands. When the Commonwealth was established, Commonwealth Act No. 1 (known as the National Defense Act) created the Philippine Military Academy, patterned after West Point. World War II interrupted the further development of an official military. The academy reopened in 1947 and moved to Fort del Pilar, about 10 kilometers outside Baguio City.

The focus of the military has been internal security, specifically, dealing with the Communist insurgency (the New People's Army) as well as a Muslim insurgency (Moro National Liberation Front) in the south. External security was provided by the United States, which continued to maintain almost two dozen military bases throughout the Philippines, including Clark Air Base and Subic Naval Base, two of the largest U.S. bases outside the United States.

It was during the Marcos dictatorship that the role of the military took a decisive turn. When martial law was declared, various military officials were placed in political positions, marking the beginning of the politicization of the Philippine military. The corruption that marked Marcos and his cronies was also evident among the top officials of the military. With the assassination of Ninoy Aquino in 1983 orchestrated by the military, mid-level officers, all graduates of the Philippine Military Academy, and in particular a group from the class of 1971, formed RAM—Reform the Armed Forces Movement. These officers had not been in the military prior to martial law and had not experienced military subservience to civilian government.

A revolt by RAM triggered the events of the EDSA Revolution. When it became evident that Marcos would "steal" the election in February 1986, members of RAM planned a coup. Word got out and General Ver moved to arrest them. The officers and their political mentor, Juan Ponce Enrile, the minister of defense, fled to Camp Aguinaldo, where they were joined by General Fidel Ramos, vice-chief of staff of the armed forces. They seized the two main military installations in Quezon City, Crame and Aguinaldo. Enrile acknowledged that the elections had been rigged and he had requested help from Cardinal Sin. Sin, using Radio Veritas, called on the faithful to

President Gloria Macapagal-Arroyo salutes while passing an honor guard during a ceremony marking the 15th anniversary of the EDSA Revolution, one month after she became president as the result of EDSA 2. (Library of Congress)

protect Enrile, Ramos, and the members of RAM from being destroyed by Marcos's forces. When the dust settled, Marcos had left the country and Corazon Aquino was president. The military could claim a major role in the EDSA Revolution, the event that launched People Power.

Not all military officers supported or were satisfied with the presidency and policies of President Aquino. At least seven coup attempts took place during her six-year term. None was successful, but they were indicative of a different vision for the role of the military in the Philippine democracy.

Again, in 2001, when events known as EDSA II led to the ouster of President Joseph Estrada and the swearing in of President Gloria Macapagal-Arroyo, certain generals claimed that they were responsible. They maintained that the consequences of EDSA II were not the result of a Supreme Court decision regarding Estrada's corruption or the turning out of thousands of Filipinos, but rather a military coup.

THE EDUCATIONAL SYSTEM

Teaching and learning have been part of Philippine society from pre-Hispanic times. Yet the notion of organized and institutional education as imported by colonial masters took hold in the Philippines. When the Spaniards settled in Manila, to their amazement, they found a population with a literacy rate higher than that of Madrid. The indigenous population had a system of writing known as *baybayin,* which they used primarily for writing letters. A syllabary rather than an alphabet, it consisted of three vowels and fourteen consonants. Each consonant carried with it a vowel value. The friars recognized the value of *baybayin* and built printing presses to produce materials exclusively for the local population.

When the Spaniards set up educational institutions in the Philippines, Filipinos were excluded. It was not until the late eighteenth century that Spanish schools and colleges were opened to Filipinos, and then only to the children of the local elite. From this, the local elite gained the title *ilustrados,* enlightened ones, because they had access to education within the Spanish colonial system, which was a Western-style system. This education separated them from the "uneducated" masses.

Yet, in his *Las Islas Filipinas,* published in Madrid in 1820, Tomas de Comyn noted that "if by general instruction of a country, one understands[,] as in Europe, the large relative number of those who know how to read and write, the Philippines can hold its own compared to nations which are considered advanced." An explanation was given some fifty years later: "The majority of the *indios* who know how to read and write did not learn [how to do so] in schools. It is a recreation in which they indulge which enables them[,] in a short time, to write and draw letters simultaneously. Those who live in rural communities far from the public school[s] usually begin their writing exercises with [a] bamboo pen on a banana leaf."

The arrival of the Americans changed the availability of organized and formal education to the masses. Stories were

*Embroidery class at Paco School in Manila, between 1900 and 1923.
(Library of Congress)*

told about American soldiers who, when not fighting in the
field, taught Filipino children how to read and write. In light
of the policy of Benevolent Assimilation, teachers were sent
from the United States to educate and civilize Filipinos. When
more than five hundred American teachers sailed for the
Philippines on the U.S. Transport *Thomas* in August 1901,
they came to be known as "Thomasites." The group on the
Thomas was the largest group of American teachers sent to
the Philippines, although not the first. By 1902, more than
1,000 teachers had reached the Philippines. By 1909, some
4,000 elementary schools were scattered throughout the
Philippines. But the Americans were divided about approach
and emphasis. Some favored vocational training, others an
academic education. American policies shifted back and
forth, depending on those in power. But both approaches had
problems and failed to achieve the results their proponents
had anticipated. Two things did result: (1) English became the
dominant tongue; and (2) there was, in the words of Stanley
Karnow, "an almost compulsive appetite among Filipinos for
education—or at least the appearance of being educated."

Children in an elementary school in Kalibo, Panay, 1986.
(Paul A. Souders/Corbis)

Entering school at the ages of six or seven, students in the Philippines face six years of elementary school and four years of high school. Because those who finish high school do so at the ages of fifteen or sixteen, it is practical for them to continue their education if funds are available. The Americans established not only the elementary and secondary schools, but higher education as well. The University of the Philippines was established in 1908. In addition, Filipinos, who came to be known as *pensionados,* those receiving a pension (which was to pay for their education), were sent to the United States for college.

After independence, in the aftermath of World War II, there was a strong move to rebuild educational institutions. Many war veterans, as well as those who had been unable to attend school during the Japanese Occupation, wanted to complete their education. By 1948, enrollment in private colleges was twice that of the pre-war period. By 1957, the Philippines ranked second among 121 nations in its ratio of enrollment in higher education. Only the United States, which had the G.I. Bill for veterans, ranked higher.

The educational system was based on the American model in which a student had to earn a specific number of credits in order to graduate. Students were required to pass objective written exams rather than oral presentations. Because of economic hardships, textbooks were almost nonexistent. Thus, class notes and memorization were the key components. When taking exams, students had to reproduce the professor's words as given in class, a policy that allowed for little creativity. Students were faced with a high degree of specialization in their courses, and general education suffered as a result of the emphasis on specialized professional courses. Freshmen and sophomores enrolled in courses for their majors in order to prepare for government licensing examinations. (The results of such exams are still published in daily newspapers in the Philippines.)

Statistics of 2000 show more than 39,000 elementary schools, almost 36,000 (91 percent) being public. On the other hand, 41 percent of the high schools are private. At the higher educational level, 73 percent of colleges are private institutions. These numbers point to the economic burden education has become for many families; yet parents continue to make economic sacrifices for the education of their children.

MANILA

In *Manila, My Manila,* a loving tribute, the late Nick Joaquin noted: "Manila happenings have a national effect. . . . When Manila sneezes, the Philippines catches a cold." Without question, Manila is the center of the national life—politically, culturally, and economically. Located on the east side of Manila Bay at the mouth of the Pasig River, what was once the community known as Manila has now spread to include a much larger area, yet it keeps the familiar name.

There are different theories about where Manila got its name. Some say that it was from the plant *nilad,* a water plant with star-shaped flowers that grew in the area. *May nilad* means that there is *nilad.* Others say that the name comes from *May dila,* meaning "with a tongue," because the original settlement was located on a strip of land at the mouth of the Pasig River. Much of what is now Manila rests on sand and silt dumped by the Pasig River. Joaquin noted that even the names of some of the cities reflect this: Makati, a place of tides, and Mandaluyong, a place of waves.

When the Spaniards settled in the Philippines, Manila and surrounding population centers were under the authority of the sultan of Brunei. Once reinforcements arrived, the Spaniards made their move. In 1571, they took Manila and made it their headquarters in the archipelago. They built a fort on the promontory known as Maynila. Made of wood, it was not sufficient for the Spanish needs and thus was replaced by stone between 1591 and 1593. The enclosed area came to be known as *Intramuros,* the city within the walls. The walls were 4.5 kilometers long and encompassed 64 hectares of land. This structure included a moat, eight gates, ten bulwarks *(baluartes),* three small bulwarks *(baluartillos),* two redoubts *(reductos),* and three ravelins *(revellins).*

The walls are still there and are certainly worth a visit. Inside the walls are found the San Agustin Church, which was built in 1606 and has survived all the disasters that have hit Manila; the Monastery of San Agustin, which is now a museum of religious art; the Manila Cathedral; Fort Santiago, where prisoners were kept, including the national hero, Jose Rizal, until his execution; and five reconstructed colonial houses, located on Juan Luna Street. But this is not simply a place of historic buildings: It has become a location for outstanding restaurants that specialize in open-air buffets on weekends. The moat was turned into an eighteen-hole golf course that is still in use.

Already a center for trade, particularly with the Chinese,

Manila continued to dominate the economy of the archipelago. The instituting of the Manila Galleon did nothing to reduce that status. Political matters were handled in Manila, as were serious ecclesiastical affairs. Most Spaniards refused to live outside the safety of the city walls, and with the exception of the missionary friars, they found no reason to do so. The local people and Chinese merchants lived outside the walls in their respective towns. Thus, it became the center of the Spanish presence and culture in the Philippines. In the eighteenth and nineteenth centuries, Manila began to spill over into neighboring towns of Bagumbayan, Binondo, and Tondo. But it was *Intramuros* that retained a sense of Old Manila with its Spanish architecture, churches, government offices, and private residences.

Today, Manila is part of a larger entity known as the National Capital Region (NCR), also known as the Metro Manila Region (MMR). This region consists of thirteen cities and four municipalities. Some of the city names are familiar: Caloocan, Makati, Mandaluyong, Malabon, Pasay, Pasig, and Quezon City. Although its land area measures 636 square kilometers, one in five Filipinos in the archipelago live in "Manila."

Generally, when people speak of Manila, they are referring to Metro Manila or what is now designated the National Capital Region. More than the capital, Manila is the center of the nation and the city of institutions. Historically, Manila was where most Spaniards chose to live. As such, it was the center of the colonial regime, with all its institutions—church, government, education, finance. When the Americans took over, Manila retained much of its importance as the center of institutional life—economically, culturally, and politically. The same is true today. David Steinberg notes that "the city offers people of all backgrounds the vehicle, educational resources, and job opportunities for upward mobility."

It has grown to be the major population center. In 1903, 3 percent of the national population lived in Manila, increasing to more than 5 percent in 1939, and 8.5 percent in 1958. Today, 20 percent live in the National Capital Region, certainly an area encompassing more than it did in 1903, but still an indication of the region as a population center.

Today, this city of extremes remains the center of business and finance, and, by some estimates, is responsible for more than half the GNP, making it a magnet for those seeking to advance economically. Two-thirds of the country's cars and trucks are located in Manila. National, international, and multinational corporations have offices in Manila. Almost all insurance, banking, communications, and advertising are based in Manila. Although other cities, for example Iligan, Cagayan de Oro, General Santos on Mindanao, and Cebu on Cebu Island, have experienced economic growth, Manila remains the economic center.

Manila is the education center and the main campuses of major universities are found there. The University of the Philippines, Diliman, Ateneo de Manila University, University of Santo Tomas, and De LaSalle University are leaders of education not only in the Philippines but in Southeast Asia in general, and they attract the best and the brightest of the nation. (Branches of UP and Ateneo are found in major cities.) Most of the universities in the Philippines are found in Manila.

More than half of those living in Manila were born elsewhere, having moved either for economic or for educational reasons. Thus the capital has become a melting pot for the various cultures found in the Philippines; the melting pot has also created a national culture that transcends regional differences. The movie industry and television are vehicles for transmitting this evolving culture throughout the archipelago. Information, in all forms of media, originates in Manila.

People visiting the Philippines for the first time or after a long absence experience a double shock of sorts: the unfamiliar and the familiar. When one walks out of the Ninoy Aquino International Airport in Manila (this is the way almost everyone arrives in the Philippines, although Cebu, Davao, Clark,

Subic, and Laoag are also international gateways), one is assaulted by the humidity and a variety of sights, sounds, and smells. The unfamiliar is expected and a part of what makes going to a new place exciting and worth the effort. It is the familiar that is unsettling. Although one does see evidence of the problems facing most third-world cities, Manila is clearly a modern city and parts of it are affluent. In Makati, one finds world-class hotels and restaurants, shopping centers, high-rise office buildings and condominiums, and extravagantly luxurious homes. Some have compared this part of Manila to well-to-do communities and cities in the United States. With its international community and modern facilities, it is cosmopolitan. And beyond the ubiquitous McDonald's, American chain restaurants such as California Pizza Kitchen, TGI Fridays, and Outback Steakhouse do a thriving business. The unfamiliar tends to be the institutional aspects of Manila, in that institutions may not operate as expected, and these can be disconcerting.

But there is also the other end of the economic spectrum. The hundreds of thousands who have moved to Manila to find their fortune, or simply a better way of life, often end up in slum areas around Manila. In Steinberg's words: "The miles of slums, warrens of tin huts, and planking over open sewers . . . are the lot for most Filipinos in Manila." Most slum dwellers are squatters who lack such essential services as water and electricity. They are forced to drink water either from the government-supplied tap in the market or from polluted waterways nearby. The urban poor are always present in Manila, even in affluent sections; most of them are either unemployed or work as street vendors.

Manila is the cultural center of the nation. High culture is symbolized, represented, and presented at the Cultural Center of the Philippines (CCP). With two resident ballet companies—Ballet Philippines and Philippine Ballet Theater—the Philippine Philharmonic Orchestra, and a resident theater company—Tanghalang Pilipino—and other resident companies, the Cultural Center is in many ways the cultural hub of the Philippines.

Popular culture also originates from Manila. People across the archipelago watch television programs that originate in Manila, the home of five major television networks. The growth of cable television has allowed the networks in Manila to send signals to community antenna TV (CATV) in the provinces. Manila is now one of the most advanced urban centers in Asia in the area of cable television. The programming is geared to urban interests, and many provincial stations serve as replay or relay stations. The commercial orientation is seen in the fact that 50 percent of total programming is made up of variety shows, soap operas, and situation comedies, that is, shows that attract advertisers. In recent years, however, the networks have not only made serious efforts but real gains in seeking to provide creative programming, including educational programming for elementary school children.

The seat of the government—all three branches—is based in Manila. The presidential palace, *Malakanyang,* located on the Pasig River, was once home to the Spanish governor general, and, later, the American governor general, and it has been the presidential palace since Commonwealth days. The Senate, House of Representatives, and the Supreme Court are also located in Manila. Those seeking to conduct government business must go to the capital.

References

Agoncillo, Teodoro A. *History of the Filipino People.* 8th ed. Quezon City: R. P. Garcia Publishing Co., 1990.

Anderson, Gerald H. "Providence and Politics Behind Protestant Missionary Beginnings in the Philippines." In *Studies in Philippine Church History,* edited by Gerald H. Anderson. Ithaca: Cornell University Press, 1969.

Burnham, Gracia, with Dean Merrill. *In the Presence of My Enemies.* Wheaton, Ill.: Tyndale House Publishers, Inc., 2003.

Clifford, Mary Dorita. "*Iglesia Independiente:* The Revolutionary Church."

In *Studies in Philippine Church History,* edited by Gerald H. Anderson. Ithaca: Cornell University Press, 1969.

Clymer, Kenton J. *Protestant Missionaries in the Philippines 1898–1916: An Inquiry into the American Colonial Mentality.* Urbana, Ill.: University of Illinois Press, 1986.

Elwood, Douglas J. "Varieties of Christianity in the Philippines." In *Studies in Philippine Church History,* edited by Gerald H. Anderson. Ithaca: Cornell University Press, 1969.

Joaquin, Nick. *Manila, My Manila.* Makati City: Bookmark, 1999.

McCoy, Alfred W., ed. *Anarchy of Families: State and Family in the Philippines.* Quezon City: Ateneo de Manila University Press, 1995.

Maggay, Melba Padilla. *Understanding ambiguity in Filipino communication patterns.* Quezon City: Institute for Studies in Asian Church and Culture, 1999.

Mendoza, Susanah Lily L. *Between the Home and the Diaspora: The Politics of Theorizing Filipino and Filipino American Identities.* New York: Routledge, 2001.

Phelan, John Leddy. *Hispanization of the Philippines: Spanish Aims and Filipino Responses, 1565–1700.* Madison, Wisc.: The University of Wisconsin Press, 1959.

Sanders, Albert J. "An Appraisal of the *Iglesia ni Cristo.*" In *Studies in Philippine Church History,* Gerald H. Anderson, ed. Ithaca: Cornell University Press, 1969.

CHAPTER 4

Philippine Society and Contemporary Issues

Since 1986, when Ferdinand E. Marcos was driven from office and from the Philippines as a result of the EDSA Revolution and the phenomenon of People Power, the Philippines has been undergoing significant changes, but not without difficulties. The elite that maintained power before Marcos wanted to return to their ascendant positions of power. Those who had gained wealth by their close association with Marcos wanted to keep it. But many others wanted to move in a new direction and avoid the mistakes of the past without forgetting it. Various issues are important components in the process of forging a new and dynamic direction for the future.

THE FAMILY

The one institution that might be said to predate the colonial intrusion and interruption is the family. Yet to speak of the family immediately suggests a Western structure, whereas kinship better defines the nature of relations in Philippine societies. The foreign presence did have an impact. In the face of colonial control, as Filipinos sought mechanisms to help them survive, the family as defined and delineated by Catholicism became an important institution. The result was, according to Jean Grossholtz, that the family is "the strongest unity of [Philippine] society, demanding the deepest loyalties of the individual and coloring all social activity with its own set of demands" (cited in McCoy 1995, 1).

Shortly after their intrusion into the archipelago, the Spaniards began to analyze social structures in the Philip-

Family and home at the turn of the century. (Library of Congress)

pines. They found the family to be the basic unit in society. Modern writers, basing their findings on Spanish reports, have described Philippine societies as being at the kinship stage at the time of the Spanish intrusion. In one of the earliest studies done of Tagalog society (1589), the basic political unit was said to consist of the family, which was made up of parents and children, relations, and slaves. Thus, family consisted of more than blood relations.

The family in pre-Hispanic Philippines followed the patterns found in much of Southeast Asia. Monogamy was the norm, and easy divorce was available to both parties. When parents divorced, their children were divided between them. Descent was traced bilaterally, that is, through both parents' lines. The focus was not on the nuclear family but a wider kinship group. And with the presence of a foreign power, after generations of experience, Filipinos learned to rely on family for all types of support. Through all empires and republics, the Filipino family has survived.

The services the family provides include employment, capital, education, socialization, medical care, and shelter for the

Family in the central part of the Philippines.
(Bennett Dean; Eye Ubiquitous/Corbis)

disabled and elderly. Above all, it seeks to impart values to each generation. This was recognized in the Philippine Civil Code, written in 1936, as the constitution of the Philippines during the Commonwealth period. Article 216 of the Philippine Civil Code states: "The family is a basic social institution which public policy cherishes and protects." The code went on to instruct state officials to recognize the family's role in society. Article 219 declares: "Mutual aid, both moral and material, shall be rendered among members of the same family. Judicial and administrative officials shall foster this mutual assistance." But this can be considered more than a nuclear family can reasonably accomplish.

Kinship was the basis of identity in pre-Hispanic society, and the community provided that sense of kinship. The Spanish intrusion meant upheaval and dislocation for many areas of the archipelago. Yet, with the intruders came a new mechanism for extending kinship. *Compadrazgo*, godparenthood, created ritual kinship. Ritual kinship is created through the

Roman Catholic Church and requires sponsorship at baptisms and confirmations; sponsors at weddings are optional. *Compadrazgo* was first introduced by the Spaniards as a visible symbol of reconciliation between the conquerors and the conquered (Phelan 1959, 78). Magellan served as sponsor at the baptism of the Cebuano leader Humabon, and Legazpi served in the same capacity almost fifty years later for Tupas, the leader of Cebu. But the power of this mechanism was recognized and the Audiencia in 1599 (early in the Spanish presence) issued an ordinance forbidding Chinese converts from serving as godparents. The Chinese were accused of accumulating godchildren to use as false witnesses. The actual spread of *compadrazgo* is difficult to trace. The relationships created by such rituals were not used as the basis of identification until well into the eighteenth century. Godparenthood did emerge as a significant part of social relationships with the rise of the *ilustrado* class.

An example of the relationships created by *compadrazgo* can be seen as a result of a child's baptism in which at least four sets of relationships can be created: first, between the godparent, *ninong/ninang* (Tagalog, from the Spanish *padrino/padrina)* and the godchild, *inaanak* (Tagalog) or *hijado/hijada* (Spanish); second, between the godparents, if there is more than one godparent: *compadre/comadre,* co-godparents (Spanish); third, between the godparent and the parents of the godchild: *compadre/comadre,* co-parents (Spanish); fourth, between the godchild and the children of the godparents: *kinakapatid,* godsister or godbrother (Tagalog). Although the focus is often on the *compadre* and/or *comadre* relationships, the others are not ignored. These relationships present opportunities for extended kinship systems.

Ritual kinship is a survival value based on the core value of the importance of family relationships. To help them survive under Spanish colonial rule, Filipinos looked for mechanisms having some point of commonality with indigenous values. Godparenthood was one such example. It should not be for-

A family works together in planting rice. (Jeremy Horner/Corbis)

gotten that kinship is the core value. As Yasushi Kikuchi has noted, "The Filipino type of kinship group is, therefore, a generational corporate group devoid of lineal or vertical continuity but expanded horizontally within each generation" (cited in McCoy 1995, 9).

In other words, kinship in the Philippines is not primarily vertical but horizontal and expands within each generation; these relationships create an ever wider safety net of fictive relationships within each generation rather than from generation to generation. Even when Filipinos reach a position where such a mechanism is not necessary for survival, it has been retained to reflect connection and respect.

CORRUPTION

Although the place of family and relationships is rooted in pre-modern Philippines, they continue to be important in present-day Philippines, a nation that exists as a part of the modern world. Real problems have resulted. If decisions are made based on personal or familial relationships rather than legal or economic principles, something has to give. One result is corruption, at least from a Western perspective. If one expects a government official to perform a service defined by the office simply because that is the duty of the official, one may be disappointed and frustrated. What is required is one of two possibilities. The first is to find someone who has a relationship with that official to serve as an intermediary. Money or goods known as *lagay* will change hands. The second is the direct approach—to create a relationship with the official by means of what some might call a bribe. And, indeed, it might be a bribe. But it also fits within the cultural context of the importance of relationships. What one does is not merely for oneself, but for the family, perhaps for friends, and therefore whatever needs to be done for the benefit of others is not wrong. Nepotism is not frowned upon but accepted as the way things are.

To attempt to get something done, from getting a driver's license to obtaining permits for doing business, requires "gifts." Navigating the labyrinth of governmental bureaucracy, daunting as it is, is made "easier" by the presence of a middleman or agent. The final result, in the short term, may be getting what one needs. Over the long haul, the results are debilitating to society as a whole, partly because they have become accepted as the way things are done. As David Steinberg writes: "By a thousand big and little strokes, the society, the economy, the nation itself gets distorted" (Steinberg 2000, 7).

The roots of political corruption can be traced back to the Spanish system of governance. The governor-general was appointed by the Crown to be its supreme representative in the Philippines. Chosen because they were friends or supporters of the king, these men were not always qualified or dedicated to the task. It was understood that each would profit, through graft and corruption, from "service." Petty officials throughout the archipelago also sought to make their for-

Shacks along the river in the slums of Tondo in Manila.
(Paul A. Souders/Corbis)

tunes, which meant bribery and a neglect of instructions from the center of Spanish power in the Philippines, Manila. Filipinos came to see public service as a means for private gain. And given the importance of family, it was a means of gaining financial benefits for one's family. Thus, it is understood that one will seek to advance his or her own and the family's interests instead of that of the community. Such behavior is contrary to the modern notion of nation building.

One of the consequences of corruption is poverty. The Philippines has a wealth of natural resources along with one of the most educated populations in the world. Yet, the Philippines is marked by great poverty among a significant portion of the population. As the late Benigno Aquino wrote:

> Here is a land in which a few are spectacularly rich while the masses remain abjectly poor. Here is a land where freedom and its blessings are a reality for the minority and an illusion for the many. Here is a land consecrated to democracy but run by an entrenched plutocracy. Here is a land of privilege

and rank—a republic dedicated to equality but mired in an archaic system of caste.

The divide between the haves and the have-nots is great. More than half the rural population is poor, bearing a disproportionate share of the poor. More than 75 percent of the poorest 30 percent live in the rural areas. They are tenant farmers, landless agricultural workers, fishermen, and forestry workers. Many of their communities are unable to meet or provide basic needs such as potable water and health services. Almost 40 percent of households in eleven provinces do not have access to safe water, and high rates of malnutrition continue in twelve provinces, some in the richest regions, in terms of resources.

The urban poor usually live as squatters in slum areas. These areas often lack the most basic of necessities—running water, electricity, and sewage facilities. More than half of these poor work in the informal sector as vendors, selling goods on the street. Others work at service and repair work, construction, and petty production. Children under the age of fifteen and women make up almost 60 percent of the employed urban poor.

TERRORISM

After September 11, 2001, terrorism became a preoccupation with the United States and many of its allies, including the Philippines. For decades, various insurgencies had plagued the Philippine government. Generally, they fell into one of two camps: Communist and Muslim. Most of the groups involved now have been declared terrorist organizations. Internationally, the focus is on Islamic groups.

In 1968, Muslim leaders in the southern Philippines founded the Moro National Liberation Front (MNLF). Its stated goal was full independence, but the realistic outcome would be increased autonomy. When Ferdinand Marcos

Members of the group Abu Sayyaf outside a mosque on Jolo, where they were holding hostages. (AFP/Getty Images)

declared martial law, he moved against the MNLF, requiring Muslims in the south (but also all Filipinos) to surrender their firearms. By 1974, the MNLF had 50,000 to 60,000 "soldiers" in the field. Various OPEC nations sympathized with the Muslims of the southern Philippines. With financial support and weapons from wealthy Islamic states, the MNLF was well supplied. At one point, two-thirds of the Philippine armed forces were stationed in the Muslim areas, draining needed resources from the Philippine government. In 1977, Marcos granted autonomy to certain regions in Mindanao, autonomy that was expanded in 1981. The mainstream Muslim resistance got what it wanted and only occasional outbreaks of violence against Christian communities and/or Philippine government forces took place. In addition, the Arab states hired and imported thousands of Filipinos to work as domestic helpers, construction workers, and in other low-level occupations. Much of the money earned by these workers was remitted to the Philippines, providing an infusion of cash for a weakening economy.

But the MNLF did not speak for all Muslims in the southern Philippines, and new groups began to challenge the authority of the Philippine government and the presence of Christian communities in the south. One such group is known as Abu Sayyaf, which means "bearer of the sword." Founded by Abdurajak Janjalani, who fought as a mujahedin in Afghanistan against the Soviets, it began its campaign of terror in 1991, with bombings, grenade attacks on Christian groups and congregations, and abductions of priests, nuns, and teachers. In 2000, the group gained international attention with the kidnapping of foreigners and the holding of journalists who were reporting on the situation.

Abu Sayyaf has had strong ties to the al Qaeda network, and has agitated for the creation of an independent Islamic state in the southern Philippines. Some of its members claim to have trained in Afghanistan. Their plans have included assassinating Pope John Paul II during his last visit to the Philippines and blowing up twelve American airliners in one day—both several years before the events of September 11, 2001. But the death of Janjalani in 1998 impacted the Islamic nature of Abu Sayyaf. Splintering into three groups, their focus has been primarily murder and kidnapping. The money they have made from collecting ransom, $25 million alone from Libya, has provided finances that have helped recruiting and, in turn, has enabled them to expand their activities. The character of the group has changed from that of one driven by ideology or religion to that of individuals motivated by greed. This is clearly spelled out in Gracia Burnham's book, *In the Presence of My Enemies*. Gracia and her husband, Martin, missionaries in the Philippines, were kidnapped on May 27, 2001, from a resort on the island of Palawan, and were held by members of Abu Sayyaf for one year and eleven days. On June 7, 2002, an encounter with Philippine troops resulted in

Missionaries Martin and Gracia Burnham during their time as captives of the Islamic terrorist group Abu Sayyaf. Gracia was later rescued. Martin killed. (Reuters/Corbis)

Gracia's rescue, but the death of her husband. Although ransom had been paid, the Abu Sayyaf was not satisfied and wanted more. Burnham's account of their ordeal is chilling and clearly demonstrates that the danger Abu Sayyaf represents is real.

THE DIASPORA

The diaspora is a significant aspect of Philippine society. The statistics are less than exact, but it is estimated that 8 million Filipinos live outside the archipelago. That compares to approximately 4 million Americans, excluding military personnel, living outside the United States. By the year 2020, close to one in three Filipinos will live abroad.

Based on historical records, we know that Filipinos were migrating and working in other countries since before the time of the Spanish intrusion. The first Spanish ship to return to North America from the Philippines had Filipinos working aboard, some of whom died and were buried in what is now Santa Barbara, California. Later on, a community of Filipinos who had escaped Spanish ships was established in Louisiana. It would seem that Filipinos have been leaving the archipelago to work abroad for at least the last five centuries.

The first step in the move abroad has often been a migration to Manila, where there are better opportunities for education and work. Having been uprooted from one's home community and province, and having obtained better training, individuals are more likely to consider a further move. Filipinos were once able to travel to the United States without passports or visas because their country was considered a part of the United States. Some came to work as laborers in the sugar-cane fields of Hawaii and the farm lands of California. Laws intended to control the populations of Japanese and Chinese later affected Filipinos as well. When the Philippines gained independence in 1946, those seeking to immigrate to the United States had to deal with the reality of a quota limit. In 1965, the United States Congress raised the quota on Filipinos, opening the door for a new wave of immigrants, specifically those who were college-educated or had professional skills. Because those with education and skills were more likely to seek a better life abroad, a "brain drain" occurred.

Martial law made immigrating abroad a much more attractive option, particularly for those who opposed the Marcos regime. With college degrees and the ability to speak English, Filipinos became desirable workers in many countries. As the political and economic situation continued to deteriorate, Filipinos looked for work abroad. Even those with college degrees and professional skills found that they could earn more doing menial labor or working as maids (known as domestic helpers, or DHs) than they could working in their given professions in the Philippines.

The result is not only a diasporic scattering, but a drain on

*A group planning to immigrate to Canada attending an orientation
seminar. More than a million Filipinos are expected to leave for
temporary work abroad. (AFP/Getty Images)*

the ability of the country to make economic progress. There
are positive aspects to the diaspora, however. Many, if not
most, of those in the diaspora send money back to family
members in the Philippines. It is estimated that at least $6 bil-
lion is remitted to the Philippines annually. Without this
money, the Philippine economy would be adversely affected.
In addition, some Filipinos who have gained new skills abroad
have begun to return home, if only for short stays, to share
what they have learned. This phenomenon, which is still in its
early stages, has come to be known as "brain gain"—in contrast to brain drain.

The Philippine Overseas Employment Administration
(POEW), a part of the Department of Labor, was established
in 1982. Its mission is "to ensure decent and productive
employment for Overseas Filipino Workers." The POEA seeks

Returning overseas Filipino workers and foreign tourists at the immigration counter at the international airport in Manila. (AFP/Getty Images)

to connect workers with employment opportunities abroad. OFWs, as they are known, leave the country and seek to earn higher wages than they could in the Philippines and send money home for their families. But most Filipinos abroad do not go through the POEA and lack the protection and benefits that it provides. As a result, Filipino workers are sometimes mistreated and taken advantage of, often because they are in a given country illegally.

The diaspora is important for an additional reason. Those Filipinos who live abroad influence Philippine economics, politics, and culture, and will continue to do so. First-generation immigrants are familiar with the state of the Philippines; sometimes painfully so. Some of them plan to retire in the Philippines; those who don't, usually still have family there. But above all, there is still a sense of connection, even obligation, to do something for the land of their birth and their countrymen. Various projects, mostly small, have arisen to take on this task.

Many second-generation Filipinos of the diaspora, wherever they were born or raised, try to understand what it means to be a Filipino. For some, the process and sense of awakening can be so profound that it is labeled "the born-again Filipino experience." Active members of the diaspora attempt to expand the definition and understanding of an evolving reality—being Filipino. Sometimes naïve, sometimes cynical, but almost always curious and willing to pursue the study of their parents' homeland and what they have begun to view as the land of their roots, these children of the diaspora want to make a difference through their education and experience, limited though it may be.

As the Philippines continues to develop, the diaspora will be a significant part of that process.

THE ARTS

Filipinos love to create and to perform. Whether it is singing, dancing, giving speeches, theater, or any other creative activity, Filipinos are there. Many of the art forms were brought by outsiders, but some, such as dancing and singing, are indigenous. Dances were not originally performed for an audience but were part of rituals and ceremonies. Songs, on the other hand, were not only a part of such rituals and ceremonies but also a part of everyday life. Spanish chroniclers noted that workers enjoyed singing while they performed various tasks.

In the modern world, Filipinos have adopted Western dance while preserving indigenous folk dances. Folk dances are now performed for an audience, which presents such activities in a different light. Filipino American college students have sought to reconnect with their heritage by learning and performing dances. Through student organizations for Filipino Americans, they have created what is generally called a "Philippine Culture Night," or PCN, providing a venue to perform for family and friends.

Whatever the latest dance craze is, it will probably be adopted in the Philippines. When Filipinos get together with family and friends, it is not unusual for a karaoke or videoke machine to be present. This provides an opportunity for those present to show off their real or imagined singing skills. Although some take this more seriously than others, laughter is almost always a constant.

The Philippines, past and present, is marked by a wealth of artistic production. To outsiders, these artistic endeavors might be categorized as either indigenous or borrowed, exotic or accessible. Such views are not unusual. For example, at the 1904 St. Louis World Fair, although some Filipinos were on exhibit in what could be called a human zoo, paintings and sculptures created by other Filipinos in the Western tradition were also on display—but not in the arts portion of the fair. That is, some were viewed, literally, for their foreignness, yet the works of others were taken as mainstream.

Literature

Philippine literature has both oral and written components, with oral literature being indigenous by nature, and written literature the consequence of extensive cultural influence from both colonial regimes and contact with other cultures.

Oral literature

Indigenous literature may be categorized by the ethnic groupings found in the Philippines. Riddles, various poetic forms, folk tales, and epics are the major oral literary forms found among the various ethnic groups. Folk tales include myths, legends, and fables. Myths deal with the deities and spirits that have interacted with the people of the islands. There are different creation myths for many of the ethnic groups. In one account, a bird, tired and not finding anywhere to perch, started a conflict between the sky and the sea. The sky threw stones at the sea and thus the islands were formed. A well-known account of the first man and woman tells of a bird finding a piece of bamboo floating in the sea. When it pecked at the bamboo, the first man and the first woman appeared at the same time. The man, *Malakas,* or strong, and the woman, *Maganda,* or beautiful, became the parents of the human race. Other folk tales seek to explain various aspects of nature, such as why the pineapple has many "eyes." Legends deal with more recent events than do myths. Interestingly, they tend to show evidence of the cultural impact of the Spanish presence. Feared supernatural beings are known by Spanish names, such as *engkanto, dwende,* and *capri.* Fables or short stories that seek to convey a moral lesson. Many of these also appear to be indigenized forms of fables from other cultures.

Each ethnic group in the Philippines appears to have an epic that is the defining story of that group. Although these stories have universal themes, they express the cultural values of a given people. Among the more familiar epics are the *Hudhud* of the Ifugaos, the *Ulalim* of the Kalingas, and the *Kudaman* of Palawan. Those most affected by the Spanish presence, such as the Tagalogs, have lost all trace of their epic, but others, such as the Ilokanos, have included Spanish aspects in their epic, *Biag ni Lam-ang* (The Life of Lam-ang). These epics have the following characteristics: The story is about a supernatural or heroic person of ancient times; it is based on oral tradition; it is composed in verse; and it is sung or chanted.

Epics still have a place in the life of cultural minorities and are sung during times of gathering, such as weddings and wakes. They entertain the community with the heroic deeds of their ancestors. They also convey the customs and beliefs of previous generations, often providing examples for the next generation to follow. The most important value expressed in the epics, despite their different emphases—romance, combat, or migration, for example—is the family as the central and foundational social unit.

Written literature
Philippine written literature can be found in many of the Philippine dialects, in Spanish, English, and even Chinese. Although the local population was literate at the time of the

Spanish intrusion, this skill was not used to compose or record literary forms; those remained as oral literature. Spanish influence led to the use of writing for recording literature. The earliest works that have survived tended to be religious. However, some of the conventions of indigenous poetic forms were used, such as the *talinghaga,* which employed a seven-syllable-line structure. But as time went on, Spanish poetic structures were used, even when the poetry was in an indigenous language.

Although the Tagalogs possessed no epic that survived the Spanish intrusion, a new epic took its place—the *Pasyon* (Passion). In verse form, the story is told of the events that led to the Passion of Christ. This epic is sung or chanted during the religious season of Lent. Other religious epics were composed and remain popular to the present. In a real sense, they form a bridge between indigenous oral literature and the written literature impacted by the Spanish presence and evangelistic efforts.

Not all poetry during the Spanish period was religious in nature. The *awit* and the *korido* employ different numbers of syllables per line, but both deal with the same subject: metrical romances. They tell stories of chivalry, based on European stories. The most famous work of that period is *Florante at Laura* (Florante and Laura), a metrical romance written by Francisco Baltazar, or Balagtas, as he has come to be known. Interestingly, it takes place in Albania during the medieval period. More than three hundred of these romances have survived to the present.

Secular poetry continued to develop during the second half of the nineteenth century and found a place in the stirrings of nationalist pride, from Andres Bonifacio's "Pag-ibig sa Tinubuang Lupa" (Love for the Native Land) in 1896 to Jose Rizal's "Mi Ultimo Adios" (My Last Farewell) composed before his execution at the hands of the Spaniards in 1896. The reader should note that the poem by Bonifacio was written in Tagalog, but that by Rizal was in Spanish. This illustrates well the reality in Philippine literature that an author may use either an indigenous language or a foreign language.

Rizal was not the first Filipino to write a novel, but it was his pair of highly political novels, written in Spanish, *Noli Me Tangere* (Touch Me Not) in 1887 and *El Filibusterismo* (Subversion) in 1891, that marked the emergence of the novel as a literary form in Philippine literature. Known popularly as *Noli* and *Fili,* these novels tell the story of oppression under the rule of the friars. The first novel introduces the main character of both novels, Crisostomo Ibarra, a young man recently returned from studying in Spain. Rizal describes how he seeks to improve the lot of his people, only to face the overt and covert opposition of the friars, particularly Padre Damaso, who was responsible for the death of Ibarra's father. There is romance and tragedy in the life of Ibarra and his love, Maria Clara. The novel ends with the lovers being separated. The second novel is a sequel, with Ibarra disguised as Simoun, a mysterious stranger who on the one hand seeks to abet the corruption in the government and on the other to aid an armed rebellion against the Spanish authorities. In both cases, he has the same goal: to achieve the freedom of the Filipino people.

The place of these novels in Philippine history cannot be overestimated. It can be argued that they achieved at least two significant results: the exile and ultimately the execution of Rizal and the Philippine Revolution.

After the Americans took the Philippines, literature, both poetry and prose, continued to be written in Spanish. The essay as a literary form came into its own during the American period, with most being written in Spanish and having some political agenda. The leading essayists of that period included Claro M. Recto, Teodoro M. Kalaw, and Epifanio de los Santos.

With Americans using English as the medium of instruction, a twofold change occurred in the language of Philippine literature. On the one hand, more and more works were pro-

duced in English. On the other, there was a growing movement towards the vernacular. All literary forms, traditional
and modern, were employed, both for writing in formal
English and in the vernacular. Some of the best-known writers, such as the poet Virgilio Almario, known as Rio Alma,
blended indigenous forms with modern devices such as irony
and detachment; his "Doktrinang Anakpawis" (Doctrine of
the Working Class) is an example.

During the American period and after, a generation of writers emerged who wrote in English, some of whom had lived in
the United States. Names such as N.V.M. Gonzales, Nick
Joaquin, Bienvenido N. Santos, and Carlos Bulosan are but a
few of the well-known English writers of that generation.
Their stories tell of life in the Philippines as well as life in the
United States.

Music

As with other aspects of the arts, Philippine music has both
indigenous as well as foreign elements, that is, Spanish and
American influences. These elements include the rhythms,
styles, and instruments used. Indigenous musical instruments
differ from region to region. Common types of instruments
found include flutes, mouth organs, and gongs.

Spanish accounts record that Filipinos would often sing
while working, as was their custom. These songs were not
written down because the Spanish friars considered them
obscene. Much of what we know of pre-Spanish music comes
from the ethnic and cultural minorities, those least affected
by Spanish influence. Responsive and solo singing are the two
major types found. In the first, one may hear two groups
singing back and forth, a group answering a single singer, or
two singers engaged in a "song debate." The soloist is
employed to recount the epic and other stories of importance
to a particular people.

Catholicism and particularly its rituals strongly impacted
the character of Philippine music, but indigenous elements—

themes, rhythms, structure—have survived. The chanting or singing of the *Pasyon* during the season of Lent has a Filipino character to it.

In the nineteenth century, musical instruments such as the piano, string instruments, and others began to make their way into Philippine music. The children of wealthy Filipinos were given instruction in Western music. Bands were put together to play for town celebrations. In rural areas, groups of those playing stringed instruments formed *rondalla,* a band of stringed instruments.

The American period saw a shift to American songs, melodies, and tunes. Because of the American presence, access to such music was not difficult. After Philippine independence, technology made it even easier to keep up with the latest in American popular music. Filipino singers sought to imitate what they heard from American hits. Even today, the latest hits from the United States are heard on Philippine radio. Western forms continue to influence Philippine music; rock, rap, and heavy metal have performers and fans in the Philippines.

It was not until the 1970s that popular music in the Philippines became Filipinized. OPM, original Pilipino music, began with the vernacularization of lyrics and then moved to the composing of songs in the vernacular. During the 1980s, Filipino composers and performing artists came into their own. Names such as Ryan Cayabyab and Freddie Aguilar became household names in the Philippines. But their success was not limited to the Philippines. Aguilar's "Anak" (Child), which tells the story of an ungrateful son who has forgotten what he owes his parents, became a hit throughout Asia, and was translated into a number of Asian languages. And traditional musical forms such as the *kundiman,* the love song, enjoyed a resurgence and became a part of modern cinema music. The evolution of Philippine music continues with folk musicians such as Joey Ayala, who uses indigenous instruments and music as vehicles for his lyrics.

The Cultural Center of the Philippines (CCP) has been

responsible for the dramatic increase of new works—symphonic, chamber music, and ballet music—by Filipino composers. Filipino operas have also been written and produced under the auspices of the CCP.

Theater

Theater as a concept is not indigenous to the Philippines. The rituals, dances, chants, and singing that marked pre-Spanish culture had a theatrical component, but were not theater in the sense of a performer or performers and an audience. When the Spanish friars began their work of evangelizing and teaching the local population the Catholic faith, they found that theatrical presentations and dramatizations were more effective than preaching. Religious plays were performed during certain holy days. The *Panuluyan,* a Christmas play, reenacted the search for shelter by Mary and Joseph. This involved the people of the town as the characters went from house to house, finally finding shelter in the church. The *Salubong,* an Easter play, centered around the meeting of Mary and the resurrected Jesus. Jesus and Mary meet in front of the church. Both of these plays involved the whole community. The *Sinakulo,* the Passion play, was performed for the town in front of the church. People brought their own benches and would attend all nine nights to complete the series. But not all plays brought to the Philippines were religious in nature. The Spaniards also brought "secular theater" (plays having a religious aspect but not primarily religious in their purpose). These included the *komedya* or *moro-moro,* a play based on the telling of a Spanish story set in medieval Spain. The stories usually dealt with how Muslims were converted, with a romantic twist and always the Christians as victorious. Filipinos were thus exposed to theater as something to be performed by actors and observed by the audience.

The debate as a literary form became popular in the Philippines, with three forms emerging among the Tagalogs. The

Karagatan, usually performed at wakes, involved guests being selected to participate in a debate in poetic form. The *Duplo* was similar to the *karagatan* in context, but different in that "professionals" were employed to participate. The *Balagtasan* emerged in the 1920s. Named after the poet Francisco Baltazar, who was also known as Balagtas, the *Balagtasan* takes on the appearance of a court proceeding. Those participating must make their case using verse.

It was the Spanish *zarzuela* that had the most significant impact on indigenous theater up to that point. Disdained by many Europeans as low-brow opera, it was the bridge that allowed for indigenous theater to emerge. Not only was this form produced in the vernacular, it was flexible enough to embrace other theatrical art forms, including debates, singing, and dancing. It also became the vehicle for nationalist and anti-colonial expression during the American and Japanese periods.

It was not until the martial law period and the work of the Cultural Center of the Philippines that writing plays began in earnest in the Philippines. Up to that point, much of what was performed on stage came from foreign sources, with notable exceptions. What is noteworthy is the creation and work of various theater groups, such as the Philippine Educational Theater Association (PETA) and Philippine Repertory, both established in 1967. The CCP has a resident theater company, *Tanghalang Pilipino,* which performs both original Filipino plays and foreign plays in translation.

Film

Of the arts, movies have the broadest appeal in the Philippines. From 1912, when the first movies were made in the Philippines, movies have been primarily viewed as a commodity rather than an art form. This explains why after more than eighty years of movie making in the Philippines, only a handful of works can be considered of enduring value. Filmmaking did not arise out of local interest, but was the result of foreign entrepreneurs. Thus, the need to keep audience interest became the driving force. The lack of capital meant outdated equipment and limited budgets; the result was movies that were passable but not of artistic value.

In 1919, Jose Nepomuceno produced the first Filipino movie, *Dalagang Bukid* (Country Maiden), based on the musical of the same name. Because it was a silent film, Nepomuceno hired a singer to sing the theme song while the movie was shown. This first movie set a pattern that would be followed for decades—employing traditional theater forms in different aspects of the film. The writings of the previous century, particularly those by Balagtas and Rizal, were important sources of material for the movies.

Unlike other art forms that used English or Spanish, the Philippine film industry could and did make movies in the vernacular. In this arena, there would be no competition from American films, and they could not hope to compete with American films for lack of resources. Thus, although one finds many twentieth-century titles in literature in English and Spanish, movies titles and dialogue were primarily in Tagalog. But the lack of capital required that movies make a profit. Thus, the movies were geared to whatever the audience appeared to want at the moment. The foreign movies that were drawing crowds were imitated.

Because martial law sought to regulate filmmaking and limit free expression, industry paid attention to the content of a film. Having to submit a finished script, rather than relying on improvisation, opened the film industry to new talent from literature and the theater. One such move from theater to the movies involved Lino Brocka, who became one of the leading filmmakers of the 1970s. His films, including *Tinimbang Ka Ngunit Kulang* (You Have Been Weighed and Found Wanting) in 1974; *Maynila, Sa mga Kubo ng Liwanag* (Manila, in the Claws of Light) in 1975; and *Bayan Ko: Kapit sa Patalim* (My Country: Gripping the Knife's Edge) in 1985, are among the best films of the martial law period. Five of Brocka's films were shown at the Cannes Film Festival, earning him an international reputation as a filmmaker. The rise of independent films in the post-martial law years stands in contrast to the industry that continues to produce movies lacking in artistic value and points to artistic greatness in Philippine filmmaking.

Visual Arts

Seen as less contaminated by foreign influences, ethnic minorities are looked to for "indigenous" arts. Prior to and following the Spanish intrusion, indigenous visual arts have included pottery, carving, weaving, and metal crafting, most for ritual purposes or everyday use. These visual arts have gone somewhat mainstream in the second half of the twentieth century in several ways: Some of the articles continue to be needed and used in everyday life, but many of them are produced for the tourism industry, and different Filipino artists have sought to combine indigenous art forms with modern and Western art forms.

Pottery

Archaeological finds have indicated that pottery was among the oldest of the arts practiced in the Philippines. Archaeologists have uncovered on the island of Palawan a pottery burial jar that dates back to the eighth century BCE. The lid depicts two human figures paddling a boat, apparently representing the indigenous view of the afterlife. Burial jars, though not as ancient as the one just mentioned, have been found throughout the Philippines, indicating the important place pottery had in pre-Hispanic cultures. Pottery still is used for all kinds of containers. Particularly among the Ilocanos of Northern Luzon, pottery continues to be produced. The *palayok* is used for cooking, the *banga* for keeping drinking water, the *asinan* for storing salt, and the *tapayan* for use in fermenting spirits or curing fish paste *(bagoong)*. These pots are shaped and then fired in giant walk-in kilns. The earliest examples of pottery are burial jars, their covers decorated with figures. One such lid has two men rowing a boat, possibly an expression of the afterlife by those who made and used the burial jar. Pottery remains that have been uncovered demonstrate a wide variety of shapes, sizes, and decorative techniques. More recent pottery was made for everyday use, such as for cooking and storing water.

Carving

When one speaks of wood carving in the Philippines, several ethnic groups come to mind. In Northern Luzon, the Ifugaos of the Cordilleras are known for their skill in wood carving. It is believed that this art form began with the carving of the *bulul,* or a wood carving of a human figure used in religious rituals connected with the production of rice, as well as healing. This figure also began to appear on the handles of utensils and other instruments important to life. The central post of the house also displayed the human figure and was known as *kinabagat.* From this carving of the human figure, Ifugao carving branched out into geometric patterns on walls and even the making of furniture. The technique used by Ifugaos involves using sharp tools to carve, mold, contour, and etch forms and patterns. Animal figures usually stand alone, but can be carved into the surfaces of boxes, containers, and utensils. The tourism industry has prompted Ifugao carvers to move to the Baguio City area in order to be closer to the market. What they produce is usually dictated by the marketplace and has drifted from its roots as a part of the Ifugao culture. The demand has also resulted in work of poorer quality than it once was.

Woodwork is also found at the other end of the archipelago, among Muslim groups. Because of the Islamic prohibition against representational art (primarily of humans and animals), the focus is more on decorative and geometric patterns. Among the Maranao, the carved art forms are known as *okir.* Such carvings are used on the beams and side panels of houses, as well as on musical instruments—the *kudyapi,* a two-stringed lute, or the *lankongan,* the holder of the *kulintang,* which is a series of gongs. Among the more common designs is that of the *naga,* or snake, and vines and leaves.

The Tagbanua of Palawan carve images of birds, lizards, turtles, snakes, pigs, and other animals. These images are used for religious rituals, to decorate houses, or as toys for children. The wood used is a soft white wood, called *tika.* The process begins with a sun-dried piece being shaped with a small knife. The next step is for the figure to be rubbed with leaves and then blackened either with soot or by holding the piece over an open flame to burn the resin into the wood. In the final step, small designs are etched, exposing the white wood.

Weaving

Weaving was a technology that spanned the archipelago. Different techniques, materials, colors, and designs have pointed to the place of origin for various products. Filipinos for centuries have made use of a variety of materials to produce cloth for clothing, blankets, and mats from pineapple, abaca, ramie, maguey, cotton, and bark. Many of these have not survived because of the tropical climate, but accounts and even drawings from outsiders have documented the history of weaving in Philippine culture.

Some of the more primitive cloth was made from the bark of trees. To produce this cloth, tree bark was stripped and spun into thread and then woven into cloth. This same technique was later used by lowland and highland groups. Among the lowland groups of Northern Luzon, the Ilocanos are known for the blankets they produce. Known as *binacol* and *pinilian,* these homespun cotton blankets are dyed in light or dark indigo. Some have geometric designs. Among the highlanders of Northern Luzon, each of the indigenous groups is marked by their designs of cloth that is used for the *tapis,* or

A family gathers while women weave colorful mats.
(Paul Almasy/Corbis)

wrap-around skirt, for women, and the *baag,* or loin-cloth, for men. Among ethnic minorities in the south, various techniques for weaving are used to produce styles and designs unique to each group.

Metal crafts

Metal crafts are used for a variety of functions: adornment, tools, and weapons. Jewelry originally functioned as amulets and only later assumed an ornamental character. But amulets, or *anting-anting,* as they are known, continue to be produced of various materials, including metal; these are not good luck charms but objects that protect the owner and bring the desired result, depending on the circumstance.

A wide variety of jewelry is found throughout the Philippines. The T'boli in the southern Philippines are known for their almost ostentatious displays, with brass chains and bells, strings and nets of multicolored beads, and fine chains of horsehair made into necklaces, earrings, rings, bracelets, and anklets. The T'boli are also known for their work with brass.

Brass vessels of various shapes and designs are found mostly among the peoples of the southern Philippines. Such objects combine practical function with aesthetic design. From large containers to boxes for betel-nut, a wide variety can be found constructed in brass.

Metal work was also used to produce weapons, primarily bladed weapons. Again, the peoples of the southern Philippines led the way in this area. Although those north of them used a single, multipurpose machete, known as a *bolo,* groups in the south have always used a variety of blades, including the *kris barong, kampilan,* and *tabas.* It should be noted that although much of the Philippines came under Spanish control, and this control included the manufacture of weapons, part of the southern Philippines resisted this control almost to the end of Spanish rule in the archipelago. This explains, in part, the differences between the south and the rest of the islands.

Contact with Spanish culture led to new art forms, specifically painting and sculpture, and new uses for existing artistic forms. Most of the art during the early part of the Spanish presence in the Philippines was religious in nature. Stone carvings were done for church buildings, and wood carvings were used for images and other religious objects. Metal work was done for religious medallions and altar pieces. As time went on, indigenous styles were displaced by European norms, particularly for religious objects. Painting as an art form was brought in and used almost exclusively for religious purposes.

Religious holidays, including fiestas, presented opportunities for popular artistic expression, many of which remain to the present. The *parol* (Christmas lantern) is hung outside homes during the Christmas season throughout the Philippines. Representing the Star of Bethlehem, the *parol* is a light bamboo frame covered with colorful translucent *papel de hapon* (Japanese paper, as it is known), which is glued onto the frame with rice paste. Traditionally, the five-point star was adorned with "tails" hanging from two or four of the points, but modern professional parol makers have been imaginative in the shapes they have fashioned. Papier maché is used to create figures, the type and size of which depends on the festival of a given town.

Decorating the body

Among various groups, tattooing is used for ornamentation as well as to indicate status, and as with other visual art forms, tattooing is found primarily among ethnic minorities. It should be noted that such practices are not found among the generations of the second half of the twentieth century. From the Igorots of the Cordilleras of Northern Luzon to the T'boli of Mindanao, tattoos have been used as not only a means to decorate the body, but also to indicate what group a person belongs to and what he or she has accomplished. The designs and patterns as well as locations of tattoos are what transmit that information. Among such groups, wearing jewelry or other decorative ornaments is also important. Among the highlanders of Northern Luzon, seashells are used for different purposes—earrings, hip ornaments, and necklaces, to name a few. Feathers, bones, and carabao horn are also used for ornamentation. However, the mineral wealth of the Cordilleras is shown in the jewelry made of gold and other metals worn by men and women. The T'boli are marked by an almost extravagant use of jewelry—which includes multiple earrings, necklaces, bracelets, rings (for fingers and toes), and anklets—and they display their ornaments not only on special occasions but also at work and at home.

Paintings

The rise of a wealthy class of Filipinos in the nineteenth century ushered in the art of painting by the middle of the century. Portraiture came into vogue when families commissioned artists to paint individual and family portraits. The European tradition was brought to the Philippines and, in time, artists from the Philippines traveled to Europe, where they were recognized for their work. Juan Luna won a gold medal and Felix Resureccion Hidalgo won a silver medal at the Madrid Exposition in 1884. They continued to produce paintings that won recognition for themselves and their country.

The American takeover of the Philippines led the visual arts into the realm of commercial art and advertising design. Needing to portray their presence as not only benign but also for the good of the Filipinos, they geared illustrations in textbooks and publications to that end. As patrons of art, the Americans preferred landscapes and idyllic visions of Filipinos. Filipino artists obliged, but at the same time they illustrated magazines with images that satirized the American colonial system. The best-known painter of this period was Fernando Amorsolo, and Guillermo Tolentino was the dominant figure in sculpting. His best-known work is the Bonifacio Monument, popularly known as *Monumento,* and it vividly illustrates the nationalist passion that drove the struggle against colonial rule under the Spaniards.

After World War II, the artistic styles found outside the Philippines could also be found in the Philippines, and the debates about style were present as well. Different schools and styles emerged from the 1950s through the 1990s. Two important issues for Filipino artists were, in the light of independence and the reality of becoming a nation, the question of national identity and the purpose of art. That is, could they engage in art for art's sake or were they to be a part of the nation-building project? Their view of national identity would inform their choices of subject matter, content, and form. It was into this context that the various movements in the artistic world found a place with Filipino artists. Today, all styles from every school of art have proponents and practitioners in the Philippines.

On a popular level, painting is most often seen on the bodies of *jeepneys,* vehicles based on the model of the Jeep. The art form originated with the *calesa,* a horse-drawn carriage. *Calesas* were at one time the means of public transportation. The carriages were decorated with metal and paint—the *calesa* being painted one color and its borders decorated with lines, geometric patterns, or repetitive designs. Today, the hood and sides of the *jeepney* are the areas painted. Airbrushed landscapes and scenes from comic books are popular. But some owners have moved more toward chrome as the primary means of detailing their vehicles. In either case, great care is taken to decorate a *jeepney* so that it has a unique identity.

References

Burnham, Gracia, with Dean Merrill. *In the Presence of My Enemies.* Wheaton, Ill.: Tyndale House Publishers, Inc., 2003.

CCP Encyclopedia of Philippine Art. (The Multimedia CD-ROM edition).

Enriquez, Virgilio G. *From Colonial to Liberation Psychology: The Philippine Experience.* Manila: De La Salle University Press, 1994.

Fernandez, Doreen G. *Palabas: Essays on Philippine Theater History.* Quezon City: Ateneo de Manila University Press, 1996.

Gonzales, Joaquin L., and Luis R. Calingo. *Culture Shock! Succeed in Business: Philippines.* Portland, Ore.: Graphic Arts Center Publishing Company, 1998.

Hart, Donn. *Compradinazgo: Ritual Kinship in the Philippines.* DeKalb, Ill.: Northern Illinois University Press, 1977.

Hoefer, Johannes Hoefer. *Philippines Insight Guides.* Hong Kong: APA Productions, 1984.

Lopez, Mellie Leandicho. *A Study of Philippine Games.* 2d ed. Quezon City:

University of the Philippines Press, 2001.

McCoy, Alfred W., ed. *An Anarchy of Families: State and Family in the Philippines.* Quezon City: Ateneo de Manila University Press, 1994.

Meñez, Herminia. *Explorations in Philippine Folklore.* Quezon City: Ateneo de Manila University Press, 1996.

Pastor-Roces, Marian. *Sinaunang Habi: Philippine Ancestral Weave.* Pasay City: Nikki Books, 2000.

Phelan, John Leddy. *Hispanization of the Philippines: Spanish Aims and Filipino Responses, 1565–1700.* Madison, Wisc.: The University of Wisconsin Press, 1959.

PART TWO
REFERENCE SECTION

Key Events in Philippine History

PRE-SPANISH PERIOD

900

The date of the Laguna Copperplate Inscription, the earliest known document found in the Philippines. Found in the late 1980s in the Laguna region, hence its name, this document demonstrates not only the existence of a thriving society with complex political and economic structures, but also political connections between the Manila area, Mindanao, and Java.

982

Earliest mention in Chinese records of traders from Ma-i (Mindoro) bringing merchandise to China.

1001

The first Philippine tribute mission to China from Butuan (P'u-tuan) reached Beijing.

1225

Several locations in the Philippines are included in a book about the various peoples with whom the Chinese traded, written by Chao Ju Kua, the superintendent of maritime trade in the province of Fukien. The locations mentioned include Mai (Mindoro), Palaoyu (Palawan), and P'i-she-ya (the Bisayas).

1373

In response to emissaries sent by the newly established Ming Dynasty, different parts of Luzon responded five years after the Ming dynasty came to power. When a new emperor was announced in 1405, several Philippine "states" responded, including Feng-chia-hsi-lan (Pangasinan), and did so five times during the next five years.

1417

Sulu's first tribute mission traveled to Beijing with three royal personages and a retinue of 340 persons. Part of their purpose was to have Beijing designate which of the three would be given the highest position. Paduka Batara, of the east country, was chosen, but he died in China and was buried there with a tomb, memorial arch, and gateway, as was the Chinese custom for royalty.

1515

Tome Pires in his *Summa Oriental,* a history of the Portuguese in Asia, recorded the first mention by a European of the people from the Philippines. They were referred to as *Luções* (Luzones), those from Luzon; Pires noted that there was trade between Luzon, Borneo, and Malacca.

SPANISH PERIOD

1521

Ferdinand Magellan landed in the Philippines while seeking an alternate route to the Spice Islands. Although he worked for the Spanish crown on this expedition, he was Portuguese and had been part of the earliest Portuguese presence in Southeast Asia. His attempts to interfere in local politics resulted in a battle in which he was killed. One of the five ships that left Spain on this expedition continued the voyage until it reached Spain, marking the first known European circumnavigation of the globe.

1543

The fourth Spanish expedition to the Philippines, under the leadership of Ruy Lopez de Villalobos, named the island of

Leyte as *Las Phelipinas,* a name later extended to the archipelago, in honor of the crown prince of Spain, Felipe (Philip), who later became Philip II and was responsible for establishing a permanent Spanish presence in the islands.

1565

Miguel Lopez de Legazpi, commissioned by Philip II, led an expedition from Acapulco of four ships and 380 men. With Andres de Urdaneta, an Augustinian and survivor of a previous expedition, as his chief navigator, Legazpi easily made it to the Philippines and established what was to become the permanent Spanish presence in the archipelago.

1565

Six Augustinian friars traveled with Legaspi, the most prominent among them being Fr. Andres de Urdaneta, the navigator of the expedition. Thus began the one constant of the Spanish presence in the Philippines, the mendicant orders. The Franciscans followed in 1577, the Jesuits in 1581, and the Dominicans in 1587.

1571

This year saw the taking of Manila. Legazpi had built forts in Cebu, then Panay, while waiting for reinforcements, which arrived in 1566, 1567, and 1571. In an earlier encounter (1570), Spanish forces had burned much of Manila to the ground. This act opened the way for an easy conquest of the region the following year.

1565–1815

The Manila Galleon, the economic backbone of the Spanish presence in the Philippines. Because foreign ships and traders were not allowed to enter China, Manila became a neutral location for trade to take place between the Spaniards and Chinese. In exchange for Chinese silk, porcelain, and other products, the Spaniards brought silver, chocolate, and other goods from Mexico. Each Spaniard in the islands received a share of the profit from the Galleon trade.

1588

Led by the *datus,* local political leaders, in Manila, Bulacan, and Pampanga, the Tondo Conspiracy (as the Spaniards named it) sought to regain their freedom from the Spanish intruders. Contacts with Brunei and Japan resulted in a strategy in which the Japanese would provide weapons and Brunei the military forces. The plot was revealed to the Spaniards, who responded brutally.

1603

The year of the first of the periodic massacres of Chinese. The resentment that Filipinos felt as a result of economic hardships and dislocation found a scapegoat in the Chinese merchants, who controlled retail trade. The Filipinos enthusiastically cooperated with the Spaniards in occasional massacres, the most notable of which took place in 1603, 1639, 1662, and 1782.

SEVENTEENTH-CENTURY REVOLTS

1621–1622

Led by a *babaylan* (priest of the indigenous religion) named Tamblot, from the island of Bohol, this revolt sought a return to the old ways. Although 2,000 people joined the revolt, it was easily crushed by Spanish authorities. On nearby Leyte, another revolt broke out, led by the *datu* Bankaw, a man who had welcomed Legazpi in 1565. Bankaw was captured and decapitated.

1660–1661

The most significant revolt of the century, it posed a direct threat to the Spanish continued presence in Manila. It began among the people from the province of Panpanga in response to what was oppressive draft labor (*polo*). While the Spaniards and Kampangans were quick to reach a settlement, the revolt had spread to provinces north of Pampanga. Spanish forces were required in order to end the revolt.

1663

A Christianized *babaylan* named Tapar, in the province of Iloilo, proclaimed himself God Almighty. Dressing as a woman (most *babaylans* in the Bisayas were women), he used Catholic terminology to establish a new religion, combining aspects from the old religion with Catholicism. After his followers killed a Spanish friar and burned his church and house, they escaped to the mountains. Through the use of spies and Cebuano mercenaries, the Spaniards captured most of the leaders of this revolt.

EIGHTEENTH-CENTURY REVOLTS

1744–1829

The longest revolt against the Spaniards, this upsurge lasted eighty-five years. Led by Francisco Dagohoy, a leader on the island of Bohol. Dagohoy proclaimed "Free Bohol," and established a free government in the mountains with 20,000 followers. The Spaniards could not suppress the rebellion until 1829, two years after Dagohoy's death.

1745

The first revolt among the Tagalogs, consisting of conflicts between various towns in the Tagalog provinces against the haciendas owned by the various orders. The issue was the ownership of land, thus the conflict was between communities—the towns versus the haciendas. An investigation by Pedro Calderon, an *oidor* assigned to the assessment, judged the orders to be in the wrong. Little was done to correct the situation. The revolution that would occur a century and a half later can be said to have had its roots in this revolt.

1762

Diego Silang, an Ilocano from Pangasinan, along with leaders from the Ilocos region, Abra, and Cagayan, led a revolt in Northern Luzon. He proclaimed Vigan the capital of Free Ilocos and was recognized by the British, who then held the Philippines, as the legitimate head of the Ilocos government. After his assassination, his widow, Gabriela Silang, continued the revolt. She was captured and executed by the Spanish authorities.

1762–1763

The British capture and occupy the Philippines. This was the result of Spain's entering the war against Britain in support of the French.

1785

The Royal Company of the Philippines, chartered by the Spanish crown, begins direct trade between Spain and the Philippines.

NINETEENTH-CENTURY REVOLTS

1841

A *cofradia* (confraternity) founded in 1832 by a devout peasant named Apolinario de la Cruz, who was radicalized by Spanish persecution, fought Spanish authorities in two major battles. Having won the first battle, the *cofradia* was devastated in the second. De la Cruz was captured and executed on November 4, 1841.

The *cofradia, Guardia de Honor de Maria* (Mary's Honor Guard) was established in Manila in 1872 by church officials. Lacking church oversight due to its large membership, it soon became a movement embracing indigenous practices. When church recognition was withdrawn and the movement began to experience persecution from authorities, it became radicalized and militaristic. It was a significant force during the Philippine Revolution.

Both movements should be seen as precursors to the revolution at the end of the nineteenth century, as well as struggles that continued after the American conquest.

1834
The Royal Company of the Philippines is abolished and the port of Manila opened to unrestricted foreign trade. By 1870, British and American merchants dominate Philippine import and export commerce.

1855
Additional ports are opened to foreign trade.

1896
The first seminary for Filipinos for the priesthood was established in 1712. The requirement of racial purity kept Filipinos from being admitted to the various orders (Dominicans, Jesuits, etc.). By order of the king of Spain, a seminary for Filipinos was created to train men for the priesthood. However, the conflict between Spanish and Filipino priests led to revolution. See also page 194.

THE STRUGGLE FOR FREEDOM
1872
The Cavite Mutiny is seen as the turning point in Philippine history. What began as a strike by disgruntled Filipino workers at the arsenal in Cavite was perceived by the Spaniards as the beginning of a nationwide revolt. This was not the case, but Spanish authorities used the event as a pretext to arrest, exile, and even execute those they believed to be a threat to their continued control of the islands. The most famous of those falsely accused were Mariano Gomes, Jose Burgos, and Jacinto Zamora, Roman Catholic priests. They were executed by garroting on February 17, 1872, at Bagumbayan Field.

1889

The first edition of *La Solidaridad,* a newspaper established, financed, and written by Filipino nationalists, members of the Reform Movement, published in Barcelona.

1887

Jose Rizal's novel *Noli Me Tangere* is published in Berlin.

1891

The sequel to Rizal's *Noli* is published in Ghent, Belgium. *El Filibusterismo* is dedicated to Gomez, Burgos, and Zamora.

1892

Following Jose Rizal's founding of a civic organization, *La Liga Filipina,* which resulted in his arrest and exile, a secret organization named *Kataastaasan Kagalang-galang na Katipunan ng mga Anak ng Bayan* was established. It would become the driving force of Philippine nationalism leading to the revolution.

1896

A momentous year in Philippine history, it had its share of triumphs and sorrows. Three of the leaders of the Reform Movement died in this year. Graciano Lopez Jaena died on January 20; Marcelo H. del Pilar on July 4; and Jose Rizal on December 30. The discovery of the existence of the *Katipunan* forced the hand of Filipino patriots, leading to the "Cry of Balintawak." See also page 193.

1897

A meeting seeking to resolve the differences between the two major factions of the *Katipunan* was convened at Tejeros in March. Although this meeting resulted in the creation of the Republic of the Philippines, Andres Bonifacio and some of his followers left to start a rival republic. He and his brother were arrested and then executed, dealing a serious blow to the cause. Aguinaldo, the new leader of the revolution, continued the struggle and established the Biyak-na-bato Republic in November. But due to military setbacks, in December he accepted a truce with the Spaniards and voluntary exile in Hong Kong.

1898

The conflict between the United States and Spain becomes a factor in the Philippine struggle for freedom. An agreement is reached between Aguinaldo and Dewey (who would later deny any agreement) in which the United States would deal with Spain on the seas and Aguinaldo and his forces with the Spanish presence on land. On May 1, Dewey sailed into Manila Bay and destroyed the Spanish navy. Aguinaldo landed on May 19 with arms purchased in Hong Kong, as well as those supplied by the Americans. On June 12, he declared Philippine independence in Kawit, Cavite. But the Americans decided to keep the Philippines. Working out an arrangement with Spanish forces, after a mock battle on August 13, the Spaniards surrendered to the Americans. The Treaty of Paris was signed in December. The terms of the agreement stipulated that the United States would receive the Philippines in exchange for $20 million. President McKinley proclaimed the policy of Benevolent Assimilation.

THE AMERICAN PERIOD

1899

On February 4, 1899, fighting between the Americans and the Filipinos broke out, thus marking the beginning of the Philippine-American War. Two days later, on February 6, 1899, the U.S. Senate decided to retain possession of the Philippines. The margin of victory was one vote.

On March 2, 1899, the Army Bill was passed by the U.S. Congress increasing the size of the army to 65,000 for wartime strength. In addition, a volunteer force of 35,000 for the Philippines was authorized. This enabled the Americans, after a generally unsuccessful year of fighting Filipinos, to carry out an offensive in November. Although the strategy was successful, the character of the conflict was changed to that of a guerrilla war. Manuel Tinio's brigade was destroyed December 9.

1901

President Aguinaldo was captured in March, but resistance continued. The events of September 28, 1901 came to symbolize American frustrations and resulting atrocities. On that day in Balangiga, Samar, a combined attack by townspeople and guerrillas resulted in the deaths of forty-eight of seventy-four U.S. soldiers stationed there. The Americans returned with instructions to kill everyone older than ten. General Jacob F. Smith ordered his men to turn the region into a "howling wilderness." He was later court-martialed for his actions.

1901

A group of 540 American teachers traveled to the Philippines to educate Filipinos. They came to be known as Thomasites because they traveled aboard the U.S. Army Transport *Thomas*. They were not the first American teachers to work in the Philippines, but the largest group. American soldiers had already starting teaching the locals English and other subjects. By 1902, more than 1,000 American teachers were working in the Philippines.

1902

General Malvar surrendered. The United States declared a state of peace and general amnesty with the Philippine Act of 1902.

1907

First elections held under the American regime. This marks the first freely elected legislature in Asia.

1908

The founding of the University of the Philippines.

1916

The Congress passed the Jones Act, which promised Philippine independence as soon as a stable government could be established. The Clarke Amendment, which specified a four-year time limit, passed in the Senate but failed in the House.

1919

First Independence Mission from the Philippines traveled to Washington, D.C. Other such missions would follow in 1922, 1923, 1924, 1925, 1927, 1928, 1930, 1931, and 1933.

1931

The independence mission of 1931 persuaded Representative Butler B. Hare, Senator Harry Hawes, and Senator Bronson Cutting to sponsor a Philippine independence bill that came to be known as the Hare-Hawes-Cutting Bill. Passed by the Congress on December 30, 1932, the bill was sent to President Herbert Hoover, who vetoed it. Congress overrode the veto on January 17, 1933, but Philippine president Manuel Quezon rejected the bill.

1934

The Tydings-McDuffie Act was passed by Congress and signed by President Roosevelt. Essentially the same bill as the Hare-Hawes-Cutting Bill, this legislation was accepted by Quezon and the Philippine legislature.

1935

On the night of May 2, 65,000 partially armed peasants seized three communities and threatened ten others in Bulacan, Rizal, Laguna, and Cavite. Led by Benigno Ramos, the movement was against the ruling establishment, particularly Manuel Quezon and his political party, the Nacionalista Party. Among the promises made to the Filipino people were complete independence by the end of the year (no ten-year transition period), abolishment of all taxes, and the division of large land holdings and distribution to the peasantry. Although not the only uprising during the twentieth century, it clearly pointed to the problems of poverty of those in the countryside.

On November 15, 1935, the Commonwealth of the Philippines was inaugurated with Manuel L. Quezon as the president and Sergio Osmeña as vice president, as well as ninety-eight members of the National Assembly.

1941

On December 8, in conjunction with the attack on Pearl Harbor, the Japanese bombed Aparri, Baguio, Davao, and Clark Field, and landed troops at Bataan. Two days later, more troops landed at Aparri and Pandan, near Vigan. Troop landings continued through the month.

On December 26, General Douglas MacArthur declared Manila an "open city" to spare the city from being destroyed. The Japanese bombed Manila anyway.

THE JAPANESE OCCUPATION

1942

On January 2, the Japanese entered Manila and began the work of reorganizing the government.

On March 29, various peasant groups, having met in early February, seeking to form a united front to fight the Japanese, formed the group *Hukbo ng Bayan Laban sa Hapon* (Group of the Land fighting the Japanese), or HUKBALAHAP, their members known as Huks.

On April 9, General Edward King, commander of the forces numbering approximately 78,000 Filipino and American troops on Bataan, surrendered to the Japanese.

On May 6, the island fortress of Corregidor falls. General Jonathan Wainwright, having been put in command of

USAFFE forces upon the departure of General MacArthur, surrendered the entire USAFFE forces in the Philippines.

1943

On June 20, the Preparatory Commission for Philippine Independence convened to write a constitution for the Republic of the Philippines. A convention was held for the writing of the constitution.

On September 20, a legislature was elected, as provided for by the new constitution.

On September 25, Jose P. Laurel was elected president.

On October 14, the Republic of the Philippines was inaugurated and Jose P. Laurel sworn in as president.

1944

August 1, President Manuel Quezon died in New York. Sergio Osmeña, his vice president, assumes the presidency.

On October 20, MacArthur landed in Leyte, marking the beginning of the liberation of the Philippines.

1945

On January 9, Americans land at Lingayen Gulf, on the island of Luzon, and advance on Manila.

On January 30, a series of atrocities begin in Manila. Japanese troops kill 100,000 civilians.

On February 27, General MacArthur, the military adviser, turns over the reins of civil government to President Osmeña.

On July 4, MacArthur declared liberation of the Philippines achieved.

THE PHILIPPINE REPUBLIC

1946

On July 4, the Republic of the Philippines was inaugurated with Manuel Roxas as its first president.

1947

Roxas signed military bases agreement with the United States. The agreement granted the United States ninety-nine-year leases rent-free for twenty-two bases, including Clark Air Base and Subic Naval Base.

1948

On March 6, the Hukbalahap was outlawed by Roxas.

On April 15, Roxas died and was replaced by Vice President Elpidio Quirino.

1949

On April 29, Mrs. Aurora Quezon, the widow of President Quezon, her daughter, and ten others were ambushed and massacred near Bongabon, Nueva Ecija, in central Luzon. The Huks are blamed and their movement discredited. The following year, the movement renames itself "Army for the Liberation of the People."

1953

Ramon Magsaysay elected president.

1957

Magsaysay was killed in a plane crash and his term served out by Vice President Carlos Garcia, who was elected president in November.

1961

Diosdado Macapagal was elected president.

1965

Ferdinand Marcos was elected president.

1969

Marcos was reelected, the first president to be reelected.

1972

On July 7, the Constitutional Convention votes to change the form of government from presidential rule to a parliamentary system.

On August 13, Marcos proclaimed a state of emergency.

On September 22, Marcos declared martial law.

1983

August 21, Benigno Aquino returned to the Philippines and was assassinated while being led off the plane by security forces.

1985

November 3, Marcos announces "snap elections," to be held in February.

On December 2, General Ver is acquitted in the matter of Aquino's assassination.

On December 3, Corazon Aquino, widow of Benigno Aquino, announces her intention to run for the presidency.

1986

February 7, presidential elections are held. Both Marcos and Aquino claim victory.

On March 25, Aquino abolishes the legislature, revokes the 1973 constitution, and claims all legislative powers for herself.

On May 25, Aquino creates a constitutional commission, appointing its delegates.

On October 12, a draft constitution is submitted.

1987

February 7, a national plebiscite approves the new constitution.

On May 11, the election gives Aquino supporters majorities in the legislature.

On July 6, Marcos loyalists seek to establish a rival government at the Manila Hotel with Arturo Tolentino, Marcos's vice-presidential running mate, as president.

On August 28, the most significant military coup attempt, led by Colonel Gregorio Honasan, includes an attack on the presidential residence. Fifty-three civilians and soldiers are killed, and hundreds wounded. Honasan is eventually captured, but escapes.

1989

On December 1, military rebels stage coup attempt. The United States government orders jet fighters from Clark Air Base to patrol the skies over Manila and thus tilt the balance of power to President Aquino. This signals that the United States supports the elected government of the Philippines. Honasan is believed to be behind the attempt, with the support of local political leaders.

1992

Fidel Ramos elected president.

1998

Joseph "Erap" Estrada elected president.

2001

January 21, Estrada ousted and replaced by Vice President Gloria Macapagal-Arroyo.

2004

June 30, Gloria Macapagal-Arroyo is inaugurated after her election as president.

Significant People, Places, and Events

AGUINALDO, EMILIO (1869–1964). Born in Kawit, Cavite, he became the president of the first Philippine republic established in 1897. After being inducted into the *Katipunan*, he became head of the *Magdalo* faction. Successful in battle against the Spaniards, he was recognized as a leader. Based on an agreement with the Spaniards, he and close associates went into exile in Hong Kong, taking along 400,000 pesos given by the Spaniards. In Singapore, he was approached by the Americans, who were preparing to attack the Spanish presence in the Philippines. The Americans lacked ground forces that Aguinaldo had and needed his support. Believing the Americans, Aguinaldo professed altruistic motives, declaring Philippine independence on June 12, 1898, in his hometown. The Americans decided to keep the Philippines, which led to the Philippine-American War. The elite sided with the Americans, and Aguinaldo had the support of

Emilio Aguinaldo, the first president of the first Philippine republic. He fought the Spaniards and then led the fight against the Americans. (Library of Congress)

the masses. The struggle continued until his capture on March 23, 1901. Although the conflict continued for another year, Aguinaldo's capture was the death-blow to Philippine efforts to maintain their independence.

AQUINO, BENIGNO "Ninoy" Jr. (1932–1983). The victim of a political assassination, Aquino, the son of a prominent politician, began his career as a journalist. He came to the national spotlight when, on a secret mission for President Ramon Magsaysay, he convinced the Huk leader Luis Taruc to surrender in 1954. Aquino entered politics and in 1956 was elected mayor of his hometown, Concepcion, at the age of twenty-four. He became governor of Tarlac in 1961 and senator in 1967. The leader of the opposition, he was arrested one day after President Marcos declared martial law in 1972. Although kept in solitary confinement and sentenced to death after a lengthy trial, Aquino remained the focal point of the opposition. He was allowed to travel to the United States in 1980 for health reason. Upon his return to the Philippines, he was assassinated at the Manila International Airport when he exited the plane. His body lay in state for ten days, still in the bloodstained clothes he was wearing when martyred. Millions lined the route to the cemetery as funeral procession wound its way through Manila. The route was 30 kilometers and the procession lasted eleven hours. His martyrdom is seen as the main catalyst triggering events leading to the EDSA Revolution and culminating in the removal of Ferdinand Marcos and the election of Aquino's widow, Corazon "Cory" Cojuanco Aquino.

AQUINO, CORAZON "Cory" COJUANCO (1933–). Seventh president of the third Philippine Republic. From one of the wealthiest families in the Philippines and having studied in the United States, she remained in the background, raising five children while her husband, Benigno "Ninoy" Aquino Jr., involved himself in a successful political career. It was after her husband's assassination that this devout Catholic housewife came to represent and symbolize the moral opposition to the Marcos dictatorship. Initially reluctant, she became the opposition's presidential candidate in a "snap election" called by Marcos in November 1985. The results of the election were contested because both Marcos and Aquino claimed victory. A military revolt led to the events of the EDSA Revolution. Marcos left the country and Aquino claimed that her government's legitimacy was based on the EDSA Revolution rather than the contested election. She announced a provisional constitution, appointed a commission to write a new one, and presented that constitution to the people for ratification in February 1987, one year after the ESDA Revolution.

AQUINO, MELCHORA ("Tandang Sora") (1812–1919). Known as the "Mother of the Revolution," she supplied *Katipuneros* with food, as well as nursed the sick and wounded during the early battles of the Revolution. She was arrested and deported to Guam by the Spaniards and then repatriated by the Americans six years later in 1903. Her story is one of many of Filipinas who actively participated in the Revolution. Freedom fighters Gregoria Montoya of Kawit, Cavite; Agueda Kahabagan of Santa Cruz, Laguna; and Teresa Magbanua of Pototan, Iloilo, were each known as the Joan of Arc of their respective regions. Trinidad Tecson of San Miguel, Bulacan, fought as a common soldier and, while recovering from a leg wound, served as a nurse. Women who had financial resources assisted the cause as well. Nazaria Lagos from Duenas, Iloilo, built a military hospital at her hacienda where she cared for the wounded.

BATAAN DEATH MARCH. After fighting the Japanese valiantly for more than three months, American and Filipino forces had been decimated by disease and the lack of food. On April 9, 1942, General Edward P. King surrendered. This affected 70,000 American and Filipino troops. The Japanese forced them to march from Bataan to San Fernando,

Pampanga, where they were put in box cars and transported to a prison camp—a journey for some of more than 90 miles (140 kilometers). The summer heat, the lack of food and water, and health problems ranging from malaria to dysentery made the march almost impossible for many. Those who could not march due to weakness were usually shot, bayoneted, or beheaded. Of the 70,000 men who began the march, more than 10,000 died, with about 54,000 reaching Camp O'Donnel. The cruel treatment of American and Filipino soldiers resulted in so many deaths that this episode in Philippine history came to be known as the Death March. Coming after a humiliating defeat, the cruelty of the march served as a rallying point and helped cement a bond between Americans and Filipinos.

BONIFACIO, ANDRES (1863–1897). Although not the founder of the *Katipunan,* his leadership left its mark and shape on the revolutionary movement. Coming from difficult economic circumstances, he educated himself and read widely. In 1892, he attended the founding of *La Liga Filipina,* which was led by Jose Rizal. Rizal was arrested three days later and this led Bonifacio and associates to create the *Katipunan.* In 1895, Bonifacio became the legitimate leader of the movement, and his actions led to a tremendous expansion in its membership. Recognized as the leader of the revolution, he chaired a meeting in March 1897 to attempt to heal the breech that had developed between two factions of the *Katipunan.* The meeting resulted in the establishment of the Republic of the Philippines, with Emilio Aguinaldo as president. Bonifacio was elected director of the interior, but that position was questioned by some. He declared the results of the election null and void, adjourned the meeting, and left. Failing to gain the support of many others, he established a rival republic in Naik. Bonifacio and his brother were captured by forces loyal to Aguinaldo. They were found guilty of treason and executed by firing squad. The driving force of the revolution was gone.

CAVITE MUTINY. On January 20, 1872, payday for the workers at the Cavite Arsenal, workers discovered a new deduction in their already small wages. Others working in the artillery corps and government shops had lost exemptions. This led to what has been called a strike, in which both Filipinos and Spaniards were killed. The Spaniards viewed this "strike" as political and part of a larger national movement leading to a revolution. Those viewed as opponents of the Spanish presence were arrested, although they had nothing to do with the events in Cavite. Some were exiled, while others, including the famous trio of Filipino priests, Gomez, Burgos, and Zamora, were publicly executed as enemies of the state. 1872 is viewed as the turning point in Philippine history.

THE CRY OF BALINTAWAK. When the existence of the secret society, the *Katipunan,* was discovered by Spanish authorities on August 19, 1896, Andres Bonifacio summoned the leaders to meet at Balintawak to discuss what steps should be taken to deal with the crisis. Five hundred members of the *Katipunan* met there. Although the exact details of the next few days are in dispute, at some point, when asked whether they would fight the Spanish to the death, all agreed to do so. Bonifacio had them tear up their *cedulas* (personal identity papers) and they shouted, "Long live the Philippines" *(Mabuhay Filipinas).* This event marked the beginning of the Philippine Revolution.

DEL PILAR, MARCELO H. (1850–1896). A younger brother of one of the Filipino priests exiled to Guam in the aftermath of the Cavite Mutiny, Marcelo finished a law degree at the University of Santo Tomas. He established the newspaper *Diariong Tagalog* in 1882, and it became a vehicle for criticizing the friars for their mistreatment of Filipinos. Forced to leave the country to avoid arrest, Marcelo traveled to Spain, where he became one of the pillars of the Reform Movement there. He succeeded Graciano Lopez Jaena as the editor of *La Soli-*

daridad in 1889, using the name Plaridel. The paper closed in 1895 because of a lack of financial support. By that time, the reformer del Pilar advocated revolution as the solution to the oppression in the Philippines. He died of malnutrition on July 4, 1896.

EDSA REVOLUTION/PEOPLE POWER. EDSA is the acronym for Epifanio de los Santos Avenue, a major thoroughfare in Metro Manila. After the results of a "snap election," in which Ferdinand Marcos and Corazon "Cory" Aquino were the main candidates, were called into question, a military revolt led by two major figures in the Marcos regime broke out. Taking refuge in Camp Aguinaldo, along EDSA, they appealed to Cardinal Sin for support. He called upon the faithful to protect the rebels. Between 1 and 2 million people filled EDSA and prevented the military forces still loyal to Marcos from reaching the rebels. From February 22 to the 25, "People Power" supported those who had broken away from the Marcos dictatorship. Marcos left the country that night and spent his last days in Hawaii. Some have seen the EDSA Revolution as a revolution, others as merely a return to power of the oligarchy whose power had been clipped during the Marcos years. It has served as a paradigm for other popular uprisings, including EDSA II, which resulted in the deposing of President Joseph Estrada and his being replaced by Gloria Macapagal-Arroyo; and EDSA III, which failed to achieve any political change even though it was a larger gathering than EDSA II.

ESTRADA, JOSEPH EJERCITO (1937–). Known as "Erap" (*pare* spelled backwards; *pare,* short for *kumpare,* is used as a term of familiarity), the third president after the end of the Marcos dictatorship, he was born Joseph Ejercito, the eighth child of a lower-middle class family. His siblings earned college degrees, but he went into acting. Taking the name Joseph Estrada, he usually played the hero who successfully challenged the rich and powerful. His political career began when

Joseph Estrada, president from 1998 until he was removed from office in 2001. (Reuters/Corbis)

he became mayor of San Juan during the Marcos dictatorship. Later, he served as a senator for one term and then ran in 1992 as an independent candidate for vice president and won. He cultivated a flamboyant image as the father of ten children, three by his wife. He was known for his mangling of English. In 1998, Estrada became president with support from the rural peasants and urban poor. His presidency came to an end on January 21, 2001, as the result of EDSA II.

GARCIA, CARLOS (1896–1971). The fourth president of the third Philippine republic, he became president upon the death of President Ramon Magsaysay, served out his term, and then was elected to a single term in 1957. A high school teacher, Garcia entered politics in 1925, serving as congressman of his district on the island of Bohol, and later as governor of Bohol. When he was elected president in 1957, his vice-presidential candidate was defeated by the candidate from the opposition, Diosdado Macapagal. To deal with the economic difficulties facing the Philippines, Garcia sought economic independence from foreign dominance with the "Filipino First" policy, encouraging Filipinos to buy local products instead of imported American goods. Garcia's administration was marked by corruption, the issue that led to his defeat by Macapagal. A delegate to the 1971 constitutional convention, he was elected its president on June 11, 1971. Garcia died three days later.

GOMBURZA. This acronym refers to three martyred Roman Catholic priests who were executed by strangulation on February 17, 1872. In response to a work strike in Cavite thought to be the precursor of a national revolt, Spanish authorities arrested Filipinos they believed were opposed to the Spanish presence. Included in this group were Fr. Mariano Gomes (aged eighty-four), Fr. Jacinto Zamor (aged thirty-seven), and Fr. Jose Burgos (aged thirty-five). Although there was no evidence of any involvement on their part in what was essentially a spontaneous work action, the priests were found guilty of treason. It is worth noting that the Catholic Church did not defrock them before their executions and they were allowed by the archbishop to go to their deaths in their priestly garb. It is believed that their deaths marked the genesis of the separatist movements that would emerge years later.

JACINTO, EMILIO (1875–1899). Although one of the *Katipunan*'s youngest members, he came to be known as the "Brains of the *Katipunan*." Having studied law at the University of Santo Tomas, he became a close associate of Andres Bonifacio. Jacinto composed the *kartilla,* the membership pledge of the *Katipunan.* He was made editor of the society's newspaper, *Kalayaan,* Tagalog for "freedom." It was his writing that influenced thousands to join the movement in 1896. Later that year, he attempted to rescue Rizal, but failed to convince him to escape. Jacinto was wounded and captured by Spanish forces; he died at the age of twenty-three.

KATIPUNAN. The Tagalog word for association, this group's full name was *Kataastaasan Kagalang-galang na Katipunan nang mga Anak nang Bayan* (The Highest and Most Respectable Association of the Sons of the Land). It was founded on July 7, 1892, after the arrest and exile of Jose Rizal, who had organized *La Liga Filipina* on July 3. In light of the crackdown on Rizal and his organization, the futility of seeking reforms through peaceful means was evident, and it was decided that a secret society should be founded. Those who joined signed their membership papers with their own blood. It had political, moral, and civic aims, with the political aim being separation from Spain. It was not until 1895, when Andres Bonifacio became the leader of the movement, that its membership significantly expanded. It was the discovery by Spanish authorities of the existence of the *Katipunan* that led to the beginning of the Philippine Revolution.

MABINI, APOLINARIO (1864–1903). Although born into a poor family, he was educated at home and later won a scholarship to the Colegio de San Juan de Letran. Mabini went on to pass the bar exam after graduating in law from the University of Santo Tomas. Shortly after this, he contracted polio, which resulted in paralysis. Mabini later became a political advisor to President Aguinaldo. Known as the "Brains of the Revolution," he was captured by the Americans in December 1899 and exiled to Guam for refusing to take the oath of allegiance. He took the oath in February 1903 so that he could return to the Philippines. Mabini died of cholera three months after returning from exile.

MACAPAGAL, DIOSDADO (1911–1997). The fifth president of the third Philippine Republic, he defeated Carlos Garcia in 1961. He received a law degree and later a doctorate in economics. Macapagal was elected vice president in 1957, serving under Garcia, who was from the opposing political party. Ironically, he replaced Garcia as president of the constitutional convention after Garcia's death. Macapagal is remembered for changing the date for celebrating independence from July 4, the date the Americans chose in 1946, to June 12, the day President Emilio Aguinaldo declared independence in 1898. Macapagal was a strong supporter of the U.S. efforts in Vietnam.

MACAPAGAL-ARROYO, GLORIA (1947–). The fourth president after the Marcos dictatorship, she came to power as the result of EDSA II. The daughter of former President Diosdado Macapagal, like her father, she held a doctorate in economics. After a decade of teaching economics, she entered politics. She was elected a senator in 1992 and vice president in 1998. She was a staunch supporter of the United States after the events of September 11, 2001.

MAGSAYSAY, RAMON (1907–1957). The third president of the third Philippine Republic, he was well known as a guerrilla leader during the Japanese Occupation. Magsaysay was elected to Congress and later was appointed secretary of defense during the Quirino administration. Viewed as responsible for defeating the Huk insurgency, he was elected president in 1953 by a large margin. Known for his willingness to deal with the common folk, he was a contrast to other Filipino leaders. He died

Ramon Magsaysay, president from 1953 until his untimely death in 1957. (Time Life Pictures/Getty Images)

in a plane crash during the last year of his term and was succeeded by Carlos Garcia.

MARCOS, FERDINAND (1917–1989). The sixth president of the third Philippine Republic, he came to dominate the nation for more than two decades. Marcos came to national prominence when he was arrested for the assassination of his father's political rival. After being found guilty, he wrote his own appeal, took the bar exam, and finished first in the nation. His conviction was overturned. Marcos was touted as an outstanding guerrilla leader during the Japanese Occupation, but this would later be called into question. Marcos was elected to three terms in the Congress and then to the Senate, where he became president of the Senate. His marriage to Imelda Romualdez, a beauty queen from the Visayas, was seen as strengthening and advancing his political career. In 1965, when Macapagal reneged on a pledge to step aside and support Marcos's candidacy for the presidency, Marcos joined the opposition, the *Nacionalista* Party, and became their candidate. When the Catholic vote split between Macapagal and Raul Manglapus, Marcos won. In 1969, he became the first president to be reelected. On September 22, 1972, he declared martial law, which remained in place until 1981. These years were seen as the era of the Marcos dictatorship—or the conjugal dictatorship, because Imelda Marcos wielded ever-growing power. The assassination of Ninoy Aquino, his strongest political rival, marked the decline of Marcos's hold on power. In February 1986, after a presidential election he claimed to have won and the events of the EDSA Revolution, he left the country to live in exile in Hawaii until his death.

QUEZON, MANUEL L. (1878–1944). The president of the Commonwealth until his death in Saranac Lake, New York. He studied law at the University of Santo Tomas until the Philippine-American War broke out. Quezon served as an aide to President Emilio Aguinaldo. His life in politics began in

1905, when he ran for governor and later as a member of the Assembly. Serving as a Philippine Commissioner, Quezon lived in the United States for nearly eight years, during which time he pushed for legislation in the U.S. Congress. In the 1920s, he became the leading political figure in the Philippines, setting the stage for his election to the presidency in 1935. After the Japanese invasion, he set up a government in exile in the United States.

RAMOS, FIDEL (1928–). Eighth president of the third Philippine Republic, Ramos was a military man who later entered politics. Born into a well-to-do family, Ramos received his education at West Point and the University of Illinois. In the Philippine army, he served in Korea and Vietnam. During the Marcos dictatorship, he was the head of the Philippine Constabulary (now the Philippine National Police). Ramos was also the vice-chief of staff of the armed forces. A close associ-

Fidel Ramos, president from 1992 to 1998. (Embassy of the Philippines)

ate of Marcos, he joined Juan Ponce Enrile and those in the military opposed to Marcos, events that led to the EDSA Revolution. In the Aquino administration, he served first as chief of staff and then defense minister. In 1992, Ramos was elected president with 23.5 percent of the vote. Ramos was faced with an energy crisis as well as economic problems. He sought to end both Communist and Muslim insurgencies and formed a National Unification Commission to oversee this. Ramos was later able to reach an agreement with the Moro National Liberation Front and end the insurgency. Toward the end of his term, his supporters sought to change the constitution to allow Ramos to run for a second term. Cardinal Sin and former President Aquino demonstrated publicly in opposition to this. The constitution was not changed.

RIZAL, JOSE (1861–1896). Jose Rizal was considered by many to be the national hero of the Philippines. Born into a well-to-do family, Jose received a bachelor's degree from Ateneo de Manila and studied medicine at the University of Santo Tomas. Based on instructions from his older brother, Paciano, Jose changed his surname from Mercado to Rizal to avoid drawing the attention of the Spanish authorities. He had an amazing intellect: He spoke, read, and translated twenty-two languages; he was also a physician, an ophthalmologist, a surgeon, a writer, a painter, and a sculptor. He studied in Spain after leaving the Philippines. In Europe, he wrote two novels, *Noli Me Tangere* (Touch Me Not, 1887) and *El Filibusterismo* (The Subversive, 1891), in which he pointed out in detail the unjust rule of the friars and, by extension, the Spanish government in the Philippines. He was arrested and exiled to Dapitan on Mindanao shortly after his return to the Philippines. In 1896, after the discovery of the existence of the *Katipunan*, Rizal was put on trial for treason and sedition. He was found guilty and executed by firing squad on December 30, 1896.

ROXAS, MANUEL A. (1892–1948). The first president of the third Philippine Republic, he earned a law degree from the University of the Philippines in 1913 and taught law before entering politics. Roxas was elected to Congress in 1922 and later would succeed Sergio Osmeña as Speaker of the House in 1934. When the Philippines was given independence in 1946, he was elected president. Roxas died of a heart attack at Clark Field Air Base in April 1948 and was succeeded by Elpidio Quirino.

Language, Food, Etiquette, and Customs

LANGUAGE

As mentioned in the introduction, the Philippines has the fourth largest English-speaking population, behind those of the United States, the United Kingdom, and India. There are in fact two official languages in the Philippines, English and Tagalog, both holdovers from the colonial era. Beyond the official languages the Philippines is marked by the linguistic diversity one might expect of an archipelago spread out over such a large area. Figures vary, but generally it is accepted that there are eleven languages and eighty-seven dialects spoken in the Philippines. Nine out of ten Filipinos count one of the following as their first language: Tagalog, Cebuano, Ilocano, Hiligaynon, Bicolano, Waray-Waray, Kapampangan (or Pampangan), and Pangasinan. These eight languages have their roots in the Malay and Polynesian languages, and are related to modern-day Indonesian and Malay. Some of these languages are closer or more similar to others; for example, it is easier for Ilocanos and Pangasinans to learn each other's language than it is for them to learn any of the other six languages. Those who speak the major Bisayan languages—Cebuano, Ilonggo, and Waray-Waray—find it easier to communicate with each other than with those from other language groups.

When the Spanish friars began to do missionary work in the Philippines, they were dismayed to find that there was no *lingua franca,* a common tongue, used throughout the islands. The linguistic diversity was not unexpected, but their experiences in the New World created the expectation that

217

one language would be used throughout the region. Without this *lingua franca,* it was decided that the various linguistic and ethnic groups would be divided up among the religious orders, all the orders having a significant presence in the Manila area and the surrounding provinces, which were Tagalog. Most Spaniards lived in Manila, and only handfuls of friars lived in rural areas and learned the local dialects. The friars who learned the local dialects and who were supported by the *Patronato Real,* that is, the Spanish Crown, became the legal intermediaries between Manila and the rural population. The result was that rather than the local dialects blending in some manner toward a *lingua franca,* they all remained distinct and separate. Spanish became the one language used throughout the islands, but few could speak Spanish.

When the Philippine Revolution broke out, it did so among the Tagalog provinces. There are a number of reasons for this, discussed in the first chapter. What is important here is that Tagalog gained an ascendant position as the language to be used among the revolutionaries. For example, the *Katipunan* required that all discussions be held in Tagalog, and their writings were in Tagalog. Other provinces and linguistic groups did join the revolution, but it remained in the minds of many as a Tagalog event. When it came time to write a national constitution, the issue of a national language emerged. The Biyak-na-Bato Constitution, one of the first in the Philippines, signed on November 1, 1897, stated in Article 8 that Tagalog would be the national language of the republic.

But the Malolos Constitution, written the next year, stated in Article 93: "The use of languages spoken in the Philippines shall be optional. Their use cannot be regulated except by virtue of law, and solely for acts of public authority and in the courts. For these acts the Spanish language may be used in the meantime." Thus, the language brought by the colonial presence became the closest equivalent to a national language. The American presence brought another language that would dominate. English became the medium of instruction when the Americans set up an extensive educational system, and the ability to read, write, and speak English was the key to advancement. The University of the Philippines was founded in 1908, but it was only in 1938, after the establishment of the Commonwealth, that Tagalog language and literature classes were offered.

The constitution of 1935, written by the Philippine legislature and approved by the U.S. Congress, stated in Article 14, Section 3: "The [Philippine] Congress shall take steps toward the development and adoption of a common national language based on one of the existing native languages. Until otherwise provided by law, English and Spanish shall continue as official languages." The "native language" chosen was, of course, Tagalog, although the two other major languages, Ilocano and Bisaya, were spoken by larger numbers of Filipinos.

By the time of the writing of the constitution of 1973, two official languages were recognized: English and Filipino—based on Tagalog (Article 14, section 3). Filipino had emerged as an indigenous *lingua franca* during testimony given at the Commission on National Language for the constitutional convention in 1971. Dr. Cecilio Lopez, emeritus from the University of the Philippines, argued that "a new urban vernacular had spontaneously developed" in the Manila area. Based on Tagalog grammar, with vocabulary from English, Spanish, and all major dialects, this new *lingua franca* was called Filipino. His theory was not supported by many, but the idea remained. After the EDSA Revolution, the new constitution stated boldly in Article 14, Section 6: "The national language of the Philippines is Filipino." But the reality of the presence of English is found in Section 7: "For purposes of communication and instruction, the official languages of the Philippines are Filipino and, until otherwise provided by law, English." Thus, the colonial legacy remained.

In the 1990s, attempts were made by the government to make Filipino the medium of communication, whether in government activities or in education. Two hundred college executives asked that Filipino be the main medium in the classroom, rather than English. This did not become a reality, however. But in those areas where the use of Filipino could not be legislated, such as in the media (with the exception of daily newspapers), Filipino flourished.

The continuing problem is that English is seen as essential to economic progress because it opened the Philippines to communication with the rest of the world, facilitated foreign commerce, and made Filipinos desirable employees for international firms both in the Philippines and abroad. Thus, the debate about the place of English in Philippine society remains. As recently as September 2004, certain areas of Manila, and particular campuses, were designated as English-only areas.

The wide use of English has provided economic benefits for Filipinos. They are able to work in English-speaking countries, and American companies, as well as multinationals, have set up offices/branches in the Philippines. Successful Filipinos are generally fluent in Filipino and English. Filipinos who come from non-Tagalog regions probably speak a given local language or dialect at home, Filipino in ordinary conversations when in Manila, and English for business and international relations.

But Filipino as a national language is important. It provides a sense of identity as well as national pride. Different scholars point to the EDSA Revolution as the point at which the use of Filipino became a symbol of national pride. Although many visitors to the Philippines like the fact that English is so widely used, there should be an awareness that Filipino is the national language. Efforts should be made to learn to use it as much as possible.

Below are some useful phrases in Filipino, along with pronunciation suggestions:

Hello (informal)	*Kumusta (Coo-moose-TAH)*
Hello (formal)	*Kumusta po kayo (Coo-moose-TAH po kha-yo)*

I am (My name is)	*Ako si (A-KO-see)*
Good morning	*Magandang umaga po (Ma-GUN-dang oo-ma-GA po)*
Good afternoon	*Magandang hapon po (Ma-GUN-dang HAP-pon po)*
Good evening	*Magandang gabi po (Ma-GUN-dang ga-BEE po)*
Thank you	*Salamat po (Sah-LA-mat po)*
Thank you very much	*Maraming salamat po (ma-RAH-ming sah-LA-mat po)*
You are welcome	*Walang anuman po (Wa-LUNG a-noo-MAN po)*
Cheers	*Mabuhay (Mah-BOO-high)*
Good-bye	*Paalam na po (Pa-A-lahm na po)*

Those visiting the Philippines and hearing Filipino will probably notice at least three things about the language. The first is the presence of words that are either Spanish or Spanish in origin. For example, the greeting "Hello" is *Kumusta*, which is based on the Spanish *como esta*. Spanish linguistic influence is more noticeable in religious terms and words used in measurement, such as in counting and telling time. The second is the presence of English. In fact, English and Filipino (based on Tagalog) are often so interwoven in conversation that what some call Taglish results. Those who are fluent in both pick and choose a word or phrase from either language. There are no set rules. Lastly, Filipino has the ability to turn any word, or so it often seems, into a verb by adding the prefix *mag*. *Magtaxi* means to take or ride a taxi. *Magkape* (meaning *kape*, coffee) is to have coffee.

Beyond the fact that different dialects are spoken throughout the Philippines, there are characteristics in pronunciation that seem to mark the speech of those from various regions. Ilokanos are known not only for their double consonants and the resulting sounds but for trilling their R's. In addition, Ilokano does not have the glottal stop at the end of words, unlike Tagalog. Thus, their pronunciation marks them as

Ilokanos. And although certain Ilokano words are the same as in Tagalog, with the difference that the H at the beginning of a word is dropped, people from Pampanga seem to drop H's at the beginning of words in both Filipino and English. The Bisayans are most noted for their pronunciation of vowels. E's become I's, and O's become U's. Thus, *may* (my) comes out as *me* (me) when spoken by someone from the Bisayas. The result is a variety of "styles" of speaking Filipino. In addition, Bisayans are known for their peculiar pronunciation of English words that end with "tle." Thus, bottle is pronounced "bah-toll." These regional variations are the source of humor, but serve to color the national language with a diversity reflecting that found in the population.

Examples of greetings in Ilokano:

Good morning	*Naimbag a bigatmo (Nah-im- BUG a bee-GUT mo)*
Good afternoon	*Naimbag a malemmo (Nah-im-BUG a mall-IM mo)*
Good evening	*Naimbag a rabiimo (Nah-im-BUG a ro-BEE-e mo)*
Thank you	*Agyamanak (ug-YAH-ma-knock)*
Thank you very much	*Agyamanak unay (ug-YAH-ma-knock OO-nigh)*
You are welcome	*Awan ti agyaman (awe-ONE tee ug-YAH-mon)*

Examples of greetings in Cebuano:

Good morning	*Maayong buntag (Mah-EYE-yung BOON-tug)*
Good afternoon	*Maayong hapon (Mah-EYE-yung HAP-pon po)*
Good evening	*Maayong gabii (Mah-EYE-yung ga-BEE-ee)*
Thank you	*Salamat (Sah-LA-mat)*
Thank you very much	*Daghan kaayong salamat (dog-HAN ka-EYE-yung sah-LA-mat)*

You are welcome   *Maayong pag-abot (Mah-EYE-yung pug-AH-boat)*

Slang

That Filipinos love to play with language is shown in the various forms of slang found in Filipino. The vocabulary and grammatical rules can be borrowed from Spanish, English, Filipino, and various Philippine languages and dialects. One form of Philippine slang is known as *swardspeak,* which evolved in the Manila area among the gay and theater communities, but is also attributed to the gay community in the diaspora. Several examples will show how this slang borrowed freely from various sources. *Bagets* is a term used to refer to a young person. It is based on the Filipino word *bago,* or new, which is then made to sound "Spanish" as *bagito* and then finds it final form as *bagets,* which one could argue is an "English" form. Thus, the form and meaning are different from the original word but still connected in different ways. *Biyuti* is taken from the English word "beauty," and although *biyuti* can mean beauty, it can also refer to health, personhood, fate, and other things. In this case, pronunciation and meaning differ from the original English. *Bru* is taken from the Spanish *bruja,* meaning witch, but is used as a term of endearment for a girl or woman. *Kebs* or *queber,* meaning "I don't care," represents "English" and "Spanish" forms taken from the Filipino *kibit,* which means a shrugging of the shoulders to indicate doubt, contempt, indifference, and so forth.

Slang is not codified, nor is it uniform. Different segments of the population use their own expressions but at the same time embrace those of other groups. The diaspora will undoubtedly add new vocabulary and ways of expression as part of Filipino slang.

An Ancient Script

As mentioned in the chapter on history, the Tagalogs had a writing system known as *baybayin*. Although some refer to this system as *alibata,* this name was a twentieth-century invention. Consisting of between fifteen and seventeen "letters," *baybayin* was a syllabary, not an alphabet; each symbol or letter represented a syllable. Thus, the twelve to fourteen consonants also had one of three vowels.

Based on Spanish reports, Tagalogs (and by extension other ethnic groups) wrote on palm leaves and bamboo using a stylus made of metal. The reason that we have to rely on Spanish accounts is that such writings by the Tagalogs have not survived, one of the reasons being the types of materials

The Lord's Prayer written in baybayin *as printed in the* Doctrina Christiana, *1593. (Reproduced for ABC-CLIO)*

used, but also because they were not meant to survive. Spanish reports indicate that the technology of writing was not used for recording history, laws, or anything else, because law and governance were based on tradition. Songs and chants were one of the primary methods of keeping alive stories, legends, and myths, which were sung or chanted while planting, harvesting, or rowing or during ceremonies, such those for mourning the dead. The skill of writing seems to have been used for one purpose only writing letters, specifically, love letters. (This practice continues among the Mangyan, an ethnic minority on the island of Mindoro.)

During the twentieth century, *baybayin* became a symbol of pride of a literate past and entered the popular culture, particularly among Filipinos of the diaspora. Many Web sites give descriptions of this system of writing, including some sites that allow one to transliterate into *baybayin*. AOL has *baybayin* as one of the fonts available for its users. Tattoos in *baybayin* are particularly popular among younger Filipinos of the diaspora.

FOOD

When it comes to food in the Philippines, there are various opinions. For those on the outside looking in, Philippine cuisine seems out of place. As one writer put it, "Even in matters of food, the Philippines seems out of place. No fiery curries, no spicy satays" (Hoefer 1984, 25). All seem to agree that Philippine cuisine is marked by outside influences. As one Filipino writer summarized: "Drawing origins from various cultures but displaying regional characteristics, Filipino food was prepared by Malay settlers, spiced with commercial relations with Chinese traders, stewed in 300 years of Spanish rule, and hamburgered by American influence in the Philippine way of life" (Monina A. Mercado, cited in Hoefer 1984, 101). But for insiders, food and eating in the Philippines is much more than that. "Food punctuates his [a Filipino's] life, is a touchstone to his memories, is a measure of his relationships with nature, his fellowman, with the world" (Fernandez 1986, 20). As with everything else in the Philippines, there is great variety in the cuisine, and that variety is marked further by regional permutations, resulting in a seemingly endless cornucopia of delicacies and delights.

Rice

Rice, as in other Asian countries, is the staple of diet in the Philippines. More than that, it is the symbol of life. It is a part of every meal, including breakfast, with the rice from the previous night's dinner being fried lightly with garlic. Rice is a bland food, and the dishes eaten with it provide the contrast. Yet it is a necessary backdrop for each meal, providing bulk as well as the background for the various flavors presented. More than twenty varieties of rice are grown in the Philippines. Some are known for their color or scent, others for their flavor.

Different strains of rice found in the rice market in Baguio City. (Corel Corporation)

Rice has a variety of uses beyond being the backdrop of a meal. The water from washing rice can be used for the broth of *sinigang;* it can also be fermented into wine. Rice can be used to make a variety of desserts. Rice flour is used to make rice "cakes," such as *bibingka* (baked), *puto* (steamed), and *palitao* (boiled). *Malagkit,* sweet rice or sticky rice, as it is known, is used to make different kinds of *suman* or *kakanin.* The various recipes use coconut as an important ingredient.

Fish

Fish is important to the Philippine diet—all kinds of fish, prepared in many different ways. The archipelago has a great variety when it comes to seafood. In addition, freshwater fishponds produce more than twenty varieties of fish, crab, shrimp, and oysters. These two sources provide protein. *Bangus,* a freshwater milkfish, is one of the most popular fish. Numerous recipes use *bangus* as the main ingredient.

Sawsawan *and Eating*

In the cuisine of many places in the world, the taste is decided by the cook. To add any kind of seasoning would be an insult. This is not so in the Philippines, at least among the Tagalogs. The practice of using *sawsawan,* the dipping sauce, allows the one eating to have as much say in the flavoring of the food as the cook. The simplicity of Philippine cuisine allows this, as does the mindset of Filipinos. The cook is not the superior of those who are eating. He or she does not dictate the exact flavor of a dish. The cook knows how sour the *sinigang* should be cooked, but allows, and even expects, the flavor to be "embellished, enhanced, adjusted, and adapted to the individual tastes by means of the *sawsawan* or dipping sauce" (Fernandez 1986, 27). Thus, the center of the table will be set with small bowls or saucers of soy sauce—some with *kalamansi* juice (a local citrus fruit similar to lemon in taste and func-

A typical scene at the fish market. (Leslie Laddaran)

tion), *patis* (fish sauce), *bagoong* (anchovy or shrimp paste), vinegar, *achara* (pickled fruit or vegetables with grated green papaya), and other *sawsawan*. A list of fifty-two dips is listed in *The Complete Sawsawan Guide,* compiled by Mila S. Enriquez and Dez Bautista (Cordero-Fernando 1992, 56–57).

Basic Flavorings

Philippine cooking is said to be simple. Here is a list of the basic methods of cooking:

Adobo: cooked in vinegar, soy sauce, and garlic
Guisado: sauteed
Sinigang: boiled with a sour fruit or vegetable
Paksiw: cooked in vinegar and garlic
Ginataan: cooked in coconut milk
Nilaga: boiling fish, meat, or poultry
Inihaw: broiled over charcoal

Two styles of preparing food stand out, not only for their taste, but also because they do not require refrigeration. *Adobo,* because of the vinegar, and *sinigang,* because of the souring ingredient, do not spoil easily, a real concern in a tropical environment. Both are said to taste better the day after or several days after they have been cooked. Generally, *adobo* is made with chicken and pork, but can be made with other meats as well. *Sinigang* is not limited to meat but can also be cooked using fish. There are a number of souring agents that can be used in preparing *sinigang,* included *sampaloc* (tamarind), *camias* (an indigenous fruit), *guavas,* or *kalamansi.* The recipe below calls for radishes to sour the mix.

If the Philippines had a national dish, it would probably be *adobo.* It is not only a dish but a style of cooking, with many variations possible; one cookbook has at least thirteen recipes, including one for bamboo shoots, another for squid, and still another for okra. Almost anything can be cooked *adobo* style. Here is a basic recipe:

Adobong Manok *(Chicken Adobo)*
1 3-pound chicken, cut into serving pieces
1/2 cup soy sauce

3/4 cup white vinegar
1 or 2 cloves of garlic, crushed
2 bay leaves
1/2 tablespoon peppercorns

Bring the chicken to a boil together with the soy sauce, vinegar, garlic, bay leaves, and peppercorns and simmer for half an hour. Remove the chicken pieces from the pot and broil them for ten minutes. Let the sauce in the pot boil until it is reduced by half. Add salt to taste. Cover the broiled chicken pieces with the sauce. Serve hot. (Serves six) (Alejandro 1985, 51)

Sinigang na Isda (Boiled Fish)
8 cups water
1/2 cup lemon juice
1 cup chopped onion
2 cups diced ripe tomatoes
2 cups radishes, left whole
2 pounds sea bass or bluefish (shelled shrimp, fresh croaker, whitefish, or squid may be substituted) cut into fillets
3 long, fresh, hot green peppers
1 1/2 pounds watercress or spinach
fish sauce or salt and pepper to taste

In a saucepan, bring to a boil the water, lemon juice, onion, and tomatoes. Simmer for fifteen minutes. Add radishes and fish and bring to a boil. Simmer till radishes are tender, yet crisp. Add the hot peppers and watercress or spinach. Add fish sauce or salt and pepper to taste. (Serves four to six) (Alejandro 1985, 142)

Influences

The various influences on Philippine cuisine are sometimes difficult to trace, yet other times are obvious. Malay influence is found in many recipes that are now considered indigenous, such as those using coconut or coconut milk. Chinese influence is pervasive, beginning with *pansit,* a noodle dish. There are different kinds of *pansit,* depending on the type of noodle used, as well as the ingredients cooked with the noodles. *Miki* (made from wheat flour and sold fresh, not dried), *bihon* (rice noodles), and *sotanghon* (translucent noodles) are but a few of the kinds of *pansit* found in Philippine cuisine. In addition, there are regional variations, such as *pansit Malabon,* which includes oysters and seafood. A typical Philippine cookbook will list between half a dozen and a dozen recipes for *pansit. Lomi* and *mami* are noodle dishes with broth. *Lumpia* is a local version of egg rolls. *Siomai* and *siopao* are made with meat encased in dough, local versions of Chinese dumplings.

What has been called Spanish influence in Philippine cuisine should be seen as influences from Mexico. It has been estimated by one author that about 80 percent of the dishes prepared in the Philippines can be traced back to this influence. The names of dishes indicate their origins, names such as *apritada* (a meat recipe with tomato sauce and vegetables), *menudo* (pork and liver stew), *empanada* (meat turnover), *pochero* (a meat stew with vegetables and tomato sauce), *pan de sal* (sourdough bread rolls), and *chicharron* (fried pork rind or skin), to name but a few.

Regional Tastes

Each area of the Philippines has it own variations of the dishes common to the archipelago. For example, Bikolanos, the people of the Bikol area (the southeast part of Luzon) are known for their cooking with coconut milk. The Kapampangans, or Pampangos, are known for their prowess in the kitchen, but their style of cooking is but one of many found in the Philippines.

A variety of snacks. (Leslie Laddaran)

Desserts

Most of the desserts found in the Philippines are imported. From *leche flan* (a milk-and-egg custard) and *lengua de gato* (a thin sweet pastry) to a variety of rice cakes, the recipes have come from elsewhere. But there are indigenous desserts as well. *Guinataan,* a sweet stew of rice or rice balls, coconut milk, and sugar, can be made with corn, sweet potatoes, taro, or other ingredients. *Halo-halo* is probably the most popular dessert, being "the ultimate warm weather refreshment" (Alejandro 1985, 231). The name *halo-halo* means "mixed mixed," and that is what it is—a combination of a variety of ingredients. It is made by filling the bottom half of a tall glass with a tablespoon (or more) of a choice of sweetened fruit or vegetables. These include *langka* (jackfruit); *makapuno* (young coconut meat), kidney beans, garbanzo beans, sweet potato, *ube* (a local purple yam), and fried bananas. Then crushed ice is added to fill the glass. Evaporated milk is then generously poured over the ice. The mixture can then be topped with a scoop of ice cream, a piece of *leche flan,* or anything else one desires. There is no wrong way to make *halo-halo;* it is up to the one creating it.

Fruits

The Philippines has a rich variety of fruit, many unknown to those who have never been to the islands. Fruit is an important part of the life of Filipinos. Beyond the food and nourishment, as well as stimulating tastes, the various kinds of fruit serve as markers of the calendar. There is no word in Filipino for time. The word *tiempo* or *tiyempo* (as it is pronounced) is from Spanish. The word used prior to contact with the Spaniards, and long afterwards as well, was *panahon,* or season. The year is experienced in terms of what fruits are "in season." The fruits found in the Philippines include bananas, mangos, papayas, pineapples, and citrus—such as grapefruit and tangerines, jackfruit, guavas, durian, santol, lanzones, and rambutan.

THE CENTRAL PLACE OF RELATIONSHIPS

At least two things should be kept in mind with regard to Philippine social customs and interpersonal relationships. First, every person is considered worthy of respect. Failure to show appropriate respect reflects badly on both parties. Second, relationships are important, bringing with them a sense of connection and obligation, and often the basis of identity. These two aspects are closely related.

The late Virgilio Enriquez mapped out eight levels of interaction in Philippine society. Ranging from basic civility *(pakikitungo)* to being one with *(pakikiisa),* all levels of personal interaction come under the heading of *pakiki-pagkapwa. Kapwa* is the Tagalog word for fellow being, and *pakiki* is a prefix denoting cooperation. Some see *kapwa* as referring to others, but it is the unity of the self and others, a recognition of shared identity. Although in Enriquez's formula people are divided into two categories, outsiders *(ibang tao)* and insiders *(hindi ibang tao)*, all are under *pakiki-pagkapwa* and thus worthy of respect. When rejecting the requests of a beggar, for example, one should say, *"Patawarin po"* (Forgive me, sir).

A sense of respect and connection can be shown in various ways. In the national language, Filipino, a statement or question is ended with *po* when addressing one older than oneself, or *ho* when addressing someone of the same or younger age. Although dictionaries give "sir" or "madam" as the English equivalents of *po* and *ho,* in reality, they serve as honorific titles, markers of respect. Another way of showing respect is to include the appropriate title before a person's first name. The choices of what title should be used include those reflecting age, those indicating familial relationship, and those showing affection by using titles from other spheres of life. In the northern part of Luzon as well as in the Bisayas, *manong* and *manang* are commonly used when addressing a person older than oneself. Coming from the Spanish *hermano* (brother) and *hermana* (sister), *manong* is used for a male who is older and *manang* for a female who is older. It is not unusual for those close in age to compare birth dates to reckon who is to be called *manong* or *manang.* In work situations, the English titles "Sir" and "Ma'am" are often used before a superior's first name, as in Sir Dennis or Ma'am Irma.

Within families, the children address their older siblings with terms of respect. Again, in Northern Luzon and in the Bisayas, *manong* and *manang* are used. Among the Tagalogs, *kuya* is used for an older brother and *ate* for an older sister. Specifically, *kuya* refers to the eldest brother and *ate* to the eldest sister. *Diko* is the second eldest brother, *sanko* the third, *siko* the fourth; for sisters, the order is *ditse* for the second eldest sister, *sanse* for the third, *dete* for the fourth. When there are more siblings, *manong* and *manang* are used. Rela-

Large families are part of Philippine society.
(Catherine Karnow/Corbis)

tionships created by the church rituals of baptisms and weddings bring with them another set of titles: *compadre* and *comadre, ninong* and *ninang.* Those outside the family may use familial titles, such as *tito/tita* (uncle/aunt) or *lolo/lola* (grandfather/grandmother). Among friends, titles vary, but they are generally borrowed from other relationships and they are not used in the same sense: Sometimes they are used seriously, sometimes playfully.

The reader may have noticed that almost all titles indicating respect and relationship/connection come from outside the Philippines. From Spanish *manong/manang* derived from *hermano/hermana, tito/tita* from *tio/tia,* and *lolo/lola* from *abuelo/abuela,* while from Chinese has come *kuya/ate,* etc. Even the use of the titles such as "sister" and "brod" (from brother) has developed from various aspects of American Protestantism. Again the distinction between surface and core values is helpful. The core value is respect for one's fellow person *(kapwa).* The surface value is reflected in the connections and relationships created and in the titles used. Thus, the origin of the titles is not significant, but the bonds they signify and the obligations they entail are.

Interestingly, this distinction (between core values and surface or survivor values) was not taken into account by American social scientists in the development of Philippine social science. Instead, the American view presented the vision of a passive society with the values of *hiya* (shame), *utang na loob* (gratitude for a debt that cannot be repaid), *pakikisama* (yielding to the will of the majority [this was one of the eight listed by Enriquez, but as a level of adjusting]), *bahala na* (literally, *whatever,* but implying a certain fatalism), and *amor propio* (sensitivity to personal affront). American sociologists went on to list three "evils" by Filipino standards: *walang pakikisama* (one inept at the level of adjustment); *walang hiya* (one who lacks a sense of propriety); and *walang utang na loob* (one who lacks adeptness in reciprocating by way of gratitude). Enriquez and others have argued that these values were surface values and came into being in reaction to a colonial presence. In addition, one could argue that American sociologists selected values that best reflected a conquered people. Enriquez went on to argue that the Americans used *utang na loob* to perpetuate the colonial mentality of Filipinos as well as a sense of obligation to the Americans, choosing to overlook other psychosocial concepts tied to the concept of *loob* (what is inside), such as *kusang loob* (initiative) and *lakas ng loob* (guts). Although the case made by Enriquez is persuasive, it could be argued that the survivor values have become so entrenched that they almost represent core values in the thinking of many Filipinos, even today. It is the combination of core values and survivor values that creates the sense of obligation inherent in all relationships, no matter how superficial.

The concept that every person is to be treated with respect and have a sense of relationship has social consequences, but not in the ways found in the West. For example, individuality is subordinate to the will of the group. The consensus of the group is necessary. As one seeks to show respect to the person to whom he or she is speaking, a direct "no" can be considered offensive. By saying "yes," one can mean anything from a positive to a negative, which is indicated by other factors, such as a lack of enthusiasm. Decisions are made from a relational perspective.

SURNAMES

Many surnames in the Philippines have foreign origins: some Spanish and others Chinese. The cause of the Spanish origin is twofold: Some are the descendants of Spanish families; others had a Spanish surname chosen for them in one of the fascinating stories of Philippine history. On November 21, 1849, Narciso Claveria y Zaldua, governor general of the Philippines, issued a decree regarding the surnames of the local population. The first part of the decree read in part: "The natives in general lack individual surnames which distinguished them by families. They arbitrarily adopt the names of saints, and this results in the existence of thousands of individuals having the same surname." The resulting confusion affected every aspect of administration, including religious, because the degrees of consanguinity could not be determined with any accuracy, parochial records being of little help. Claveria had a catalogue of surnames prepared (from "the vegetable and mineral kingdoms, geography, arts, etc.") and sent to the governors of each province. The appropriate officials were to send to each town the necessary number of surnames, and they were to take care that "the distribution be made by letters, in the appropriate proportions." But in some provinces this did not happen.

The regulations regarding surnames were complicated, and even today have been misunderstood. Claveria's decree stipulated not everyone had to select a new surname:

"Natives of Spanish, indigenous, or Chinese origin who already have a surname may retain it and pass it on to their descendants. . . . Families who can prove that they have kept for four generations their surnames, even though it may be the name of a saint, but not those like *de la Cruz, de los Santos,* and some others which are so numerous that they would continue producing confusion, may pass them on to their descendants; the Reverend Fathers and the heads of provinces are advised to use their judgment in the implementation of this article."

The results can be confusing to the historian doing research and care must be taken to examine surnames based on the particular province in question. For example, the *principales* in the Bikol region had names primarily Spanish and religious in origin such as *de la Cruz* and *de los Santos.* On the other hand, the *principales* of Pampanga had names that were Kapampangan in origin and were most likely not affected by the decree. The fact that the local Spanish friar had the final say in the matter has to be taken into account.

The results in the province of Ilocos Sur (see below) reflect what occurred in other provinces, although contrary to the instructions given. In certain provinces, including Ilocos Sur, the governor apparently sent a page of the catalogue of surnames, or the pages of a particular letter, rather than sending a complete copy of the catalog to each of the major towns. Thus, instead of having a distribution from each letter of the alphabet, a town would generally receive one letter. Some nationalists have seen this as an attempt by the Spanish regime to keep track of the local population. But the lack of uniformity in how this decree was implemented indicates otherwise.

Letters of Last Names and Towns
A: Vigan, West Filipinos
B: Santa Catalina
C: Narvacan/Cabugao
D: Santa Maria
E: Santiago and San Esteban

F: Vigan, East Mestizos
G: Candon
I/Y: Sinait
M: Bangar
O: Balaoan
P: Bantay
Q: Caoayan
Ra: Santa Catalina
Re: San Vicente
T: Santo Domingo
U/O: Masingal
V: San Juan

Chinese surnames are the result of intermarriage and are common enough. One of the best known is that of Jaime Cardinal Sin. A Chinese mestizo, he carries the Chinese name of his father, Sin. Some Chinese surnames, mostly from Chinese immigrants who came to the Philippines before the beginning of twentieth century, have been camouflaged into Spanish-sounding names, such as Tuason from Son Tua, Cojuangco from Ko Wang Ko, and Lopez from Lo, one of the most common names in China. In the twentieth century, Chinese immigrants, who either intermarried or became naturalized citizens, were more likely to keep their Chinese surnames.

GIVEN NAMES AND NICKNAMES

Both given names and nicknames may seem strange or strange sounding to the Western ear, but they are perfectly natural and acceptable in Philippine society. Some given names are composites, that is, a combination of syllables from several names, such as Luzviminda, from Luzon, Visayas, and Mindanao; or they are a combination of parents' names, such as Jomar, from Jose and Maria. Some families name their children in an orderly fashion, each one beginning with the same letter or following a particular theme.

Most nicknames are given at an early age, and remain throughout adulthood. Others may be given or taken in the adult years. Such nicknames could be categorized as those that have been called "door bell names," for example, Bing, Bong, Ding, Dong, Ping, or a combination of two such names; fruit names, for example, Apple, Cherry, Peaches, as Apple Pie, Cherry Pie, and so forth; or duplicating syllables, for example, Nene, Lynlyn. Among the most common nicknames are Baby, for girls, and Boy, for, well, boys. "(H)ere in the Philippines, wonderful imagination and humor is often applied to the naming process, particularly, it seems, in the Chinese community. My favourites include Bach Johann Sebastian; Edgar Allan Pe; Jonathan Livingston Sy; Magic Chiongson, Chica Go, and my girlfriend's very own sister, Van Go" (Mathew Sutherland).

HOSPITALITY

Filipinos are a hospitable people. This trait is more apparent in the rural areas than in the urban centers, that is, in places where traditional ways survive and are practiced more. Guests in Filipino homes are given the best food and the best accommodations that a family can offer, even if it means deprivation for that family. One tourist guidebook notes that "many backpackers claim they never had to sleep out in the open unless it was by choice wherever there was at least a farmer's or a fisherman's hut nearby" (Hoefer 1984, 295). A visit to someone's house requires that the guest be offered a snack and something to drink; the guest must accept the offer. When the guest enters the house, it is not uncommon for someone to be sent out the backdoor to a nearby *sari-sari* store to buy something to offer the guest.

It is not unusual for foreign guests to be fed and shown around town, and even perhaps be given a place to stay. But one must be careful on two fronts. First, one must not take advantage of this hospitality. Second, hospitality brings with it a sense of reciprocity and therefore an obligation or obligations to respond when given the opportunity. Such reciprocity in the Philippines creates not merely an obligation but a bond, a relationship. It should be noted that as one enters into a relationship with a Filipino or Filipina, that person's family and extended family becomes a part of that relationship; it is therefore entirely appropriate to use the same designations for the parents, grandparents, aunts, and uncles as does the person with whom you have the relationship.

SPORTS AND GAMBLING

Filipinos love sports and endless kinds of competitive activities. It should be noted that when it comes to play, the word *laro* is used, as in *Laro tayo* (Let's play), and competitive games may be called *labanan*. *Labanan* can also be used to describe conflict, fight, rivalry, and contest, coming from the root word *laban*, which means to fight. These two words illustrate the two sides to games in the Philippines. On the one hand, games can be a form of socialization and can serve to demonstrate or build stronger relationships. On the other, games can be competitive to the point of physical conflict. Often, the line between the two is thin and can easily be crossed. Gambling presents a middle ground; that is, there is competition, sometimes fierce competition, but the conflict is "played out" in the arena of gambling.

One of the best-known activities in this area is cockfighting, which is highly competitive and driven by gambling. In the earliest European account of Filipinos, Antonio Pigafetta, the official chronicler who traveled with Magellan, recorded how certain peoples in the islands bred and raised fighting cocks for the sole purpose of pitting them against other cocks. He remarked that much of a family's wealth could be bet on the outcome of a fight, with the family either losing its fortune

Training and preparing cocks for the arena. (Library of Congress)

or gaining one. Although the Spaniards later sought to eradicate this great "evil," it remains a significant part of Philippine culture.

Cockfighting generally takes place in an arena called a cockpit. The roosters used in the fights are expensive birds that are bred and trained. The care given to each of these is remarkable. There are no programs drawn up. Contests are agreed upon in a corner of the cockpit. Those in the audience place their bets with *kristos,* who stand in the ring. Using a form of sign language, bets are placed with no paper record—every bet is committed to memory. Before the contest begins, each rooster is equipped with a razor-sharp blade, one chosen by the owner, tied to one leg. The two birds fighting are placed face-to-face and then released. Contests often last mere seconds before one of the two participants is crippled or killed.

One of the most popular forms of gambling in the Philippines is an illegal lottery known as *jueteng* (pronounced "wheh teng"). The name comes from the Chinese words *hue* (flower) and *eng* (to bet) and the game came into existence in the Philippines during the Spanish period. The rules of the game are simple. The bettor places a wager on two numbers between one and thirty-seven. *Bolitas,* small wooden numbered balls, are put inside a rattan container. One *bolita* is rolled out and then a second, the two numbers representing the winning combination. The lottery can be played in backyards or in homes, the locations of which are known in the community. *Cobradores* are the individuals who take the bets, announce the winning two-number combination, and deliver the prize money to the winner(s). The *cobrador* not only collects bets, but also solicits them, sometimes going to peoples' homes to do so. Winnings can be delivered to one's home as well. The *cobrador* can also be a source of gossip and information in the community.

One of the reasons that *jueteng* continues to enjoy immense popularity is the fact that one can bet as little as 1 peso (less than U.S.$0.02) and as much as 200 pesos (less than U.S.$4). A 1-peso bet can bring in anywhere from 400 pesos (less than U.S.$8) to 1,000 pesos (less than U.S.$20). As with any lottery, the players believe that they have a realistic chance at winning.

Although *jueteng* is popular, it is illegal. Yet it continues to be the main form of gambling in the Philippines. It has been estimated that *jueteng* operators make as much as 65 million pesos a day (over U.S.$1 million). The system continues to operate almost completely unhindered because police and government officials look the other way, for a price. Payoffs are given to local, provincial, and national officials. In fact, allegations that President Estrada had received millions of pesos in *jueteng* money were some of the reasons for his impeachment. His successor, Gloria Macapagal-Arroyo, has also been plagued with difficulties related to *juetang* money because her husband and son have received large sums from the *jueteng* system. These allegations have threatened to destabilize her administration.

There are many indigenous games in the Philippines, but

perhaps among the best known is *sungka*. The game can be played indoors or outdoors, but is often played during the rainy season when most people stay indoors. The *sungka* board, or *sungkaan*, is a little less than three feet long and about six inches wide. There are two parallel rows of seven equidistant holes running the length of the board. The holes, two inches in diameter and hollowed out to about an inch in depth, are about half an inch to an inch apart. Each hole is called *bahay*, or "house" in Filipino. At each end of the board is a large hole about five inches in diameter, known as *ulo*, or head. Two players are given forty-nine tokens, which may be pebbles, cowrie shells, tamarind seeds, or other seeds. The board is placed between the two players with the row closest to a player being his or hers. The large hole *(ulo)* to the player's left belongs to him or her. The object of the game is to end up with the most tokens in one's *ulo*.

Basketball is the most popular team sport, in part because the necessary ingredients are relatively simple: a goal, which can be made of any variety of metal objects, and a ball.

A basketball game in the province. (Paul A. Souders/Corbis)

Throughout the Philippines, makeshift goals as well as regulation basketball courts can be found. Competitions exist at almost every level and can take place almost year-round. Volleyball, which requires little formal equipment—something resembling a net, and a ball—is also popular. Boxing is the sport in which Filipinos have enjoyed international success. As a result, boxers are viewed as heroes. Chess is popular and an arena in which Filipinos have done well. Mahjong is also popular, but accessible only to those who have the financial means. For those with the financial means, tennis, golf, and various types of racing—horse, bicycle, and motor—are an important aspect of recreation.

COMMUNICATION

One major difference that is usually noticed about Americans and Filipinos in terms of communication is that Americans are seen as direct and blunt, in both verbal and nonverbal communication, but Filipinos are not. In Philippine society, direct confrontation is generally avoided. Where a question prompts a negative answer, a negative answer is not given, but something less direct. Instead of saying that one cannot be present at a particular event to which he or she has been invited, one will answer, "I'll try." In this way, the one inviting is not offended or embarrassed and neither is the one who was invited. Yet there is an understanding that the one invited will probably not be present. This method of communication can be frustrating for Americans and other Westerners, who may see it as hypocrisy, or, worse, as lying. They fail to appreciate that the one being "evasive" is in fact trying to spare their feelings.

On the other hand, for all the claims that Americans are "so frank," Filipinos are much franker, but only in certain areas of conversation. For example, Filipinos are much more likely to comment on the physical features of friends, as in, "Boy, you've really put on weight," but in the local vernacular. Or comments can be made about skin color, such as "You've gotten darker," in a culture that prizes fair skin. For those visiting from abroad, this "directness" can be disconcerting, if not painful and offensive. But no offense is intended. Rather, the comments are intended to show interest.

BODY LANGUAGE

In verbal communication, various factors come into play as to the meaning and intent of what is being said. The context, the tone, and intonation can be strong indicators about the significance of the words used. Body language is also important. As with other aspects of Philippine culture, there are differences between regions and ethnic groups, but certain practices are common. Subtlety is an important mark of body language, and the absence of subtlety can indicate a lack of sophistication and that one is from the province and not the city. One can greet both friends and strangers by nodding or by raising the eyebrows. Meeting friends will likely lead to conversation and physical greetings can then include shaking hands. Between women, embraces and bussing can be acceptable. Eye contact is more sensitive and tricky in that prolonged eye contact can be seen as aggressive and/or rude.

Smiling is an important part of body language, and a very common part of life in the Philippines. However, smiles are not limited to pleasant or humorous situations. Smiling can be used to cover up embarrassment, discomfort, nervousness, and even sadness. Filipinos love to laugh and humor is an important part of life. Friends enjoy making jokes at the expense of each other, all in good fun, generally.

When gesturing for someone to approach, it is impolite to point or use the index finger. Neither should one use a beckoning gesture with the palm up; this is the way one calls a dog, not a person. One should turn the hand with the palm down. Again, subtlety is an indicator of status. Often, when asked where a particular location is, Filipinos might point with pursed lips or by using their eyes and a nod to indicate direction or location.

Physical contact between individuals of the same gender in public is not considered inappropriate. Thus, one may see two men holding hands or two women holding hands, or each with an arm around the other. PDAs, or public displays of affection, between members of the opposite sex are more common than in the past, but usually such displays are found more often in urban settings than in rural areas.

HOLIDAYS

Holidays in the Philippines fall into one of three categories: general, or those celebrated by other cultures such as New Year's Day and Valentine's Day; religious; and historical with political implications.

Most towns have a patron saint and celebrate with a yearly *fiesta,* or feast, planned to coincide with the day of that saint; the *fiesta,* a lavish and expensive festival, lasts for two to three days. Food and drinks are generously provided for neighbors and visitors alike. Musicians, performers, and others are engaged to provide entertainment. The seemingly mandatory beauty contest, the contestants usually sponsored to improve their chances of winning, is a highlight of the *fiesta.*

Religious holidays celebrated throughout the Philippines include the following: Three Kings is the last day of the Christmas season and falls on January 6. With Three Kings, one still has an opportunity to give gifts and visit family and friends. Lent, which begins on Ash Wednesday and continues until Palm Sunday, Holy Week, Good Friday, and Easter. Holy Week, including Palm Sunday and Easter, is the most important religious season in the Philippines. Unlike others around the world who also celebrate this season, Filipinos tend to focus much more on the events before Easter, particularly Good Friday. November 1 is All Saints Day and a time for families to go to cemeteries and visit the graves of loved ones.

Schoolchildren march in a parade during the festival called
"Kasadyaan" in the city of Tacloban. (Reuters/Corbis)

Beforehand, arrangements are made for the area around the
graves to be cleaned up and the graves whitewashed. Food is
brought and the family has a meal at the grave in remem-
brance of those who have died and in a sense sharing the meal
and family gathering with them.

Historical holidays tend to revolve around political events
or figures. The most recent comes from the EDSA Revolution—February 22–25: People Power Days. This is held to
remember the events that led to the ouster of Ferdinand Marcos and a return to democracy. June 12 is Independence Day,
based on President Emilio Aguinaldo's declaration of independence in 1898. National Heroes Day, also known as
Andres Bonifacio Day because this was his birthday, falls on
November 30. Rizal Day is the last major holiday of the year,

falling on December 30, the day Dr. Jose Rizal, the national hero, was executed by firing squad by the Spaniards.

References

Abella, Domingo. *Catalogo Alfabetico de Apellidos.* Manila: National Archives Publication, 1973.

Alejandro, Reynaldo. *The Philippine Cookbook.* New York: Perigee Books, 1985.

Canonigo, Cristina S. *Conversational English-Cebuano Made Easy.* Manila: JUCIP BOOKS, 1999.

Cordero-Fernando, Gilda. *Philippine Food and Life.* Manila: Anvil Publishing Co., 1996.

Enriquez, Virgilio G. *From Colonial to Liberation Psychology: The Philippine Experience.* Manila: De La Salle University Press, 1994.

Fernandez, Doreen G. "Food and the Filipino." In *Philippine World-View,* edited by Virgilio G. Enriquez. Singapore: Institute of Southeast Asian Studies, 1986.

Gonzales, Joaquin L., and Luis R. Calingo. *Culture Shock! Succeed in Business: Philippines.* Portland, Ore.: Graphic Arts Center Publishing Company, 1998.

Hoefer, Johannes Hoefer. *Philippines Insight Guides.* Hong Kong: APA Productions, 1984.

Lopez, Mellie Leandicho. *A Study of Philippine Games.* 2d ed. Quezon City: University of the Philippines Press, 2001.

Manalansan IV, Martin F. *Global Divas: Filipino Gay Men in the Diaspora.* Durham, N.C.: Duke University Press, 2003.

Meñez, Herminia. *Explorations in Philippine Folklore.* Quezon City: Ateneo de Manila University Press, 1996.

Sutherland, Matthew. "A Rhose, by Any Other Name." http://www.pinoyuk.com/Featurettes/124.aspx.

Philippine-related Organizations

The country code for calling the Philippines is 63, and is followed by the city code, 2 being that for Manila. However, cell phones are everywhere; in fact, they outnumber land-line phones five to one. To reach someone on his or her cell phone, dial 63 for the country code, then a three-digit number beginning with 9, and then follow with the seven-digit number. (Often, when giving out a text number, a 0 precedes the 9. This 0 is not to be included when calling from outside the country.) Text messaging, or texting, is the most common method of communication on cell phones. In fact, the Philippines is known as the texting capital of the world. One reason for the popularity of texting is that it is much cheaper than calling; one minute of calling costs ten times as much as one text message. Most users of cell phones belong to one of two systems, Globe or Smart, and rather than pay a monthly fee, they buy cards and add "load" to their phones.

BUSINESS AND ECONOMIC ORGANIZATIONS

The United States and Japan are the two largest trading partners with the Philippines, accounting for 36 percent of exports and 40 percent of imports. Other important trading partners include Singapore, Taiwan, China, Hong Kong, and various ASEAN members. Various countries have associations in the Philippines. What follows is a partial list:

American Chamber of Commerce of the Philippines (AMCHAM)
2nd Floor Corinthian Plaza
Paseo de Roxas St.

Makati City
Tel.: 818-7911 to 13
Fax: 811-3081
Web site: www.amchamphil.com.ph

Australian-New Zealand Chamber of Commerce (Philippines) Inc.
7/F Oakwood Premier, Glorietta 4
Ayala Center, Perea Street
Makati City
Tel.: 755-8840, 755-8841
Fax: 755-8843, 755-8844
Web site: www.anzcham.org

British Chamber of Commerce of the Philippines
c/o The British Embassy Manila
17/F, L.V. Locsin Building
6752 Ayala Avenue, corner Makati Avenue
Makati City
Tel.: 580-8359, 816-7116
Fax: 893-9073, 815-6233

Canadian Chamber of Commerce of the Philippines
Unit 1406 Antel 2000 Corporate Centre
121 Valero Street, Salcedo Village
Makati City
Tel.: 843-6457, 843-6466
Fax: 843-6469
Web site : www.cancham.com.ph

European Chamber of Commerce of the Philippines
19th Floor PS Bank Tower
Sen. Gil J. Puyat, corner Tindalo Street
Makati City
Tel.: 759-6680 to 89, 759-6694, 816-1709
Fax: 759-6690, 845-1395, 815-2979
Web site: www.eccp.com

Federation of Filipino-Chinese Chamber of Commerce and Industry
6th Floor Federation Center
Muelle de Binondo St.
Manila
Tel.: 241-9201 to 05
Fax: 242-2361, 242-2347
Web site: www.ffcccii.com.ph

Filipino-lndian Chamber of Commerce (Philippines), Inc.
Rm. 1803, Cityland Condominium Tower I
6815 Ayala Avenue
Makati City
Tel.: 844-7222, 814-0918
Fax: 844-6983

Japanese Chamber of Commerce and Industry of the Philippines
6th Floor Jaycem Bldg.
104 Rada St., Legaspi Village
Makati City
Tel.: 892-3233, 816-6877
Fax: 815-0317

Korean Chamber of Commerce Philippines, Inc.
204 CCH Bldg., 136 Alfaro St., Salcedo Village
Makati City
Tel.: 840-1716, 840-1718
Fax: 894-0712

Official Spanish Chamber of Commerce Industry & Navigation in the Philippines, Inc.
2658 or 2652 Maytubig Street
Malate, Manila
Tel.: 404-1072
Fax: 404-7073

Philippine Chamber of Commerce and Industry
14/F Multinational Bancorporation Centre
6805 Ayala Avenue
Makati City
Tel.: 843-3374, 843-3176, 843-4098,
843-4133, 843-4128
Fax: 843-4102, 843-4103
Web site: www.philcham.com

Taiwan Chamber of Commerce (Philippines), Inc.
2nd Floor, Room 203 Global Tower
Mascardo St., corner M. Reyes St.
Makati Bangkal
Makati City
Tel.: 819-0323
Fax: 843-1851

ASIAN DEVELOPMENT BANK

With headquarters in Manila, the Asian Development Bank is a multilateral development finance institution dedicated to dealing with and reducing poverty in Asia and the Pacific. Founded in 1966, it is now owned by sixty-three members, mostly from the region. ADB has twenty-six offices around the world, with eighteen resident missions throughout Asia.

Headquarters:
6 ADB Avenue
Mandaluyong City 1550
Tel.: [63] (2) 632 4444
Fax: [63] (2) 636 2444
Web site: http://www.adb.org

PHILIPPINE EMBASSIES

The Philippines has an ambassador in the United States, with the embassy located in Washington, D.C., and consulates (general) in Chicago, Honolulu, Los Angeles, New York, San Francisco, San Jose (Northern Mariana Islands), Tamuning (Guam), and San Diego.

Philippine Embassy
1600 Massachusetts Avenue NW
Washington, D.C. 20036
Tel.: (202) 467-9300
Fax: (202) 328-7614

Philippine Consulate General
3600 Wilshire Boulevard
Los Angeles, CA 90010
Tel.: (213) 487-4527
Fax: (213) 386-4063

PHILIPPINE GOVERNMENT

The main Web site for the Philippine government with links to the various departments: www.philippines.gov.ph

EMBASSIES IN THE PHILIPPINES

United States:
Embassy of the United States of America
1201 Roxas Boulevard
Manila
Tel.: [63] (2) 523-6300
Fax: [63] (2) 522-4361
Web site: http://usembassy.state.gov/manila

Japan:
Embassy of Japan
2617 Roxas Blvd.
Pasay City
Metro Manila

Tel.: [63] (2) 551-5710
Fax: [63] (2) 551-5784
Web site: http://www.ph.emb-japan.go.jp

Australia:
Embassy of Australia
Level 23, Tower 2
RCBC Plaza
6819 Ayala Avenue
Makati City
Tel.: [63] (2) 757-8100
Fax: [63] (2) 757-8268
Web site: www.australia.com.ph

European Union:
Delegation of the European Commission in the Philippines
7th Floor, Salustiana D. Ty Tower
104 Paseo de Roxas, Legaspi Village
Makati City
Tel.: [63] (2) 812-6421 to 30
Fax: [63] (2) 812-6687
Web site: http://www.euphil.org

Singapore:
Singapore Embassy
35th Floor, The Enterprise Center
6766 Ayala Avenue, corner Paseo de Roxas
Makati City
Tel.: [63] (2) 751-2345
Fax: [63] (2) 751-2346
Web site: www.mfa.gov.sg/manila

Spain:
Embassy of Spain
5th Floor, A.C.T. Tower
135 Sen. Gil Puyat Ave.

Makati City 1227
Tel.: [63] (2) 818-5526, 818-3561, 818-3581
Fax: [63] (2) 810-2885
Web site: www.mae.es/consulados/manila

Annotated Bibliography of Recommended Works

A wealth of literature on the Philippines is available and two factors make it readily accessible to readers in the United States. The first is that most Filipino scholars do their writing in English. English was so long the language used in the educational system in the Philippines and those doing work on various aspects of the Philippines wrote in English. Second, works published in the Philippines are easily available. For example, Philippine Expressions is a mail-order source of literature published in the Philippines and the United States. The University of Hawaii Press is a distributor for various university presses in the Philippines. Amazon.com also carries many works written by Filipinos and published in the Philippines. The advent of e-commerce has produced a number of businesses and Web sites that specialize in material on the Philippines. A few notable examples are www.kababayan central.com, www.koleksyon.com, www.myAyala.com, and www.philbook.com.

HISTORY

David Joel Steinberg's *The Philippines: A Singular and a Plural Place,* 4th ed. (Boulder, Colo.: Westview Press, 2000), 272 pages, is probably the best concise overview of the Philippines. Included in his presentation of the Philippines are chapters titled "A Singular and a Plural Folk," dealing with the ethnic diversity, and "The Religious Impulse: Global and Local Traditions," describing the syncretism in Philippine religious life. Although the work is not primarily historical, the coverage is more than adequate for a good grasp of Philippine history. Teodoro A. Agoncillo's *History of the Filipino*

People, 8th ed. (Quezon City: R. P. Garcia Publishing Co., 1990), 637 pages, is the most widely used textbook of Philippine history in the Philippines. It presents a detailed history, but there are gaps in Agoncillo's account that reflect his ideological and philosophical bents. Agoncillo deals with social, religious, and economic aspects of Philippine life as well as the history of the Filipino people.

There are many works about the early Philippines, that is, beginning with the Spanish intrusion. Two characteristics of the works should be noted. Most of them were written by non-Filipinos, and many of them, although strong works in their own right, generally tend to focus not on the local population but on the Spanish intruders, their history, and their institutions. Among such books are Martin Noone's *The Islands Saw It: The Discovery and Conquest of the Philippines* (Manila: Historical Conservation Society, 1986), 476 pages; Nicholas P. Cushner's *Spain in the Philippines: From Conquest to Revolution* (Quezon City: Ateneo de Manila University Press, 1971), 272 pages; *Landed Estates in the Colonial Philippines* (New Haven: Yale University Southeast Asia Studies, 1976), 145 pages; William L. Schurz's *The Manila Galleon* (1939; reprint, Manila: Historical Conservation Society, 1985), 364 pages; and Horatio de la Costa's *The Jesuits* (Cambridge, Mass.: Harvard University Press, 1961), 702 pages. Exceptions to this pattern include John Leddy Phelan's *The Hispanization of the Philippines: Spanish Aims and Filipino Responses, 1565–1700* (Madison: University of Wisconsin Press, 1959), 218 pages, and the many works of the prolific William Henry Scott. Although *Hispanization* was written more than forty years ago by a Latin American historian who never visited the Philippines or learned any of its languages or dialects, it remains one of the most significant works on the period, in part, because of its focus on the local population. Phelan opened the door to social histories of Filipinos. One of the few to follow Phelan's lead was Scott. Using Spanish sources, he sought to find as much as he could about Filipinos. His books include *Cracks in the Parchment Curtain* (Quezon City: New Day Publishers, 1982), 300 pages; *Prehispanic Source Materials for the Study of Philippine History,* rev. ed. (Quezon City: New Day Publishers, 1989); *Looking for the Prehispanic Filipino* (Quezon City: New Day Publishers, 1992), 172 pages; and *Barangay: Sixteenth-Century Philippine Culture and Society* (Quezon City: Ateneo de Manila University Press, 1994), 306 pages, which was published after his untimely death in 1993.

One of the marks of works on the Philippines is that they tend to be regional in nature, that is, a particular island, province, or ethnic group is the focus. Certain scholars have become associated with the area of their research. For example, John A. Larkin on Pampanga (a province just north of Manila); Robert Bruce Cruikshank on Samar; Rosario Mendoza Cortes on Pangasinan (a province in central Luzon); and Glenn May on Batangas (a Tagalog province southeast of Manila). These works tend to cover the Spanish colonial period, certain aspects being dealt with in more detail than others.

The period leading up to the Philippine Revolution and the Revolution itself is well documented, researched, and written about by Filipino scholars. One should begin with Reynaldo C. Ileto's invaluable *Pasyon and Revolution: Popular Movements in the Philippines, 1840–1910,* 6th ed. (Quezon City: Ateneo de Manila University Press, 2003). Using sources normally overlooked, Ileto presents the Filipino peasants' worldview and how they understood the events prior to, during, and after the revolution. His collection of essays, *Filipinos and Their Revolution: Event, Discourse and Historiography* (Quezon City: Ateneo de Manila University Press, 1998), 300 pages, is also interesting reading. In one of the essays, he takes on one of the most controversial books ever written about that period. Glenn May's *Invention of a Hero* (Madison, Wisc.: University of Wisconsin Press, 1996), 200 pages, which was released during the centennial of the beginning of the revolution, calls into question much of the historical data and writing by and about Andres Bonifacio, the leader of the *Katipunan* and central figure at its inception. Agoncillo produced a series of more conventional works on the revolution, including the foundational works *The Revolt of the Masses* (1956; reprint, Quezon City: University of the Philippines Press, 2002), 451 pages, and *Malolos: The Crisis of the Republic* (Quezon City: University of the Philippines Press, 1960), 831 pages.

It is only natural that the American period in the Philippines is the focus of much research in this country. Perhaps the best-known recent work on the Philippines in the United States, however, is by the journalist Stanley Karnow. *In Our Image: America's Empire in the Philippines* (New York: Random House, 1989), 494 pages, is a sentimentalized presentation of America's rule in the Philippines. It is well-researched and has much to commend it, but presents real dangers as well. His view of the taking and keeping of the Philippines by the United States is problematic, to say the least. The three-part video series with the same title, produced by PBS and narrated by Karnow, is fascinating for all the historical images and interviews with individuals who have since died. A good counterbalance to Karnow is *The Philippines Reader: A History of Colonialism, Neocolonialism, Dictatorship, and Resistance,* edited by Daniel B. Schirmer and Stephen Rosskamm Shalom (Boston: South End Press, 1987), 425 pages. These editors are as selective in their presentation as Karnow. Then there is the off-beat but informative *The History of the Burgis* by Mariel N. Francisco and Fe Maria C. Arriola (Quezon City: GCF Books, 1987), 200 pages. The book contains numerous cartoons and photographs. Some of the text is in Tagalog, but most of it is in English and accessible to an American audience.

If there is one part of the American period more widely written about than others, it is World War II. Bataan, Corregidor, and Douglas MacArthur are names that are a part of

American history. So much has been produced, but as with so much of Philippine history, the focus is not on Filipinos. There has been a recent resurgence in writing on the period. Among new titles are *Ghost Soldiers,* by Hampton Sides (New York: Doubleday, 2001), 342 pages, which details the operation to rescue American POWs from a camp at Cabanatuan; *We Band of Angels,* by Elizabeth M. Norman (New York: Random House, 1999), 327 pages, which relates the experiences of American nurses during the war, and *Conduct Under Fire: Four American Doctors and Their Fight for Life as Prisoners of the Japanese: 1941–1945,* by John A. Glusman (New York: Viking, 2005), 588 pages, which is written by the son of one of the doctors and recoints what these men went through as prisoners of war. Again, the focus is on the Americans. The two-volume work by Agoncillo on the Japanese occupation is titled *The Fateful Years: Japan's Adventure in the Philippines, 1941–45* (1965; reprint, Quezon City: University of the Philippines Press, 2001), 1008 pages. Brutal in its honesty, it is one of the most thorough studies of the period.

Manila, My Manila (Makati City: Bookmark, 1999), 366 pages, by Nick Joaquin, was written at the request of then Mayor Mel Lopez, who wanted a popular history of Manila for the people of Manila. The first edition, published in 1990, was distributed exclusively in the city's schools. Not a historian, Joaquin was considered by many to be the most distinguished Filipino writer in English. He was declared a National Artist in 1976. Among the best known of his works is the novel *The Woman Who Had Two Navels* and the three-act play *A Portrait of the Artist as Filipino.* There are inaccuracies in some of the historical data, but there can be no doubt that this was a labor of love because Joaquin presented this moving tribute to the city he loved. Several works that present a more academic examination of the history of Manila include Robert R. Reed's *Colonial Manila: The Context of Hispanic Urbanism and Process of Morphogenesis* (Berkeley: University of California Press, 1978), 129 pages, and Manuel A. Caoili's *The*

Origins of Metropolitan Manila: Social and Political Analysis (Quezon City: University of the Philippines Press, 1999), 295 pages.

INSTITUTIONS

There are many books on religion in the Philippines, most of them written from a sympathetic point of view. That is, most books written on aspects of the Catholic Church in the Philippines are not as objective as one might hope. There are exceptions, such as the work of John N. Schumacher, S.J., but the reader should beware. One of the most helpful guides to how Catholicism changed in the Philippines is John Leddy Phelan's "The Philippinization of Catholicism," a chapter in his book *Hispanization of the Philippines.* A good overview is Gerald H. Anderson's *Studies in Philippine Church History* (Ithaca: Cornell University Press, 1969), 421 pages, a collection of essays by various authors, edited by Anderson. With the exception of the essays by the Dominican Aragon and the Jesuit de la Costa, the essays on the whole present a well-rounded view of the church in the Philippines. The best book on the beginning of the Protestant missionary work in the Philippines is Kenton J. Clymer's *Protestant Missionaries in the Philippines 1898–1916: An Inquiry into the American Colonial Mentality* (Urbana, Ill.: University of Illinois Press, 1986), 267 pages. Clymer examines the mainstream Protestant denominations and their efforts and mistakes in seeking to evangelize the Philippines. Shelton Woods's *A Broken Mirror: Protestant Fundamentalism in the Philippines* continues the project by looking at the work of groups that did not exist when the Philippines was taken but came into being as a part of the fundamentalism phenomenon. Both works deal with the impact of the missionary movement on the Filipino people and culture.

SOCIETY

Pacto de Sangre: Spanish Legacy in the Philippines (Manila: National Historical Institute, 2003), 190 pages, edited by Virgilio S. Almario, discusses Spain's impact on Philippine society. Produced by "The Philippine-Spanish Friendship Day Committee," it tends to overlook the negative aspects of Spain's time in the Philippines, but the artwork and photographic reproductions make this book a must have. *An Anarchy of Families: State and Family in the Philippines* (Madison, Wisc.: University of Wisconsin Press, 2004), 552 pages, edited by Alfred W. McCoy, examines the connections between the two institutions of the family and the state, specifically, the relationship between a strong institution (the family) and the weak state. Although the essays tend to focus on particular families, such as the Dimaporos of Maranao and the Pardo de Taveras of Manila, for example, they serve to demonstrate the place of the family in Philippine politics. *The History of the Burgis* by Mariel N. Francisco and Fe Maria C. Arriola, mentioned above, is helpful in presenting the evolution of Philippine society from pre-Spanish times to the present. Donn Hart's *Compadrinazgo: Ritual Kinship in the Philippines* (De Kalb, Ill.: Northern Illinois University Press, 1977), 256 pages, presents a detailed examination of the history, development, and place of ritual kinship (godparents, etc.) in Philippine society. Virgilio G. Enriquez's works deal with Philippine psychology and relationships based on Filipino paradigms, not those of the West, and are especially insightful. *From Colonial to Liberation Psychology* (Quezon City: University of the Philippines Press, 1992), 169 pages, is a good place to start. His untimely death has left a hole in the field of Philippine psychology.

FOOD

One name comes to mind when thinking of literature on Philippine cuisine: Doreen G. Fernandez. An academic, her approach was not limited by that fact. Instead, when reading her work, one gets a real sense that this is someone who enjoyed food—researching and writing about food, talking about food, and eating. Sadly, her untimely death has robbed us of her expertise. But the legacy left behind does her honor. Anything by Fernandez on food is worth reading. An equally outstanding work is *Philippine Food and Life* by Gilda Cordero-Fernando (Manila: Anvil Publishing Co., 1996), 191 pages. This book explores the regional (on the island of Luzon) approaches to cooking by presenting recipes from fourteen provinces on Luzon. Also worth noting is *The Philippine Cookbook* by Reynaldo Alejandro (New York: Perigee Books, 1985), 256 pages. Alejandro provides a basic approach and a good beginning to the issue of Philippine cooking. The Web sites mentioned previously have a wide selection of books on Philippine cuisine, including cookbooks on the various regional styles of cooking.

THE ARTS

In dealing with the folk literature of the Philippines, the eight-volume set compiled by Damiana L. Eugenio and published by the University of the Philippines Press, though not exhaustive, is the most complete collection available. The volumes include *Legends, Epics, Proverbs, Myths,* and *Folk Tales.* A much more accessible work is *Explorations in Philippine Folklore* by Herminia Meñez (Quezon City: Ateneo de Manila University Press, 1996), 159 pages. Meñez deals with a wide variety of topics that fall under the broad designation of folklore. From the place of women warriors in various epics to the monsters in folk tales, this book presents a good exposure to various aspects that make up Philippine culture.

An invaluable resource for background and information about Philippine art is the CCP Encyclopedia of Philippine Art, a double CD-ROM produced by the Culture Center of the Philippines. The material is divided into eight categories: Peoples of the Philippines, Philippine Music, Philippine Dance, Philippine Literature, Philippine Architecture, Philippine Visual Arts, Philippine Film, and Philippine Theater. Doreen G. Fernandez's *Palabas: Essays on Philippine Theater History* (Quezon City: Ateneo de Manila University Press, 1996), 264 pages, is a collection of her writings about the development of theater in the Philippines. Of particular interest is her work on the place of theater in Philippine society as subversion, from the early American period and the Japanese occupation to the time of martial law.

In the visual arts, a number of coffee table books deal with specific aspects of the arts in the Philippines. *Sinaunang Habi: Philippine Ancestral Weave* (Pasay City: Nikki Books, 2000), 312 pages, by Marian Pastor-Roces, is a marvelous visual presentation of the weaving done from one end of the Philippines to the other. This book makes the case that this technology was one of the cultural aspects that united the islands of the archipelago now known as the Philippines. *Philippine Ancestral Houses* (Quezon City: GCF Books, 1980), 263 pages, by Fernando N. Zialcita and Martin I. Tinio, is a good pictorial presentation of Philippine architecture; and Augusto F. Villalon's mammoth *Lugar: Essays on Philippine Heritage and Architecture* (Makati City: Bookmark, 2001), 474 pages, is a more technical and complete work on the subject.

LITERATURE

The Philippines has a rich literary tradition and some of it is accessible, either through translation or because the works were written in English. The necessary starting point is Jose Rizal's two novels, *Noli Me Tangere* (Makati City: Bookmark, 1996), 452 pages, and *El Filibusterismo* (Makati City: Bookmark, 1996), 342 pages (or the *Noli* and the *Fili,* as they are familiarly known in the Philippines). Both are required reading for all high school and college students in the Philippines. Although written in Spanish in the late 1800s, a number of

English translations have been produced. The most recent and by far best translations were done by Soledad Lacson-Locsin, and although published in the Philippines, they are available in the United States. The novels tell the story of Crisostomo Ibarra, who at the beginning of *Noli* has returned to the Philippines from studying in Spain. He has plans for improving conditions only to find forces at work who prefer that things stay as they are. The romance between Ibarra and Maria Clara is iconic in Philippine literature. *Noli* presents a look into the life and culture of Filipinos at the end of the nineteenth century, but *Fili* is a darker and angrier vision of the Philippines under the grip of the power of the friars. As one author has stated, the book is "dominated by dialogue, ideology and the angrier passions" and is a "series of meditations." Ibarra, now known as Simoun, struggles with the issue of violence as a legitimate means of revolution. Critics have argued that these books are not great literature, but that misses the point. They were revolutionary in a number of ways, particularly in galvanizing Filipinos in their struggle against Spain. *Jose Rizal, The Movie,* directed by Marilou Diaz-Abaya and starring Cesar Montano as Rizal, does a wonderful job of telling the story of Rizal's life and showing how he thought about the two novels. Subtitled, this is a must for those interested in Rizal, his life, and his work.

In the twentieth century, the wealth of Philippine literature is overwhelming and it would seem a shame not to mention all the men and women who have written poetry, short stories, novels, and the like. But space constraints allow only two novels to be mentioned. The reader is encouraged to mine the treasures to be found in the various aspects of Philippine literature. Carlos Bulosan's best known work, *America Is in the Heart* (1946; reprint, Seattle: University of Washington Press, 1975), 327 pages, deals with the harsh conditions of Filipino migrant workers in pre–World War II United States. It is part of a rich tradition of writing by Filipinos in the diaspora as they struggle with newness, homesickness, and injustice. Nick

Joaquin's award-winning *The Woman Who Had Two Navels* (1961; reprint, Makati: Bookmark, 1991), 336 pages, considered to be his masterpiece, is an intricate story of the search for identity and purpose.

For those wishing to learn how to speak either Tagalog or Ilokano, the University of Hawaii has printed practical and accessible works for that purpose. Teresita V. Ramos has produced a number of works on Tagalog. Three of her works are to be used as a starting point: *Tagalog Structures* (Honolulu: University of Hawaii Press, 1971), 176 pages; *Conversational Tagalog: A Functional-Situational Approach* (Honolulu: University of Hawaii Press, 1985), 341 pages; and *Tagalog Dictionary* (Honolulu: University of Hawaii Press, 1971), 330 pages. The first work is grammatical in its approach, the second focuses on the conversational use of Tagalog. The Tagalog dictionary is to serve as a resource. The next step for those interested in going to the next level is *Intermediate Tagalog: Developing Cultural Awareness Through Language* (Honolulu: The University Press of Hawaii, 1981), 521 pages, by Ramos and Rosalina Morales Goulet. Precy Espiritu has written a pair of books on Ilokano: *Let's Speak Ilokano* (Honolulu: University of Hawaii Press, 1984), 297 pages, and *Intermediate Ilokano: An Integrated Language and Culture Reading Text* (Honolulu: University of Hawa'i Press, 2004), 404 pages. Her approach is like that of Ramos in that she seeks to help the reader gain conversational competence rather than simply a grammatical understanding of the structures of Ilokano.

GUIDEBOOKS

There are a number of helpful guidebooks about the Philippines. The Lonely Planet's *Philippines: A Travel Survival Kit* (Lonely Planet, 1997), 528 pages, by Jens Peters, now in its sixth edition, has the strength of containing 143 maps, which can be of great help to the traveler. The big downside of this work is that it was published in 1997 and thus is dated. The reader would not know, among other things, that the peso is now half its value of 1997, and that after the events of 9/11, there has been an increase in terrorism, particularly in places such as Mindanao. These are obviously important considerations. At the same time, much of the information in Peters's work can be helpful. There is another Lonely Planet *Philippines* (Lonely Planet Publications, 2003), 448 pages, by a group of authors who revised the original book. However, it is not as good as Peters's work and not worth the money. Hans Johannes Hoefer's *Philippines* (Insight Guides, Hong Kong: APA Productions, 1984), though dated, has invaluable articles by various authors dealing with different aspects of Philippine culture and history. One of the best-rated guides is David Dalton's *The Rough Guide to the Philippines* (Rough Guides Limited, 2004), 528 pages. In addition to the comprehensive nature of the information, the author's frankness is not only refreshing but also helpful.

One more work can be included in this category, and also in the section on the economy: *Culture Shock! Succeed in Business* (Portland, Ore.: Graphic Arts Center Publishing Company, 1998), 206 pages, by Joaquin L. Gonzalez and Luis R. Calingo, has a wealth of material helpful to anyone traveling to the Philippines, but particularly for anyone planning to do business in the Philippines. Chapter titles include "Getting Your Business Started," "Present and Future Niches," "Management Matters," and "Culture, Customs and Communication."

Index

Page numbers in **boldface** denote photographs.

About the Author

Damon Woods, the son of missionary parents, grew up in Baguio City in the Philippines. Having received his Ph.D. from the University of California, Los Angeles, in Southeast Asian History, he has been a lecturer at UCLA, the University of California, Irvine, and California State University, Long Beach. Among the courses he has taught are Philippine History, Philippine Radical Tradition, Missionaries and Southeast Asia, Religion and Society in Southeast Asia, and America's Wars in Southeast Asia. His research has focused on documents written by Tagalogs in the Tagalog language in the sixteenth and seventeenth centuries.